Research in Mexican History

Research in Mexican History

Topics, Methodology, Sources, and a Practical Guide to Field Research

Compiled and Edited by

Richard E. Greenleaf

Tulane University

Michael C. Meyer

University of Nebraska

For the Committee on Mexican Studies
Conference on Latin American History

UNIVERSITY OF NEBRASKA PRESS · LINCOLN

198304

In Memoriam
Howard Francis Cline
1915-71

Contents

A map of Mexico follows page 62.

Introduction

A year before his death, Howard Cline, director of the Hispanic Foundation of the Library of Congress, suggested that the fledgling Committee of Mexicanists of the Conference on Latin American History undertake the coordination of a volume designed as a guide for the young scholar leaving the comfortable confines of his North American classroom and venturing south to research in the wilds of Mexican history. He envisioned an unpretentious book, inexpensive enough so that all could afford it, but one so replete with practical information on problems of research that every historian would carry it along in his briefcase as he crossed the border on his way south to Mexico City. The committee subsequently endorsed the project as one of the more useful services it could perform for its own constituency as well as for Mexicanists in other fields.

On the counsel of many colleagues, the scope of the project was gradually enlarged to encompass not merely a guide to research in the field but, more generically, a guide to research of the field. For this reason we solicited and received contributions outlining research lacunae to be filled, special methodological problems encountered in some areas, and descriptions of several collections of source materials outside of Mexico itself. While the core of the book remains an aid to historical research in Mexico, the inclusion of the additional information, we believe, increases the general utility and appeal of the volume, as it can be used prior to departure.

All of the contributors to this guide have put in their time in the Mexican archives. They all would like to have had such a book available to them when they began. But because we all continue to learn, not only from our own experience, but from the experience of others, because conditions change, because new collections of documents become available and others are moved from one location to another, we believe that this volume has something to offer the more seasoned Mexicanist as well.

Years of experience have shown that the young scholar arriving in Mexico for research, no matter how thorough his preparation and training, encounters certain difficulties not only in his everyday living but also in his archival travail. It would be foolhardy to try to anticipate every problem that might arise, but careful use of this volume, we believe, will minimize the frustrations of geographical and cultural dislocation. Some of the problems are amazingly recurrent and these can be easily avoided.

But this book has another purpose as well. For years our Mexican colleagues have good-naturedly responded to the signals of distress sent out by the floundering North American scholar. It is difficult for us to appreciate what our reaction would be in Lincoln, Nebraska, or New Orleans, Louisiana, if a horde of Mexicans descended upon us each summer soliciting information on Pontiac's Rebellion, Jackson's Kitchen Cabinet, the Greenback movement, or the suffragettes. As professionals we would try to help with matters within our fields of competence and we would direct them to other authorities, but our good will could well wear thin if we were called upon to change pesos into dollars, open bank accounts, provide taxi service, fix traffic tickets, and repeatedly provide information which could be readily available in some convenient form. Our Mexican counterparts have not complained and, in fact, in the pages of this guide continue as they have in the past to offer their services. But we believe that there is no reason for the North American to arrive in Mexico City without a certain backlog of practical information on doing research there.

Coordinating the efforts of some thirty-five Mexican specialists proved to be a somewhat more onerous task than we had anticipated when we agreed to assume responsibility for editing the volume. None of the articles has appeared in print previously; all were prepared simultaneously for this volume. As a result, none of the authors had the benefit of knowing the exact content of the other selections to be included. In order to avoid needless duplication we found it desirable to edit many of the contributions more heavily than would have been necessary had the number of articles been smaller or had each author known the nature of his colleagues' contributions. In addition, for the purpose of making the over-all organization of the volume more coherent, we found it necessary to divide several selections and combine others. We ask the indulgence of those contributors whose manuscripts we have taken liberties with. In all cases the changes were made with the potential user in mind. The book is divided into two main sections. Part I treats general problems encountered in researching Mexican history. It is designed as a preliminary to research in the field and contains the overviews of two seasoned veterans: Daniel Cosío Villegas and France V. Scholes. It also presents two analyses of topics in need of study and, in addition, discusses the theory and practice of several nontraditional approaches: ethnohistory, historical statistics, and oral history. Part II comprises the practical guide to research in the field. After two introductory chapters which contain information on day-to-day living in Mexico and general background on the organization and availability of Mexican archives, it describes individual archival collections in Mexico (chapter 6) and outside of Mexico (chapter 7). Chapter 8 is a description of major libraries in Mexico City, and chapters 9-11 consider the major sources for specific topics and chronological periods. The general information on hours, staff, and available facilities contained in chapters 6-8 is not repeated in chapters 9-11. The final chapter offers several specialized bibliographies, and the appendixes contain maps and other practical information the foreign researcher in Mexico might like to have close at hand.

It is customary for authors or editors to interject in their preface disclaimers of various sorts, if for no other reason than to protect themselves from the book review critics. We feel the need more than most because we are directing our effort to the community of scholars. We make no pretense of having exhausted the topic. Many archival collections are not described, some undoubtedly because we have overlooked them, and others because pressing commitments kept some potential contributors from submitting manuscripts when promised. We would applaud the effort of any other group to produce a more thorough guide which would render ours obsolete. In the interim, however, we hope to perform a service. The major archives, where most of the North Americans do their research, are covered.

Richard E. Greenleaf
Tulane University

Michael C. Meyer
University of Nebraska

Part I

The Nature of Research in Mexican History

1

Problems of the Young Scholar

A. A View from Mexico City
by Daniel Cosío Villegas

Fortunately for me, the little I can say here is based on old and repeated experience. Although I'm not really sure why, for many years a good number of young students have come, and continue to come, soliciting help and advice from me on their historical investigations. Nevertheless, my experience is limited. I talk with them as much as necessary about the subject, the sources to consult, the libraries and archives to use, as well as about the people with whom it might be useful to talk. But only rarely do I find out about the final results of all of this, because the majority of these students write doctoral dissertations which are never published. Very exceptionally one of them has felt obliged to send me a mimeographed copy of his dissertation. Even more rare is the case when one of these is printed. When one of these two exceptions occurs, I am pleasantly surprised to see the effort put in, the diligence in accumulating data, the good organization of the material and its intelligible presentation. Contrary to general opinion, especially on the part of his professors, the young North American who arrives in Mexico with the idea of researching a topic which could be considered "impossible," either because of its own nature, or because of the lack of adequate sources, is more the exception than the rule. It is true that once I received a telephone call from a student from Wisconsin asking me for the telephone number of the Archivo General de la Nación because he wanted to obtain some data by telephone. I asked him what information he was looking for, and he then told me that he wanted to find out in detail about the military engagements of Don Ramón del Valle Inclán during the Mexican Revolution. He explained to me as an excuse that he was in a terrible hurry because he had made the trip to Mexico on an old motorcycle that had given him a lot of trouble along the way. Fortunately, I was able to relieve him of his anxieties by telling him that he could now return to his school immediately, and at leisure, because Don Ramón had come to Mexico for the first (and only) time on September 7, 1921, after the military phase of the revolution had ended.

Although infrequent, the cases closest to the "impossible" subject are those which have some intrinsic interest but because of reasons unique to Mexico are very difficult or impossible to investigate. These are subjects which the students have thought about because they have heard their professors discuss them or have read about them in journals. As an example I offer the famous "decision-making process," invented by and popularized by North American political scientists some years ago.

Of course, nobody can deny the interest in finding out how and who really makes the decisions which influence a country's course of international economics and politics. But it should be agreed that by its very nature this is an internal process, even intimate; in other words, it is concealed from public view and for this reason rarely leaves a written trace. And if this happens in nations with a political life as open as in the United States, it is even more understandable that it should happen in Mexico, a country whose public life is a true mystery. But there is still more. If the difficulties are so great dealing with present-day problems that occur right under our nose, the investigation of the "decision-making process" becomes impossible when it treats an era fifty or one hundred years ago. Given this type of theme, the researcher must either give up on the enterprise or fill in the gaps left by the actual information with fantasy.

Nevertheless, the general norm is that the young North American researcher may think of an interesting subject, even a very interesting one; but here is where his difficulties can begin. The first of these is that he may not know at all, or at least not know sufficiently, if the subject chosen has already been studied by another North American; he is even less certain if it has been studied by a Mexican. Generally he has some idea of available sources but not to the point of being able to determine whether they will yield another work with at least a minimum of originality, and thus constitute a contribution to the knowledge of Mexican history. This problem is the one that has perplexed me most because it is difficult to imagine how these mistakes can be made when publications such as the *Hispanic American Historical Review*, the *Handbook of Latin American Studies*, and the *Latin American Research Re-*

view, among others, are readily available.

The second difficulty is more common. Having chosen an interesting and original topic to investigate, the young North American does not know sufficiently if the documentary sources, and even the published works, exist to support its serious study. For this reason I expect that this research guide will be of immense utility, especially if it provides clear and precise information not only on the existence of documentary sources, but also on their availability, especially those in private hands.

The third difficulty is even harder to explain, but fortunately it is not too common. In general the preparation of the young North American scholar is good: he is serious, industrious, disciplined; he can read and take notes, accumulate and organize the material he gathers; and his knowledge of written Spanish is sufficient to enable him to understand and appreciate what he finds. Nevertheless, there are some types of studies, eras, or personalities where these particular attributes alone are insufficient to assure success. I remember a recent case of a researcher interested in undertaking a significant study on Francisco Bulnes. I told him that the theme was not only interesting, but fascinating, since Bulnes was a man of unique talent and understood the political life of his country as few others. But Bulnes, I warned him, is one of the most evasive, designing, and deceitful writers that Mexico has produced. For this reason, if he, our investigator, was not used to playing with three decks at a time it would be best for him to change his subject.

And this leads me to what I consider to be the greatest failure of North American studies in Mexican history. But it is not properly attributable to the young students, but rather to his older teachers, and perhaps more than anything to the nature of being a North American. His good faith, his naiveté, his innocence are excessive, so he accepts at face value what Mexican writers say. This is particularly true of the period in Mexican history since Independence, even truer of the modern period, and still more true of the Mexican Revolution.

The young North American researcher (as well as many more seasoned ones) ignores a bit of well-known advice: before reading a historical work it is necessary to determine who wrote it. It should be added that the genuine Mexican historians of the modern and revolutionary periods are few. What is common is what, for lack of a better term, one might call the historical balladeer (*el romancero de la historia*): a narrator of events which he saw or heard about from his elders. In addition, there are historical balladeers with preconceived opinions, and consequently their stories must be handled skeptically.

Can these difficulties I have pointed out be remedied? With the exception of the last two I think they can, and without much difficulty. This guide to research will be of great help. But there is one point, which it will not treat, that I consider of special importance.

The North American Latin Americanist—in other words, the professor specializing in Latin American generalities—should not consider himself prepared to suggest, much less to approve, a research topic of one of his students interested in Mexican history without first seeking the advice of a Mexicanist, that is, a professor who has devoted himself especially to Mexican history. Even more, he should ask the advice of the Mexicanist specializing in the historical period to which the research topic corresponds. And perhaps sometime he may even decide to write to his Mexican colleagues, who are generally quite kind, even if occasionally they don't respond to the letters they receive.

B. A View from the North
by France V. Scholes

During the last forty-four years, I have made many visits (for a total of at least fifty months) to Mexico for research in national and regional archives and manuscript collections.[1] I have a vivid recollection of my first experience as a young investigator in the collections of Mexico City (October, 1927, to May, 1928). In later years, I have had ample opportunity to observe the activities, problems, and sometimes the frustrations of other young scholars from the United States, to whom I have always sought to offer help if asked. The following comments are intended to serve as practical advice to graduate students specializing in colonial history who may undertake archival research in Mexico.

The vast extent and the richness of Mexican archives provide almost unlimited research opportunities for students of colonial history, but the wealth of documentation also presents problems that may test the capacity and devotion of the young scholar as he undertakes his first research venture in these collections. The Archivo General de la Nación (AGN), Mexico City, the greatest repository of colonial manuscripts in North America, contains more than 25,000 volumes of unbound bundles (legajos) of colonial documents which are assembled, according to general or topical content, in more than 130 subdivisions (ramos) of unequal extent, varying from less than 10 to some 4,000 volumes or legajos each. For many of the ramos partial or complete inventories (printed, manuscript, and on file cards) are available, but others, including, for example, the very important Ramo de Civil (comprising 2,500 or more volumes of colonial judicial records) have not been cataloged. Moreover, it should be noted that the contents (chronological or topical) of the different ramos are not mutually exclusive. Consequently, for many research projects the investigator must utilize documentation in several ramos of AGN.[2]

Two examples will serve to illustrate this point. (1) The student whose research topic may be some aspect of colonial land tenure will probably find it necessary to make use of documents in the Ramo de Civil, Hospital de Jesús, Mercedes, Tierras, Vínculos, and other subdivisions of AGN. (2) Research topics relating to Indian affairs (for example, labor, tribute, native nobility, village government, and private or community landholding) may require research for pertinent materials in Indios, Mercedes, Reales Cédulas (Originales and Duplicadas), Tierras, Tributos, and Vínculos.

The graduate student who may be contemplating research in AGN should also have some knowledge of important lacunae in this great manuscript collection. For example: (1) The Ramo de Reales Cédulas Originales begins only with the year 1609. Copies of some royal legislation prior to that date may be found scattered through Reales Cédulas Duplicadas, but a large part of this subdivision consists of viceregal decisions and miscellaneous documents of local or colonial origin. (2) AGN does not have extensive and consecutive series (chronologically) of the letters to Crown and Council of important colonial officials: viceroys, oidores, treasury officials, local governmental agencies, bishops, prelates of monastic orders, etc. There is a ramo entitled Correspondencia de Virreyes, but it begins with documents of the mid-eighteenth century. (3) The Real Hacienda ramos of AGN provide only partial records for the fiscal history of colonial Mexico. (4) AGN does not have a comprehensive series of *residencia* records for viceregal or provincial officials. To fill in such lacunae the investigator must often research the Archivo General de Indias (AGI), Seville.

For many research topics even of limited scope, investigators may find it necessary to supplement AGN documentation by materials in other major Mexico City collections: the Biblioteca Nacional, Museo Nacional de Antropología e Historia, Municipal Archive, Archivo de Notarías, Cathedral Archive, and others. For some of these collections special inventories are available; for the notary records in the Archivo de Protocolos only meager and incomplete guides have been made. Access to the Cathedral records is difficult to gain, and this may be true also of some archives of the national secretariats (for example, the Archivo Histórico de la Defensa Nacional).

In addition to the manuscript collections of the national capital, Mexico also has a rich store of state and local archives, civil and ecclesiastical (see Carrera Stampa's *Archivalia Mexicana*).[3] Some of these cover a wide range chronologically, beginning with the sixteenth century, but often with significant lacunae. Others cover only a much more limited time span. To cite two examples with which I am familiar: The Archivo de Protocolos de Mérida, Yucatán, begins with the last decades of the seventeenth century. The colonial records in Yucatán's Archivo del Estado are very fragmentary and relate mainly to the last half century before Independence. And, finally, there is serious lack of adequate inventories, published or manuscript, for the state and local archives.

The foregoing comments would suggest that a prime requisite for a successful and fruitful first research venture in Mexican archives is a carefully defined project (e.g., a doctoral dissertation) of reasonable and manageable proportions, formulated on the basis of available information concerning the potential manuscript sources (their character, extent, and location) for each project and the time and financial resources at the disposal of the investigator. This comment is prompted in part by the fact that on several occasions I have witnessed the discouragement and frustration of young archive investigators who had been encouraged or permitted to undertake research on projects of such broad scope that they could not be encompassed in the time and with the resources available, or projects for which the major manuscript sources were in some other archive. Formulation of a suitable and manageable project calls for a measure of careful planning, including interested guidance by the student's faculty mentor (guidance that sometimes has not been given), reviews of printed inventories of archives and of manuscript collections, and, if I may stress an obvious point, reasonable proficiency in Spanish and some previous exposure to paleography, especially the processal handwriting, if the research topic may require the use of early sixteenth-century records.

Research in colonial archives will also be facilitated and expedited if the investigator has a comprehensive knowledge of the basic principles, methods, and procedures of Spanish colonial government and administration, and it would be especially helpful, if, as part of his graduate or seminar courses, he has had practical experience in reading and abstracting colonial legislative and judicial documents (civil or criminal processes, and even part or all of a *residencia*), *probanzas* of merits and services, petitions for some form of reward or office, etc., and some acquaintance with legal procedures and formalities (wills, powers of attorney, types of court decisions, and decrees for execution of name, etc.). Practice in abstracting a repetitious or a complicated *proceso* or a *probanza*—their interrogations and testimony of witnesses—and separating wheat from chaff should serve to speed up actual archive research, and knowledge of basic legal formalities should serve to facilitate exact comprehension of the language and understanding of important and crucial documentation.

It is also recommended that the young investigator, as part of the planning for his first research venture in Mexican manuscript collections, should inform himself of the extent to which such collections are available in the form of microfilm, photostat, and typescript copies in major United States libraries, for such information may well permit more efficient use of his time (usually limited) in Mexico. I have often recalled to my own students the case of a young scholar on his first visit to a foreign archive (in this case the AGI, Seville) who spent many months at considerable expense searching for and having copies made of documents that were readily available in major United States libraries. The amount of colonial documentation in Mexican, Spanish, and other foreign archives already at hand for student use in this country is enormous. Moreover, it is well known that the total corpus of documentation already available represents, all too often, duplicate copies of archival materials. It is my candid view that one or more of our scholarly foundations could perform a great service to the advancement of research in colonial history by granting substantial aid for the preparation of a union catalog of United States library holdings of microfilm, photostat, and typescript copies of documents in Mexican, Spanish, and other manuscript collections. Also the young scholar should make some effort to acquire basic information for the purposes of his research project concerning pertinent original manuscript sources in United States collections—for example, the Bancroft Library, University of Texas Library, New Mexico Records Center, Newberry Library, Gilcrease Institute, Library of Congress, etc. For it may well be that these collections contain significant items to supplement his findings in Mexico; indeed, they may contain key documents now missing from Mexican collections.

During the many visits that I have made to Mexican archives—in the capital city and in provincial centers—I have always been received with courtesy and kindness by the directors, staff, and other custodians of these collections. I remember with abiding gratitude the gracious manner in which the venerable Luis González Obregón directed me to the shelves of Inquisition papers in AGN in October, 1927, made illuminating comments concerning their contents and historical value, and, as he turned away toward his office, said quietly, "Cuidado con los ojos." Some of my best friends in Mexico have been members of the permanent AGN staff, to whom I owe a great debt for their generous and kindly assistance and continuing interest in my research projects. On numerous occasions they have freely placed at my disposal references to documents not listed in the available catalogs.

I am confident that young scholars will receive the same courtesies and considerations. But some words of warning! Do not begin your first term in the archives with any fanfare or unseemly pronouncement concerning your research project and how you propose to conduct your investigations. Approach your task with genuine scholarly humility in a manner that will enlist the respect and aid of the subordinate members of the archive staff, some of whom may have spent long years in archive service and have an intimate and detailed knowledge of the corpus of documentation. Although they may not have had formal academic training, it has been my experience that most of these veterans have an almost uncanny ability to spot a phoney investigator. I recall now an incident that occurred some twenty years ago in AGN. A pompous young United States investigator (a member of a reputable university faculty) for several days had been calling for volume after volume of documents, thumbing the pages, and calling for more. Finally, in exasperation, a veteran of the archive staff came to me and said: "This American—your *compañero*,—does not know what he is looking for; but if he did know, he would not recognize it if he found it."

In years past, many of my nonacademic friends have offered the comment that archival investigations must be an exciting and romantic experience—the experience of discovering new and important historical knowledge and truth. Most often my reply has been, in effect, that the day-by-day routine of archival research, the page-by-page examination of documents that constitutes so much of normal archival investigation, cannot be described as romantic; indeed, a better term would be sheer drudgery. It is the price that the archive investigator must pay in his search for new and significant historical data. But this routine and boring drudgery may, almost without warning, pay off with the discovery of exciting documentation, a discovery that may provide reward, almost beyond measure, for months and perhaps years of dreary, routine archival research. In my own case, these rewards have been greater than I have deserved.

In the course of his archival investigations the young scholar should, of course, be on the lookout for exciting and interesting documents relating to topics beyond, or even far afield from, his immediate research projects. The keen and eager graduate student will always find materials of this kind during his archival investigations and he should take note of such documentary sources. Indeed, the extent to which he does so may even be a measure of his scholarly competence. But these notes should be recorded for future reference, and should not divert him from his immediate research goal. To employ a golfer's language: "Keep your eye on the ball."

Archival research, carried on over a period of years, calls for continuing devotion of the heart and mind, a devotion that has substantial rewards, mainly of a personal nature. In a retrospective view of many years of research, I can say with truth and sincerity that some of the happiest years of my academic career have been those devoted to documentary investigations in Mexican archives.

―――――――

NOTES

1. I have also spent a total of forty-eight months in archival research in Spain. The remarks in this essay apply with equal force to investigations in both Spain and Mexico.

2. The best descriptive guide to the AGN is Jorge Ignacio Rubio Mañé, *El Archivo General de la Nación, México, D.F.* (Mexico: Editorial Cultura, 1940). If this edition is not available, check the same material as it appeared in *Revista de la Historia de América*, no. 9 (1940), pp. 63-169.

3. Manuel Carrera Stampa, *Archivalia Mexicana* (Mexico: UNAM, Instituto de Historia, 1952).

2

New Opportunities for Research

A. Topics in Need of Study: Colonial Mexico
by Stanley J. Stein

The historian seeking to indicate the main opportunities or themes for further research during three centuries of colonial rule in an area such as Mexico can justifiably express misgivings. Is it possible in a few pages to do more than mention the obvious? Well known is the conventional wisdom that each of Mexico's three colonial centuries has been viewed as embodying distinctive themes which furnish a character or personality to each of the centuries: the sixteenth as the century of conquest, culture contact, and demographic holocaust; the seventeenth as one of contraction or stagnation lasting until its last decades, when the eighteenth century's patterns of growth can be discerned; and the eighteenth as one of slow recovery until the rapid upsurge or flowering of the last half century before the outbreak of perhaps the most devastating colonial and civil war in any Latin American area. Equally a part of the conventional wisdom is the fashion in which the historiographical literature clusters around conquest and its immediate repercussions and upon the last decades of Spanish colonialism. With the notable exception of pioneering studies of sixteenth-century demography, the unfolding of encomienda, *repartimiento*, and debt peonage, and François Chevalier's masterly *Land and Society in ʿolonial Mexico*, it is accurate to conclude that many significant contributions of the past three to four decades have focused upon the end of the colonial period, terminating not with Independence but with the outbreak of revolution a decade earlier. Studies sweeping through three centuries of growth and development are understandably few; the most notable, Charles Gibson's *The Aztecs under Spanish Rule*, represents the fruit of de-

13

tailed scholarship in the valley of Mexico. It too awaits complementary treatment of other key regions of Mexico before a new over-all synthesis can be
undertaken.

Confronting the problem of pinpointing areas for further investigation, the
historian may first offer preliminary reflections based upon the older as well
as the more recent historiographical contributions. Obviously Mexico's trajectory over three centuries will have to be viewed within a broad historical
framework: in the context of growth and transformation elsewhere in America, especially with respect to the relatively unresearched yet comparable area
of Peru; in its relation to the flows and ebbs of Spanish and European economic change; and as part of the formation and interrelation of the structures
of the Atlantic basin between the onset of West European expansion of the
late fifteenth century and the first industrial revolution of the late eighteenth
century. In other terms, Mexico's role will need examination as part of the
vast historical process of the commercial revolution commencing along the
Atlantic coast of Africa, then spreading across the Atlantic to culminate in
the creation of the interregional economy of the eighteenth century linking
Europe, Africa, America, and the Far East. Second, historians will tend to
select as research topics those which reflect the interests of their time and
place, despite the recognition that topics often simply reflect personal idiosyncrasies.

From such considerations flows a third preliminary reflection, the possibility that future Mexican historiography may at last benefit from fruitful
cross-disciplinary fertilization. Dissatisfied with the short-term analysis, econ-
omists, sociologists, and demographers have begun to lengthen their time
span, to extend their probing into the distant past to those critical moments
that require the collection of quantitative data. What is surprising is not that
such data are indeed available and useful when handled critically, but that
historians have so long neglected this dimension of their craft. French, English, and United States historiography has been enriched by the data un-
earthed and manipulated by social scientists in the past quarter century and
by their challenging conclusions or, to be perhaps more accurate, hypotheses.
Their example will inevitably push the historians of Mexico's past away from
the craft's traditional preoccupation with politics and personality at moments
of crisis toward a new level of integrative analysis.

The preoccupation of recent decades with growth, development, and
"modernization" has dampened the earlier interest in the continuities of Mexican history. In the twentieth century the recession of ecclesiastical influence

upon politics (if not upon the social question), the acceleration of rural-to-urban migration, and the adherence to the ritual of elections and change of political figures (while political and administrative attitudes remain) have diverted attention from the colonial ecclesiastical establishment, community studies in depth, and effects of centuries of colonial administration. In fact, the unevenness of the process of modernization and the endurance of so-called bottlenecks suggest the advantages in reexamining the colonial roots of modern Mexico and its continuities. Because of lack of space, reference to cultural and intellectual history will be omitted in the following review of the colonial past.

Generally speaking, the Church has been viewed as an external force imposed upon a defeated and subject people, which is largely true. Yet there are aspects which merit further attention. First of all, the extent of syncretism of preconquest and Roman Catholic conceptualizations of existence has to be further examined and interpreted in depth; for decades in the sixteenth century, resistance to evangelization as well as active defection from Catholicism were widespread. Why, then, the apparent evaporation of antagonism and resistance in the following centuries? Over the long haul, is this traceable to the attraction of Christian attitudes and practices, of the symbolic over the real sacrifice? It may well be explained, as many have tried, by claiming that the faith of the conqueror is inescapable. Equally plausible but not incompatible is the possibility that the two profound religious currents reinforced each other to produce the pervasive religiosity evident, for example, in the mass pilgrimages to religious sites, the ubiquitous symbol of the *calavera*, and the use of hallucinogens.

Closer examination of the operation of the ecclesiastical establishment at the level of the parish may reveal a far more intimate identification between curate and community than suspected in view of the number of *criollos* who entered the formal ecclesiastical structures. How representative were Hidalgo and Morelos?

In recent years we have begun to perceive a facet of the ecclesiastical establishment long neglected although not unsuspected: the accumulation and manipulation of the large sums of the faithful placed at the disposal of the Church, in brief, the Church as banker. This role has been somewhat clarified by the renewal of historical interest in the process whereby the Spanish government attempted after 1804 to recapture both liquid and other ecclesiastical funds in Mexico and other Spanish colonies, the episode of the *consolidación de vales reales*. This episode, however, is only the tip of the iceberg, for the Church had long functioned as mortgage and investment bank and as trustee as well as philanthropic organization and supplier of social and welfare services. The ties between the ecclesiastical establishment and the laity were more than spiritual and recreational; through the endowments and legacies of the wealthy, the Church functioned as banker to the business community. As investment institution the Church called upon the entrepreneurial wisdom of the laity in placing its funds judiciously. What we do not yet know is the constitution of its boards of advisers, the reasons for their choice, the patterns of advice, the criteria in allocating funds. In the light of such colonial interpenetration of Chuch and economy, the collaboration of the Mexican Church with defenders of the status quo after Independence is not unexpected.

The Church in the Mexican colonial economy must also be viewed in another context, through the role of the Society of Jesus. The Jesuits' contribution to the growth and development of the colonial economy from the sixteenth to the eighteenth century has attracted historians' attention in recent times, broadening the earlier focus upon its educational and missionary activities. Evident is the inexorable growth of their liquid reserves and landed properties which underwrote their educational plant in the colonies, financed their extensive international operations, and made possible the mobilization throughout Western and Central Europe of extraordinarily competent talent. But we still do not understand the sources of their apparent capitalistic efficiency and skill, and their success in withstanding the attacks of disaffected laymen and opponents in the secular and regular clergy. In the perspective of Western European economic history, do they symbolize the high point of the medieval corporation with manifold and farflung interests, or the entering wedge of early modern capitalism in the Spanish variant of the Catholic world?

At the end of the eighteenth century the Church was no monolith. May we conclude that in its hierarchy, corporative functions, and mentality, its maldistribution of income ranging from the princely incomes of its prelates to the meager pittances of its rural parish priests, it was a faithful mirror of colonial society?

Before historians is the challenge of reconstructing the world of Mexico's indigenous peoples as the demands and goals of the new lords, secular and religious, and the impact of epidemic disease rapidly eroded them, their culture, and their values. In a kind of shorthand can we term the trauma of conquest, that trinity of defeat, death, and conversion, the change from a hierarchical and organized to a hierarchical and disorganized society? What was in fact preserved by indigenous peoples from the world they had lost by the holocaust of conquest and conversion, forced urbanization, and disease? Ethnohistorians advance the theory that late colonial culture is a Hispano–American Indian fusion; how then should we establish the key moments and what elements should we emphasize in the formation of a new Mexico? Is the beginning of modern Mexico the budding of a new mentality–that point in the seventeenth century when Mexicans perceived that conquest belonged to the. *peninsulares* and that they must mold the elements of their own reality to forge a new entity, mestizo Mexico? The overwhelming proportions of massive urbanization in recent decades have obscured a long perspective of the phenomenon in Mexico, specifically its colonial patterns. The formation of Mexico's colonial urban nuclei undoubtedly was the result of steady rural outmigration. Did migrants move in stages from isolated Indian communities to central market towns, and only thereafter to the large regional centers and ultimately to Mexico City? One might ask if the rural exodus represented a response to wage and other inducements, to the misery of cyclical famine, or simply to population pressure in communities losing their cultivable areas to encroaching grain and stock-raising estates. Can we trace in the economic, social, and political capillaries of urban colonial Mexico the integration of migrants into a consumption-oriented milieu, the path and rate of upward mobility, and the forging of a new culture?

The preservation of tradition has long been recognized as a mechanism for defense against cultural disorganization and external manipulation. Is it accurate to assume that Spaniards could never have mobilized the Indians' labor and other resources into an early capitalist economy without resort to the exploitative instruments of *repartimiento* of cash, seed, or goods and implements; forced mine service; and debt peonage? Assuming that forced incorporation into the new economy was unavoidable in the sixteenth century, how can we explain the uninterrupted continuation of squalor, misery, deprivation, and sheer repression which characterized Mexico's textile workshops for more than two centuries, a system in full vigor in 1810? To put the problem in a broader cross-cultural context, the English induced in another colonial area of the eighteenth century, India, an extraordinary upsurge in the output of cotton textiles apparently without employing forms of labor coercion utilized by entrepreneurs in Mexico. May the historian generalize that colonial mine owners and landlords, merchants and sweatshop operators simply maximized their mastery over legal institutions, codes, and the police power of the state to exploit native labor more profitably than market inducements would have permitted? The level of exploitative mechanisms imposed probably made it inevitable that Hidalgo's followers in the Bajío would sooner rather than later attack all wealthy Caucasoids indiscriminately, that the Mexican countryside during the War for Independence would become essentially a guerrilla sanctuary, and, in the nineteenth century, that Yucatecan Indians would react to exploitation in the Caste War.

With respect to Mexican colonial economic history, the large view must take as the point of departure the origins of the modern economy, namely, the widening circuits of the monetized capitalistic sector. Details of international trade mechanisms and the Mexican economy's response to European demand require investigation in depth, but equally important is the development of the internal economy. In regard to the nexi of international trade, we need further investigation of the mining cores as well as individual mines, the mobilization of labor, foodstuffs and animals from haciendas, the petty tradesmen, the merchants resident in towns who supplied them, and the large import-export wholesalers (*almaceneros*) of the Consulado of Mexico City and their Spanish and international connections. What were the mechanisms whereby silver mining ultimately may have determined the fluctuations of the internal as well as the Spanish and European economies?

At a slightly lower level, can we discern the development within Mexico of two fairly distinct economies, that of the mining North, which for peculiarly local reasons was more open in contrast to the predominantly closed Indian peasant economy of the South? Since recent analyses have properly called into question the concept of "dual" or "enclave" economies, it behooves us to establish the points at which the two in fact intersected, since fluctuations in mining had local repercussions on the composition and volume of total output. This is all the more necessary since in the eighteenth century there appeared two poles of economic growth, the sustained external demand for silver to expand Europe's position in the international economy, and Mexico's internal demand, which undoubtedly reflected demographic increase, in particular the apparently more accelerated growth of those social strata— mestizo, mulatto, and *criollo*—more integrated in the monetized sector. Although there is the constant complaint running through the colonial centuries that the export sector drained Mexico of hard currency needed in domestic transactions, and that the oligopolistic mechanism manipulated by Mexico City merchants and Spanish associates undersupplied and overpriced, it is evident that the conflict between external and internal demands sharpened in the eighteenth century. Is this why, when Bourbon economic policy adopted at last the major features of mercantilism in seeking to enforce the colonial compact, the policies were attacked as constraints upon internal development, e.g., the expansion of textile, wine, and olive oil production? In other terms, how did what appear to be mainly revenue-capturing devices embedded in ostensibly administrative changes—the intendancy system and the abolition of *repartimiento*, the state's assumption of tax collection responsibility in mining, tobacco, and *alcabalas*—affect local efforts to create and distribute new sources of wealth and income? Or were other Spanish vested interests the real source of opposition? The complaints of Mexico's deputies in the Cortes (1810-13) may be interpreted as efforts not to create a diversified economy but to permit the further expansion of economic activities established despite Spanish colonial constraints. In other words, historians must examine the roots of the crisis of growth at the end of a century of expansion. The Hidalgo phase of the independence struggle flowered in the most developed capitalistic sector of Mexico, the Bajío; the Morelos phase continued it from a base in Oaxaca, precisely where peasant producers had been coerced into the production of an export staple, cochineal.

The Mexican hacienda, which still awaits careful delineation beyond the period where Chevalier's study terminates, enjoyed uninterrupted growth in the eighteenth century as seasonal and cyclical price fluctuations provided hacendados repeated opportunities to absorb communal as well as small private properties. Critical comments are legion at the end of the eighteenth century about the menacing anomaly of exaggerated property concentrations dominating a countryside of land-hungry peasants. Yet—significantly—the struggle for independence which wiped out Indian tribute, *repartimiento*, the most repressive aspects of textile workshops, and the oligopoly of merchant guilds, left intact the major feature of the Mexican countryside, the hacienda, whether producer of pulque, sugar, grains, or cattle.

The structures of colonial administration are well known. What now remains to be done is to counterpose to what Latin Americans today call the formal structures of governance the real ones. At progressively ascending layers from *alcaldía mayor* and *corregimiento*, *ayuntamiento* and audiencia, to viceroy and captain general, we need to explore the socioeconomic syndromes of political power and the way interest groups shaped the execution of colonial policy. How did Mexicans enter the administrative superstructure of colonialism: were *corregimientos* and *alcaldías mayores* the preserve of poor but aggressive Spanish immigrants, while *criollos* aspired to the more status-conferring positions in *ayuntamientos* and treasury bureaus, as secretaries and clerks in the viceregal executive office, and as *oidores* and *fiscales* of audiencias? We have one major study of an audiencia in Mexico, that of Guadalajara, which covers only part of the colonial period; there is nothing comparable for the great audiencia of Mexico. Was the audiencia a bastion of peninsular interests, as deputies to the Cortes bitterly complained, or did its decisions on major issues reflect in fact alignment with *criollo* groups and as well a sustained effort to defend less privileged groups in colonial society?

To be more precise, how were colonial bureaucrats enmeshed in the interest webs of the Mexican colonial world, those predominantly *criollo*, those peninsular, and those where *criollo* and peninsular interests dovetailed: by kith, by kin, or by purely monetary involvement? No longer can historians be content merely to indicate who prepared a *consulta* or who were the members of a junta, tribunal, or *consejo* when key decisions were made. Rather, we will be obliged at least to attempt to evaluate bureaucratic points of view advanced, advice recommended, and decisions taken in the light of the possible associational context of the decision makers and interest groups involved.

Traditionally, through biography historians have tried to reconstruct the social fabric of the past. It is noteworthy that there are roughly less than half a dozen substantial biographies of Mexico's viceroys, none treating the three outstanding viceroys of the eighteenth century, Linares and the two Revillagigedos. However, biographies suffer the drawback of underscoring the unique. Here new tools of analysis applied to administrative as well as social and economic history promise to sharpen our grasp of historical reality. Through the technique of collective biography it may be possible to answer with some precision major questions about the geographical and social origins, careers, and performance of colonial bureaucrats and clergymen, military officers, and members of the higher economic and social strata. While not all questions about social change will be answered by prosopography, it may improve our understanding of the nature of the extended family, patterns of kinship, the role of marriage, and the process of social and occupational mobility of Mexico's colonial elite—bureaucratic, religious, social, and economic.

In the long run, historians of Mexico's colonial past must reexamine their analytical framework, undertake relevant cross-cultural comparisons, readjust periodization to the continuities of basic structures. In this perspective perhaps we should view the colonial phase of Mexico's trajectory terminating not with the achievement of independence in 1821, but at the moment the Mexican Revolution began, 1910.

B. Topics in Need of Study: Modern Mexico
by Robert A. Potash

Despite the steady flow in recent years of historical monographs equal if not superior in quality to the output of any period in the past, modern Mexico still offers many challenges as a field of research. The agenda of needed and useful topics, if not the same as it was when this writer reviewed it in 1960, is still very extensive. What follows does not pretend to be an exhaustive list, but a series of suggestions that reflect one person's experience and predilections.

The greatest opportunities seem to lie in the interrelated fields of economic and social history and particularly in the chaotic half century that preceded the Pax Porfiriana. At a basic level, the transportation system in this prerailroad era merits detailed study. The nature and functioning of the road network, the efforts at state and national levels to effect improvements, the introduction of new forms of freight and passenger service are all part of a story that has never been told in its entirety. A comprehensive study of transportation would help illuminate the political as well as social history of this era.

In similar vein a major contribution to the understanding of Mexican economic life in the post-Independence decades could come from a study of merchant banking. The true significance of exceptional lending institutions like the Juzgado de Capellanías or the Banco de Avío will be understood only when the alternative source of capital and credit, namely, the network of private merchants, is fully explored. Mexicans, Spaniards, and foreigners of various nations were constantly engaged in lending sums to private individuals and public authorities for a variety of purposes and under differing conditions. The time has certainly come to attempt detailed studies that would identify the individuals or companies, analyze their operations, and assess their influence on the country's development. Such studies could focus initially on individual Mexican moneymen or on foreign merchant houses, but the ultimate goal should be an integrated view of the system they represented.

Although the economic role of the Church has been subjected to serious scrutiny in recent works, there is still much to be done in this field. Jan

Bazant's excellent recent study, *Los Bienes de la Iglesia en México (1856-1875)* (Mexico: El Colegio de México, 1971), focuses on the Distrito Federal and five states, leaving a good deal of territory to be explored in similar studies. Michael Costeloe's earlier *Church Wealth in Mexico* (Cambridge: Cambridge University Press, 1967) is also limited geographically to the archbishopric of Mexico. A study of the management of Church wealth in other dioceses would indicate whether Costeloe's picture of the Juzgado de Capellanías is typical of the entire Mexican Church or whether there were significant regional variations.

The social realities of modern Mexico also offer major opportunities to the resourceful scholar. The general topic of poverty remains virtually intact, waiting to be explored if suitable sources can be uncovered. It is quite possible that data exist in municipal as well as state and national records, in ecclesiastical as well as secular sources. The records of police organizations, hospitals, and benevolent societies might be searched for information. As a special subject within the broader topic, a full-scale study might be made of brigandage. Here is a phenomenon that characterized Mexican life for much of the nineteenth century, yet there is no reliable study that explores its many ramifications.

The other side of the coin is beginning to be examined in recent studies of public security forces such as the army and the rurales. Of considerable interest from the viewpoint not only of these forces but of the general populace would be an examination of the *leva*, the forced recruitment system. Did it affect the poor primarily? To what extent was it used as a political weapon? Despite its compulsory character, did the *leva* open up possibilities for social advancement?

Depending on the location of relevant materials, much useful work can still be done in exploring the history of individual haciendas. Only a handful of such studies exist for either the colonial or the modern period. Needed is a series of individual studies that will throw light on the varied roles performed by haciendas (did they have a public security function in the nineteenth century, and if so, where?), their flexibility in the face of new forces—economic, social, and political—generated in the passage of time. Was the hacienda of 1910 a simple continuation of the institution in existence in 1810? In 1850?

For those interested in politics and political institutions, opportunities exist especially at the level of subnational history. Comparative studies might be made of political leadership in different regions and states. Attention should be paid particularly to the *jefe político* and to his functions before and during the Díaz regime. The state bureaucracies and their evolution from the time of independence also might be examined. To what extent did the transitions from empire to republic and from one form of regime to another produce fundamental changes in the ranks of officeholders who performed basic functions, for example, tax collecting? Did these changes take place within a homogeneous group as defined by class, race, education, etc.? The legislative bodies at state and national levels could also be the subject of a series of studies that would throw light on their composition, functions, and effectiveness. In this connection, for the period down to La Reforma, a useful monograph might be written under the title "The Priest as Politician: The Role of Clergymen in Mexico's Legislative Bodies."

For the student of intellectual history the study of Mexican conservatism continues to offer a challenge. The ideas of laymen as well as clergymen throughout the nineteenth century might well be explored in and for themselves as well as to provide background for the understanding of such movements as liberalism and positivism. Apart from these broad concepts, useful work can be done in exploring the attitudes of representative writers of different generations toward such topics as poverty, economic development, or foreign influences.

Although library shelves are loaded with what purport to be biographical studies, the number of first-rate biographies of Mexican personalities is surprisingly small. No good biography exists, for example, of Porfirio Díaz. With the opening to scholars of the Díaz papers at the University of the Americas, perhaps this void will soon be filled. Going back earlier into the nineteenth century, it now seems time for a more comprehensive and better balanced biography of Lucas Alamán than José Valadés produced over thirty years ago. Studies of Alamán's contemporaries would not be amiss. Certainly one candidate deserving of special attention is Francisco Pablo Vásquez, who became bishop of Puebla after a diplomatic career, and whose efforts to reconcile the economic interests of the new industrialists with traditional Church values are reflected in his correspondence with Alamán.

For the twentieth century the possibilities for biographies are limited only by the availability of adequate materials. Among the many figures who might be named, Obregón, Calles, and Cárdenas stand most in need of full-scale treatments. Now that John Womack has shown what could be done for Zapata, one may hope that other resourceful scholars will find ways of bridging the materials gap for other key individuals and produce studies of comparable interest and significance.

3

Special Problems in Methodology

A. Research in Mexican Ethnohistory

by Ronald M. Spores

Ethnohistory, as I understand and practice it, is documentary ethnology, a set of methods and techniques for reducing all classes of documentation to raw ethnographic data applicable to the study of human behavior within an anthropological theoretical framework. A document, whether written, drawn, or painted yesterday or a thousand years ago, is for the ethnohistorian what the live informant is for the ethnologist. I approach a body of documentation as I would a group of live informants. I seek information from documents just as I would seek it from living Mixtec, Tarascan, or Otomí informants or from a series of stratigraphic tests in the Nochixtlan Valley of Oaxaca. Problems can be formulated and research strategy can be planned much as for any other kind of ethnological study. Ethnohistorically derived patterns can be interpreted, described and explained within a structural-functional, evolutionary, ecological, or cultural-developmental theoretical framework, the manner of utilization of written sources depending on the theoretical interests of the individual scholar.

The ethnohistorian is in a position to search for solutions to anthropological problems and may engage in empirical research or test hypotheses as effectively as any other social scientist. Possible lines of inquiry might be as follows: What is the nature of the socioeconomic organization of a community and how may its patterns vary in relation to demographic fluctuation or technological innovation? How does a rancho, *estancia, sujeto*, or *agencia* relate sociopolitically and economically to its *cabecera, provincia*, or *municipio*, and what factors may contribute to changes in those relationships over time?

How do communities in a given area interrelate socioeconomically, and how do they relate to the larger sociocultural macrocosm? How are internal economic systems linked into interregional economic networks, and how do political institutions facilitate those linkages and interrelationships? How are families and voluntary associations constituted, and how are family patterns, intergroup relations, or political structure related to demographic fluctuation, geographical limitation, or technological innovation? Who wields political power in the community; how is that power defined and delimited; how are political leaders recruited; how do they function; and how are they turned out of office? What is the nature of the belief system in a community or region and how might it serve to encourage social cohesion among clusters of communities or between regions?

Whether with reference to modern, colonial, protohistoric, or prehistoric Mexico, all of these problems are directly or indirectly amenable to the documentary approach. It happens that the questions mentioned above have been of direct concern to me over the past decade. Original doubts that such matters could be approached through documentation have long been dispelled. The value and reliability of ethnohistoric procedures is now firmly established. I am convinced that in terms of the kinds of problems that have been of interest to me (evolving community structure, intergroup relations, and forms of government), ethnohistory is the most productive and flexible of all methodologies available to the anthropologist.

I will not dwell at length on what I perceive to be the strengths and weaknesses of ethnology and archeology as opposed to documentary ethnology. One set of techniques may be more appropriate to the solution of certain kinds of problems than another; other kinds of problems may require the application of all three methodologies, as has been the case with our long-range study of the development of the community and intercommunity relations in the Mixteca Alta of Oaxaca. At this point, however, I do wish to emphasize what I believe to be the strengths and limitations of documentary ethnology, or ethnohistory, as practiced in Mexico, and often it is useful to frame such statements in a comparative context.

First, documentary ethnology allows for consideration of long developmental sequences, some covering decades, others (as with the Mixteca of Oaxaca or the Valley of Mexico) extending from before A.D. 1000 to modern times (Jiménez Moreno 1941, 1954-55, 1959, 1966; Jiménez Moreno and Mateos Higuera 1940; Gamio 1922; Gibson 1964; Dahlgren 1954; Caso 1949, 1960a, 1960b, 1963; Caso and Smith 1966; Barlow 1949; López Austin

1961; León Portilla 1961, 1964; Cook and Borah 1963; Gorenstein 1966; Charlton 1969; Spores 1967, 1969). While archeology and historical linguistics can perhaps claim greater temporal penetration, I do not believe that they can ever provide the wealth of cultural detail possible with ethnohistorical procedures.

I cannot resist the temptation to point out that conventional ethnographic study is largely restricted to the present. That is, an ethnographer who happens to be concerned with the diachronic perspective must content himself with the recollections of his live informants, ancestral hearsay, and highly selective present-day conceptualizations about the realities of the past. If he is to verify what went on in the past, to authenticate his construct or test his model, he must turn to documentation, thereby employing the techniques (and, hopefully, the methodology) of the ethnohistorian.

Second, the documentary approach allows for detailed synchronic functional analysis at any point in time for which documentation is available (e.g., Caso 1963; López Austin 1961; Kirchoff 1954-55; Monzon 1946, 1949; Moreno 1931; Bandelier 1879; Katz 1966; Dahlgren 1954; Gorenstein 1966; Toscano 1946; Spores 1967). Ethnohistory cannot provide all of the detail that an ethnographer can observe or elicit from live informants, but it can and does provide knowledge of forms of behavior that because of their sensitive nature, or by intentional or unintended distortion or omission, might be concealed from the participant-observer. Legal and administrative records or personal correspondence relating to such matters as interpersonal or intergroup conflict, wealth, demography, crime, economic productivity, marriage and family patterns, or political function often provide depth and insight that may not be forthcoming in the field work situation. Divorce cases; investigations and trials for assault, murder, malfeasance, defamation, idolatry, blasphemy, and desertion; and suits over land and property afford access to information that may be extremely difficult to obtain from live informants. I have seen literally hundreds of such cases extending from 1540 to 1970 in the Archivo General de la Nación (AGN) and in the Archivo General del Estado de Oaxaca, and they are worth their weight in ethnographic gold. I find it curious that the armies of ethnologists, foreign and domestic, that have descended on Mexico in recent decades have made so little use of these resources.

Third, documentary ethnology can employ one of the most scientific methodologies in anthropology, for its basic data are highly susceptible to verification and authentication. An ethnologist studies a community and writes his report. Five or ten years later the community is restudied. The second ethnographer finds behavioral patterns that are substantially different from those presented in the original study. Have conditions changed? Did the first investigator present the true picture of life in the community, or was the second a more astute, more honest, more accurate observer? Is it a case of difference in training or methodology, laziness, too much dependence on the "man of action," limited sampling, dishonesty, fiction sounding better than fact, or is modernization to blame? Just what is, or was, the reality of life in Tepoztlán, Chan Kom, Tzintzuntzan, Mitla, or Zinacantan? We accept the ethnographer's word that he was objective and scientific. His conclusions seem reasonable in terms of our experience. But is that truly science? Can one go back and check, verify, and authenticate? Does reasonable mean reliable? Undoubtedly, the cultural reality will have changed. Or is it the theoretical orientation of the observer?

In this respect, documentary ethnology has certain advantages over conventional ethnology. As long as the documentation upon which a study is based is in existence, anyone can examine that exact same documentation, retrace the investigator's steps in observing the data for the purpose of drawing inferences from it, and reach his own conclusions about the reliability of those cultural inferences. In terms of replication and authentication and scientific verifiability, I believe that documentary ethnology is superior to observation-participation ethnography.

THE ANTHROPOLOGICAL USES
OF DOCUMENTARY SOURCES

Even in Mexico, with its enormous wealth of documentation, many anthropologists consider the ethnohistoric approach to be of limited or marginal ethnological utility. Large-scale, multidisciplinary projects are undertaken without consideration of documentation that could, in many cases, answer important questions and contribute vastly to resulting studies. Somehow, documents are seen as less desirable than observation-participation or "digging" in dealing with anthropological problems. There has been a general unwillingness to utilize documents, either ancient or modern, or to train students in their use.

Quite often, when documentation is employed, it is to provide a little historical background before diving into contemporary configurations or for putting the cap on an archeological sequence. Other practitioners favor the one-document approach, whereby one searches for or stumbles upon a single document relating to something of interest, say, sixteenth-century residence patterns as reflected in a single census taken in 1572 in a small town in Veracruz. The relevant portion of the document is utilized, usually without collation with any other sources for purposes of augmentation, authentication, or verification. The case is made to the satisfaction of the author and at least a segment of the anthropological community, and the patterns depicted become part of the literature (or lore) of anthropology. This is roughly equivalent to the "man of action," single-informant ethnographic technique, and suffers similar limitations. Another approach is to observe modern behavioral patterns in one area, say, Guatemala or Chiapas, then (in the absence of appropriate documentary data from the Maya area) to employ ethnohistoric materials relating to ancient custom from the Valley of Mexico (where modern patterns may be quite different) to demonstrate a patterned continuity. Surprisingly, many anthropologists willingly accept this procedure, which passes as ethnohistory.

A further tendency that is noted in the subfield of ethnohistory is the "history-as-served up" approach, where studies are limited to published formal chronicles, histories, reports, or ethnographies written as such for a variety of purposes. These sources are deservedly well known: Sahagún (1956, 1950-), Durán (1967), Díaz del Castillo (1967), Cortés (1969), Alva Ixtlilxochitl (1952), Las Casas (1966), Alvarado Tezozomoc (1944, 1949), Herrera (1947), Landa (1941), Zorita (1941), Beaumont (1932), Alegre (1956), Mendieta (1945), Pomar (1941), Clavijero (1958), Torquemada (1943), Códice Ramírez (1944), Motolinía (1950), Ximénez (1929-31), all important in their own right as ethnographic sources. The criticism that I would have is not that these are not valuable resources, but that too much reliance has been placed on them by too many scholars without consultation of archival resources. There has been an unwillingness to grapple with undistilled sources of a legal, administrative, or demographic nature that were not written as ethnographic or historical resources and to transform nonexplicit documentation into quite explicit ethnographic data.

There is on the part of anthropologists a Neanderthalish reluctance to spend long hours in archives or library or with head tucked into a microfilm reader. A kind of "code of the West" has evolved, whereby one must endure the anthropological passage rite of field work. In terms of anthropological "machismo," time spent in libraries or archives may not count as field work. In addition, there is a wearisome bias that still lingers in anthropological circles that documents have to do with history, and history and historiography are best left to historians, who for the most part are consumed with a desire to study unique and nonrepeating phenomena and with the arrangement of neat chronological sequences of events, and are given to writing about Great Men and Great Ideas. Anthropologists, on the other hand, are viewed as being devoted to a generalizing discipline that eschews interest in the unique, the nonreplicable, the nonrepeating, the simple sequences of events or the particular acts of individuals, in order to focus upon cultural processes and causation, so as to arrive at general principles regarding patterned human behavior and cultural development. The reader, probing the recesses of his own mind and interests can judge the accuracy, legitimacy, and justification of such views.

MEXICAN ETHNOHISTORICAL SOURCES AND PROCEDURES

In all honesty, I believe that insofar as Mexico is concerned, a great many problems being examined by anthropologists are susceptible to the documentary approach, and studies of problems that are not so directly amenable can be materially enhanced by a judicious use of written sources. These sources include formal ethnographic or historical descriptions written as such and documents that were created and utilized for some other purpose, legal, administrative, technical, or literary, and not intended to serve primarily ethnographic or historical functions. The ethnohistorian transforms the document into a raw resource by extracting its ethnographic content for utilization in anthropological studies.

It is well to focus on some of the problems of conducting ethnohistorical research in Mexico, with particular emphasis on archival research procedures and sources. Where does one turn for explanations, for answers to cultural queries, or, reflecting a current trend, how does one proceed to the testing of relevant hypotheses (i.e., statements of relationship among two or more variables) with documentary source materials?

There are first of all the printed sources: the conventional descriptive accounts; the published collections of documents; the catalogs, guides, and indexes for documentary archives and collections; and formal scholarly studies. Second, there are the American and European collections of documentation in original or copied forms.

It is virtually impossible to anticipate all of the problems of concern to anthropologists or to deal evenly with resources for all geographical areas of Mexico. Each area and each problem will require particular emphases, and the temporal spectrum to be considered will further serve to direct the investigator toward an appropriate orientation, set of documentation, and research regimen.

An initial response to questions of where one goes and what he does when he gets there is that this will depend on the nature of the problem, the time period to be covered, and the technical abilities of the investigator. Certain skills are required. The more skilled the individual, the more flexible his research design and the more adequate his exposure to the resources. The ability to read, interpret, and evaluate pictographic sources and conventional textual materials in modern and paleographic forms is an essential basic requirement. This is a basic technical skill that must be acquired, just as ethnographic interviewing, excavation and laboratory procedures, and theoretical orientations must be learned. One must prepare himself to read documentary sources and be able to utilize legal, fiscal, administrative, ecclesiastical, linguistic, and ritualistic sources as well as conventional ethnographic and historical sources, so as to draw the maximum of ethnographic data from masses of text that might otherwise be considered irrelevant.

It is highly advantageous to be familiar with legal and administrative formulary and customary procedures for filing claims or petitions; conducting investigations and civil and criminal litigation; census taking; administration; and implementation and enforcement of directives, rules, and regulations (Encinas 1945; Puga 1945; *Recopilación* 1943; Constitución Política de los Estados Unidos Mexicanos 1969; *Código Civil* 1970; *Código Agrario* 1969; Pérez Jiménez 1959; etc.)

A further essential is to have at least some understanding of governmental organization in colonial and republican times. Many ethnographic studies fail to consider these institutions and their possible effect on socioeconomic patterns. Further, the documentary ethnologist must have a knowledge of governmental function and hierarchy if he is to be aware of the context within which particular sets of documents were produced, or to understand why they were produced in the first place. In colonial times, the functions and relationships of viceroy, audiencia, *jueces,* the Inquisition, royal investigators, *alcaldes mayores, cabildos*, caciques, tribute collectors, and other public and private officers and institutions should be known, as should the laws, rules, and regulations under which they operated. There must, as well, be an awareness of the possible gap between ideal and actual practice.

In the national period, it is important to know and to be able to relate functions at national, state, and local levels and to be aware of changing function and relationship through time: (a) at the national level, the executive, legislative, and judicial branches and their complex bureaucratic web, particularly with reference to indigenous, agrarian, military, and economic affairs, communication, health and sanitation, welfare, education, and labor; (b) at the state level, the office of governor, the *secretario de despacho*, the attorney general's office, the legislature, offices or representatives of state and national bureaus or commissions, the military constabulary, state review courts, and the supreme court; (c) at the intermediate level, the *jefes políticos* (under the Porfiriato), the district judges, *agentes ministerios públicos*, and tax collectors; and (d) at the local level, the town council (*cabildo, ayuntamiento*) with its president, *regidores*, legal officers, secretaries, and police, the alcaldes, and various ancillary and auxilliary offices and institutions (Constitución Política de los Estados Unidos Mexicanos; Padgett 1966; *Código Civil* 1970; *Ley Federal de Reforma Agraria* 1971; *Ley Orgánica de Ayuntamientos . . . del Oaxaca* 1963; *Ley Orgánica de Ministerio Público* 1965; *Código Agrario* 1969, etc.).

At all levels there is a need to consider the interrelated functions of the Church, economic institutions, political parties, and other political, occupational, educational, and economic organizations and pressure groups. Knowledge of all these institutions can be obtained from documentary and printed sources, and, for the present period, from observation-investigation. The Mexican ethnohistorian should be thoroughly versed in Latin American historiography and have an understanding of evolving colonial and modern Mexican political, social, religious, and economic institutions. This can be derived from the works of Mendizabal, Haring, Gibson, Borah and Cook, Roys, Cosío Villegas, Bancroft, Orozco y Berra, etc. It is one thing to have a document from a particular place or time; it is quite something else to have an understanding of the institutional context in which the document originated.

No critical study of printed ethnohistorical sources can be attempted here, but brief commentary is in order. While it is a substantial undertaking, the Mexican ethnohistorian should know and be able to evaluate editions of the most useful primary and secondary sources. Printed materials that I have found to be of greatest utility can be grouped into six categories. Others might present other sources and arrange them differently, but the following tabulation (ample citations are provided in the references) provides something of a point of departure for the practicing or aspiring ethnohistorical researcher:

1. Conquerors, priests, investigator-observers, administrative reports, six-

teenth- and seventeenth-century Indian or mestizo writers: Díaz del Castillo (1967), Cortés (1969), Sahagún (1946, 1950-), Motolinía (1950), Landa (1941), Las Casas (1966), Alva Ixtlilxochitl (1952), Alvarado Tezozomoc (1944, 1949), Beaumont (1932), Chimalpahin (1965), Zorita (1941), Durán (1967), Relaciones of 1579-80 (Paso y Troncoso 1905-1906; *Revista Mexicana de Estudios Históricos* 1927-28; Conona Núñez 1958; Caso 1949; Bernal 1962b; Barlow 1945), *Códice Ramírez* (1944), Muñoz Camargo (1947), etc.

2. Early historical accounts and codifications: Herrera (1947), López de Gómara (1943), Oviedo y Valdés (1851-55), Mendieta (1945), Puga (1945), Encinas (1945), etc.

3. Compilations, collections, and later derivative ethnographic and historical works: Torquemada (1943), Clavijero (1958), Burgoa (1934), Alegre (1956), Veytia (1944), Ximénez (1929-31), Boturini (1746), Boban (1891), *Cartas de Indias* (1877), *Recopilación* (1943), Paso y Troncoso (1905-1906), *Colección de Documentos... Indias* (1864-84), *Colección de Documentos ... Ultramar* (1885-1932), García Icazbalceta (1858-66), Orozco y Berra (1960), García Pimentel (1904), Bandelier (1878, 1879), Jiménez Moreno (1959), Scholes and Adams (1938, 1955), Scholes and Roys (1948), Roys (1943), Barlow (1944, 1945a, 1945b, 1946a, 1946b, 1949), Miranda (1952), Bancroft (1886-88), Caso (1954, 1958, 1948-60, 1960b, 1963, 1966), Gibson (1952, 1959, 1964), Borah (1960), Cook and Borah (1960, 1963, 1968), Greenleaf (1962), Carrasco (1950, 1961, 1966), Padden (1966), Dahlgren (1954), León Portilla (1959, 1961, 1964, 1971), Mendizabal (1946), Paddock (1966b), López Sarrelangue (1965), the monumental *Diccionario Biográfico de Historia Antigua de Méjico* (1952), and frequent contributions in *Revista Mexicana de Estudios Antropológicos, Tlalocan, Anales del INAH, Investigaciones del INAH, Boletín del Archivo General de la Nación, Estudios de la Cultural Nahuatl*, and *Estudios de la Cultura Maya*.

4. Pictographic manuscripts: Glass (1964), Caso (1949, 1960a, 1960b, 1964), Caso and Smith (1966), Smith (1963, 1972), Burland (1966), Adelhofer (1963), Nicholson (1962), Robertson (1959, 1966), Dark (1958), Berlin (1947), Nuttall (1902), Nowotny (1961), Peñafiel (1900), León (1933), *Códice Osuna* (1947), Jiménez Moreno and Mateos Higuera (1940), Spores (1964), Leander (1967), Simons (1968), Dibble (1951), and Barrera Vásquez (1939).

5. Dictionaries, lexicons, and grammars in such major languages as Nahuatl (Molina 1966), Zapotec (Córdoba 1942), Mixtec (Jiménez Moreno 1962; Reyes 1890), Maya (Ciudad Real 1929), and Tarascan (Gilberti 1896,

1901). There is a major collection of early Mexican language materials in the Newberry Library, Chicago; also to be considered are the contributions of the modern linguists Swadesh, Barrera Vásquez, Roys, McQuown, Longacre, Johnson, Edmonson, and others in volume 5 of *Handbook of Middle American Indians: Linguistics.*

6. Bibliographical and critical sources and indices: León (1902-1908), García Icazbalceta (1858-66, 1954), Bernal (1962a), *Diccionario Biográfico de Historia Antigua de Méjico* (1952), Millares Carlo and Mantecón (1943), and Parra and Jiménez Moreno (1954).

The above is not intended to be a complete listing of printed sources of potential value to the ethnohistorian. Such a list would run into hundreds of items. These are only some of the more important works and sources. Careful library search, consultation with other scholars, and observation of references in existing studies will produce many additional sources of interest to scholars studying special problems or specific groups or areas.

ARCHIVAL RESOURCES

There are few shortcuts to learning how to find, read, interpret, and employ documentary resources in ethnographic research. It is desirable to sit at the feet of the masters of paleography and archival research: Agustín Millares Carlo, Silvio Zavala, France Scholes, Eleanor Adams, Ignacio Rubio Mañé, Woodrow Borah, Charles Gibson, Richard Greenleaf, Miguel Saldaña, Wigberto Jiménez Moreno, and others. Unfortunately, this is not always possible, and assuming that it is not, one turns to the printed word.

Abbreviated commentary on the holdings, organization, and ethnographic potentialities of archives in Mexico, the United States, and Europe can be found in the works of García Granados, Gibson (1964, pp. 609-34), León Portilla (1971, pp. 593-611), Colín (1967), and Spores (1967, pp. 245-47), among others. The most detailed general guide to Mexican archives is Carrera Stampa (1952). Bolton's guide (1913) to Mexican archives, and Chapman's guide (1919) to the Archivo General de Indias (AGI), Seville, are of marginal importance for Mexico in general but of primary importance for the northern, or Boderlands, area. Massively referenced studies based on archival sources by such scholars as Gibson, Borah, Greenleaf, Scholes and Roys, Miranda, Zavala, Chevalier, Bancroft, López Sarrelangue, and Tozzer (Landa 1941) provide excellent leads to pertinent documentation and give strong indication of the utility of certain sources and ramos. The utilization of colonial sources requires special skills, and substantial guidance to paleography is provided in Millares Carlo and Mantecón (1955).

Special indexes for specific archives or ramos have been published; among these are catalogs for the Ramo de Indios of AGN (Chávez Orozco 1951-53), Archivo Histórico de Hacienda (1940), now housed in the AGN, Archivo de Notarías, México (Millares Carlo and Mantecón 1946), the Muñoz Collection in Spain (Muñoz 1954), and *Indice de Documentos de Nueva España . . . Sevilla* (1928-31). Guides to the holdings in the AGN ramos of Hospital de Jesús, Tierras, and Reales Cédulas have been published serially in the *Boletín del Archivo General de la Nación*. Numerous bound guides and card catalogs are available in the various archives, including AGN, AGI, the Bancroft Library at the University of California, University of Texas Library, Library of Congress of the United States, University of New Mexico Library, Tulane University Library, Newberry Library of Chicago, British Museum Library, National Library of Paris, etc.

The single most valuable documentary collection for the Mexican ethnohistorian is the AGN, particularly the sections titled Tierras, Indios, Mercedes, Civil, Inquisición, General de Parte, Tributos, and Vínculos, all of which are of general utility for the colonial period. Of specialized (or more limited) use for the same period are the ramos of Historia, Clero Regular y Secular, Congregaciones, Reales Cédulas Duplicadas, Hacienda, and Provincias Internas. (Researchers interested in peoples of the Pacific, particularly the Philippines, will find unexpectedly rich ethnographic materials in the section Filipinas. Excellent materials for the western United States may be found in Provincias Internas and Historia.) There are abundant later works, most prominently presidential correspondence and materials relating to the Mexican Revolution, but the ethnographic potential of these sources has yet to be demonstrated.

Consultation of guides, catalogs, and published scholarly works points up the special strengths of the various sections of the AGN. In addition to the various printed indexes, complete or partial card or typescript catalogs are available for most ramos. The section designated Buscas contains archival correspondence, requests for copies of documents, and carbon copies of at least some of the documentation provided for patrons; this is a highly useful supplement to the indexes for tracing documentation pertaining to specific towns and individuals. The present director, Sr. Ignacio Rubio Mañé, has been most generous in his attitude toward utilization of the resources of the archive and has encouraged and facilitated the activities of both established and younger scholars. The archive honors reasonable requests for microfilm or typescript copies.

Four sections (ramos) of the AGI are most productive in ethnographic data for pre-Hispanic and colonial native cultures. These are Audiencia de México, Patronato, Justicia, and Escribanía de Cámara. Each section is capable of yielding ethnographic data of exceptional depth and detail. Sizable collections of photocopied materials from AGI may be found in such repositories as the United States Library of Congress, Bancroft Library, University of New Mexico Library, and Tulane University Library. Published collections of AGI materials are *Colección de Documentos . . . Indias* (1864-84), *Colección de Documentos . . . Ultramar* (1885-1932), Paso y Troncoso (1905-1906, 1940), and the García Icazbalceta and Scholes-Adams series.

In addition to the printed resources and original written and painted manuscript collections, there is housed in the library of the Museo Nacional de Antropología an important microfilm section containing several hundred reels of films of manuscript materials from state, local, and private archives. There are excellent materials pertaining to the colonial and republican periods for Chiapas, Guerrero, Oaxaca, Puebla, Tamaulipas, Tlaxcala, Veracruz, and Zacatecas. Although many of the manuscripts were selected and filmed quite randomly, patient consultation of these materials will yield abundant ethnographic data. Pictographic manuscript collections of the Museo have been carefully inventoried and described in detail by John Glass (1964).

Descriptions of the materials found in the various archives and most sections (ramos) within the depositories may be found in the guides mentioned and I shall not dwell on specific content. Let it suffice to say that all the archives and all the ramos contain potentially significant materials for ethnographic research, and that consultation of the guides and indexes, practical utilization of the materials, and familiarity with the many significant studies that have emerged from utilization of these materials will suggest where particular problems can best be researched. Consultation with experienced hands is essential if adequate use of archives is to be made.

Printed collections of documents containing materials pertinent to anthropological research are many and varied. Among what I have found to be the more important colonial sources are *Colección de Documentos . . . Indias* (1864-84) (together with Schäfer's two-volume guide [1946-]), *Colección de Documentos . . . Ultramar* (1885-1932), Paso y Troncoso (1905-1906, 1940), and the series edited by Scholes and Adams. For later periods, collections of reports in the INAH, the library of the Museo Nacional de Antropología, and the archives of the Departamento de Asuntos Agrarios have been of great value to my own studies. Such materials as are housed in the notary, military, municipal, and ecclesiastical archives and in the Biblioteca Nacional in Mexico City are generally of less importance to the ethnohistorian concerned with conventional anthropological problems but may hold valuable resources for certain kinds of research.

Unfortunately, there are few guides to state and local archives of the type devised by Borah for Oaxaca. Until such guides and indexes become available, the investigator is faced with the requirement of making local inquiry and largely trial-and-error exploration. I have found the general archive of the state of Oaxaca to be one of the most abundant sources of ethnographic fact that I have ever encountered, and I believe that patience and persistence in dealing with these materials will produce more anthropological data than would be possible with any other set of methods. State archives in other areas of Mexico should have the same potential.

If I had any single piece of advice for the documentary ethnologist interested primarily in twentieth-century cultural patterns, it would be to devote great effort to gaining access to state, district (where appropriate), and municipal archives in order to glean the abundant ethnographic material. There are often aggravating delays and impediments, but these can usually be overcome through patient persistence and expressions of good will, and the normally abundant returns make the expenditure of effort quite worthwhile. Additional twentieth-century materials can be obtained from microfilm collections in the Museo Nacional de Antropología. Nineteenth-century sources can be located in general state and municipal archives and in state and municipal criminal, civil, fiscal, property, and notarial records sections at the AGN, in the Museo microfilm collection, in the archives of such departments as Agrarian Affairs, Indigenous Affairs, Education, and the Interior, and in congressional and Supreme Court records.

The principal repositories for documentation of the colonial period are found in the AGN (including Hacienda and Hospital de Jesús), in the library of the National Museum of Anthropology (microfilm and pictographic manuscripts), in municipal or cabildo archives in larger centers like Mexico City, Guadalajara, Puebla, Oaxaca, Veracruz, and Mérida, in Church archives in the larger centers, in private collections (Castañeda Guzmán in Oaxaca, Condumex in Mexico City, etc.), and in the large foreign collections (on film or original) of the AGI, Muñoz Collection, Vatican, British Museum, National Library of Paris, United States Library of Congress, Bancroft Library, Newberry Library, University of Texas Library, University of New Mexico Li-

brary, Brigham Young University Library, and Tulane University Library.
The employment of documentary sources contained in these collections
together with the prudent utilization of abundant primary and secondary
materials in printed form can, in an appropriate theoretical and methodological context, be applied to a nearly endless variety of anthropological problems. The ethnohistorical approach has already produced substantial returns
in Mexican anthropology, but I believe that future contributions utilizing a
more conscious and systematic methodology will produce ever better ethnological studies which will provide models for application not only to Mexico
but to Spanish America in general and to all areas of the world where any
substantial corpus of ethnohistorical documentation exists.

NOTE

1. I would like to acknowledge research support from the Vanderbilt University
Center for Latin American Studies, the Ford Foundation, and the National Science
Foundation.

REFERENCES

Acosta, Joseph de
    1940. *Historia Natural y Moral de las Indias.* Ed. Edmundo O'Gorman.
    Mexico.
Actas de Cabildo de la Ciudad de México.
    1889-1916. 54 vols. Mexico.
Adelhofer, Otto
    1963. *Codex Vindobonensis Mexicanus I.* Graz, Austria.
Alegre, Francisco Javier
    1956. *Historia de la Compañía de Jesús en Nueva España.* Rome.
Alva Ixtlilxochitl, Fernando de
    1952. *Obras Históricas.* 2 vols. Mexico.
Alvarado Tezozomoc, Hernando (Fernando)
    1944. *Crónica Méxicana.* Mexico.
    1949. *Crónica Mexicayotl.* Mexico.

Anales de Cuauhtitlán
1945. *Códice Chimalpopoca*. Mexico.
Anales de Tlatelolco
1948. Ed. Salvador Toscano, Heinrich Berlin, and Robert H. Barlow. Mexico.
Arana Osnaya, E.
1961. El Idioma de los Señores de Tepozcolula. *Anales del Instituto Nacional de Antropología e Historia* 13:217-30.
Aubin, J. M.
1893. *Histoire de la Nation Mexicaine*. Paris.
Bancroft, H. H.
1886-88. *History of Mexico*. 6 vols. San Francisco.
Bandelier, Adolph E.
1878. On the Distribution and Tenure of Lands, and the Customs with Respect to Inheritance, Among the Ancient Mexicans. *Eleventh Annual Report of the Peabody Museum of Archaeology and Ethnology*, pp. 385-448.
1879. On the Social Organization and Mode of Government of the Ancient Mexicans. *Twelfth Annual Report of the Trustees of the Peabody Museum of American Archaeology and Ethnology*, pp. 557-699.
Barlow, Robert
1944. Los Caciques Coloniales de Tlatelolco en un Documento de 1561. *Memorias de la Academia Mexicana de la Historia* 3:552-56.
1945a. La Crónica "X." *Revista Mexicana de Estudios Antropológicos* 7:65-87.
1945b. Dos Relaciones Antiguas del Pueblo de Cuilapa, Estado de Oaxaca. *Tlalocan* 2:18-26.
1947-48. La Fundación de la Triple Alianza (1427-1433). *Anales del Instituto Nacional de Antropología e Historia* 3:147-55.
1946. Los Caciques de Tlatelolco en el Códice Cozcatzin. *Memorias de la Academia Mexicana da la Historia* 5:416-21.
1949. *The Extent of the Empire of the Culhau Mexico*. Ibero-Americana 28.
Barrera Vásquez, Alfredo
1939. El Códice Pérez. *Revista Mexicana de Estudios Antropológicos* 3, no. 1:69-83.
Barrera Vásquez, Alfredo and S. G. Morley
1949. *The Maya Chronicles*. Carnegie Institution of Washington. Pub. 585, contrib. 48.
Barrera Vásquez, A., and S. Rendón, trs. and eds.
1948. *El Libro de los Libros de Chilam Balam*. Mexico.
Beals, R. L.
1932. *The Comparative Ethnology of Northern Mexico before 1750*. Ibero-Americana 2.

Beaumont, Pablo
1932. *Crónica de Michoacán.* 3 vols. Mexico.
Bernal, Ignacio, ed.
1962a. *Bibliografía de Arqueología y Etnografía Mesoamérica y Norte de México, 1514-1960.* Mexico.
1962b. Relación de Guautla. *Tlalocan* 4:3-16. Berlin, H.
1947. *Fragmentos Desconocidos del Códice de Yanhuitlán.* Mexico.
Berlin, H., and R. H. Barlow, eds.
1948. *Anales de Tlatelolco y Códice de Tlatelolco.* Mexico.
Boban, Eugène
1891. *Documents pour servir à l'Histoire du Mexique.* 2 vols. and Atlas. Paris.
Bolton, H. E.
1913. *Guide to Materials for the History of the United States in the Principal Archives of Mexico.* Carnegie Institution of Washington. Pub. 163.
Borah, W. W.
1960. Sources and Possibilities for the Reconstruction of the Demographic Process of the Mixteca Alta, 1519-1895. *Revista Mexicana de Estudios Antropológicos* 16:159-71.
Borah, Woodrow, and Sherburne F. Cook
1960. *The Population of Central Mexico in 1548: An Analysis of the Suma de Visitas de Pueblos.* Ibero-Americana 43.
Boturini Benaduci, Lorenzo
1746. *Catálogo del Museo Histórico Indiano del Caballero Lorenzo Boturini Benaduci.* Madrid.
Burland, C.A.
1966. *Codex Laud.* Graz, Austria.
Burgoa, Fray F. de
1934. *Geografía Descripción.* 2 vols. Mexico.
Carrasco, Pedro
1950. *Los Otomíes.* Publicaciones del Instituto de Historia, 1st ser. no. 15.
1961. El Barrio y la Regulación del Matrimonio en un Pueblo del Valle de México en el Siglo XVI. *Revista Mexicana de Estudios Antropológicos* 17:7-26.
1966. Algunos Términos de Parentesco en el Nahuatl Clásico. *Estudios de Cultura Nahuatl,* no. 4.
Carrera Stampa, Manuel
1952. *Archivalia Mexicana.* Mexico.
Cartas de Indias
1877. Madrid.
Caso, Alfonso
1949. El Mapa de Teozacoalco. *Cuadernos Americanos* 8:145-81.

1954. *Instituciones Indígenas Precortesianas: Métodos y Resultados de la Política Indigenista de México.* Memorias del Instituto Nacional Indigenista, 4. Mexico.

1957. Lienzo de Yolotepec. *Memorias de el Colegio Nacional* 3:41-55.

1958-60. La Tenencia de la Tierra entre los Antiguos Mexicanos. *Memoria de el Colegio Nacional* 4:29-54.

1960a. *Interpretación del Códice Bodley 2858.* Mexico.

1960b. The Historical Value of the Mixtec Codices. *Boletín de Estudios Oaxaqueños,* no. 16.

1963. Land Tenure among the Ancient Mexicans. Tr. Charles Wicke. *American Anthropologist* 65:861-78.

1964. *Interpretation of the Codex Selden 3135 (A.2).* Mexico.

1966. The Lords of Yanhuitlan. In *Ancient Oaxaca,* ed. John Paddock. Stanford. Pp. 313-335.

Caso, Alfonso, and M. E. Smith

1966. *Codex Colombino.* Mexico.

Catálogo de la Colección de Don Juan Bautista Muñoz. 2 vols. Madrid.

Chamberlain, Robert S.

1948. *The Conquest and Colonization of Yucatan,* 1517-1550. Carnegie Institution of Washington. Pub. 582.

Chapman, Charles E.

1919. *Catalogue of Materials in the Archivo General de Indias for the History of the Pacific Coast and American Southwest.* Berkeley.

Charlton, Thomas H.

1969. Ethnohistory and Archaeology: Post-Conquest Aztec Sites. *American Antiquity* 34: 286-94.

Chávez Orozco, L.

1944. *Manifestations of Democracy among Mexican Indians during the Colonial Period.* Washington.

1951-53. *Indice del Ramo de Indios del Archivo General de la Nación.* 2 vols. Mexico.

Chimalpahin Cuauhtlehuanitzin, Francisco de

1965. *Relaciones Originales de Chalco Amaquemecan.* Ed. S. Rendón. Mexico.

Ciudad Real, Antonio

1929. *Diccionario de Motul, Maya-Español.* Merida.

Clavijero, F. J.

1958. *Historia Antigua de México.* 4 vols. Mexico.

Codex Mendoza

1938. Ed. James Cooper Clark. 3 vols. London.

Códice Chimalpopoca.

1945. *Anales de Cuauhtitlan y Leyenda de los Soles.* Trans. Primo Feliciano Velázquez. Mexico.

Códice Osuna
1947. Mexico.
Códice Ramírez
1944. Mexico.
Código Agrario
1969. 18th ed. Mexico.
Código Civil
1970. 25th ed. Mexico.
Colección de Documentos Inéditos Relativos al Descubrimiento, Conquista y Organización de las Antiguas Posesiones Españolas de América y Oceanía Sacados de los Archivos del Reino, y muy Especialmente del de Indias. 1864-84. 42 vols. Madrid.
Colección de Documentos Inéditos Relativos al Descubrimiento, Conquista y Organización de las Antiguas Posesiones Españolas de Ultramar. 1885-1932. 25 vols. Madrid.
Colín, Mario, ed.
1967. *Indice de Documentos Relativos a los Pueblos del Estado de México: Ramo de Mercedes del Archivo General de la Nación.* Mexico.
Constitución Política del Estado Libre y Soberano de Oaxaca.
1968. Oaxaca.
Constitución Política de los Estados Unidos Mexicanos.
1969. Mexico.
Cook, Sherburne F., and Woodrow Borah
1960. *The Indian Population of Central Mexico 1531-1610.* Ibero-Americana 44.
1963. *The Aboriginal Population of Central Mexico on the Eve of the Spanish Conquest.* Ibero-Americana 45.
1968. *The Population of the Mixteca Alta 1520-1960.* Ibero-Americana 50.
Córdoba, Juan de
1942. *Vocabulario Castellano-Zapoteca.* Ed. W. Jiménez Moreno. Mexico.
Corona Nuñez, José, ed.
1958. *Papeles de la Nueva España: Relaciones Geográficas de la Diocesis de Michoacán 1579-1580.* 2 vols. Guadalajara.
Cortés, Fernando
1969. *Cartas de Relación.* Mexico.
Crónica de Michoacán (See Beaumont 1932)
Dahlgren, Barbro
1954. *La Mixteca.* Mexico.
Dark, P.
1958. *Mixtec Ethnohistory.* Oxford.
Díaz del Castillo, Bernal
1967. *Historia Verdadera de la Conquista de la Nueva España.* Mexico.
Dibble, Charles
1951. *Códice Xolotl.* Mexico.

Diccionario Biográfico de Historia Antigua de Méjico. Ed. Rafael García. 1952. Granados. Mexico.

Durán, Diego
1967. *Historia de las Indias de Nueva España y Islas de Tierra Firme.* 2 vols. Mexico.

Encinas, Diego de
1945. *Cedulario Indiano.* 4 vols. Madrid.

Estudios de Cultura Nahuatl.
1959- Mexico.

Gamio, Manuel
1922. *La Población del Valle de Teotihuacan.* 3 vols. Mexico.

García Granados, Rafael
1952-53. *Diccionario Biográfico de Historia Antigua de Méjico.* 3 vols. Publicaciones del Instituto de Historia. 1st ser., no. 23. Mexico.

García Icazbalceta, Joaquín
1954. *Bibliografía Mexicana del Siglo XVI.* Ed. Agustín Millares Carlo. Mexico.
1858-66. *Colección de Documentos para la Historia de México.* 2 vols. Mexico.

García Pimentel, Luis, ed.
1904. *Relación de los Obispados de Tlaxcala, Michoacán, Oaxaca y Otros Lugares en el Siglo XVI.* Mexico.

Gibson, Charles
1952. *Tlaxcala in the Sixteenth Century.* New Haven.
1959. El Sistema de Gobierno Indígena de Tlaxcala, México, en el Siglo XVI. *América Indígena* 10: 86-90.
1964. *The Aztecs under Spanish Rule.* Stanford.

Gilberti, M.
1896. *Arte de la Lengua Tarasca ó de Michoacán.* Mexico.
1901. *Diccionario de la Lengua Tarasca ó de Michoacán.* Mexico.

Glass, John B.
1964. *Catálogo de la Colección de Códices: Museo Nacional de Antropología.* Mexico.

Gómez de Cervantes, Gonzalo
1944. *La Vida Económica y Social de Nueva España al Finalizar el Siglo XVI.* Mexico.

Gorenstein, Shirley
1966. The Differential Development of New World Empires. *Revista Mexicana de Estudios Antropológicos* 20:41-67.

Greenleaf, Richard E.
1962. *Zumárraga and the Mexican Inquisition, 1536-1543.* Washington.

Guía del Archivo Histórico de Hacienda.
1940. Mexico.

Handbook of Middle American Indians.
1964-. Ed. Robert Wauchope. Austin.

Haring, Clarence, H.
1947. *The Spanish Empire in America.* New York.

Herrera, Antonio de
1947. *Historia General de los Hechos de los Castellanos en las Islas y Tierra Firme del Mar Océano.* 15 vols. Madrid.

Historia Tolteca-Chichimeca.
1947. Ed. Heinrich Berlin, Silvia Rendón, Paul Kirchoff, and Salvador Toscano. Mexico.

Indice de Documentos de Nueva España Existentes en el Archivo de Indias de Sevilla.
1928-31. 4 vols. Mexico.

Indice del Ramo de Indios del Archivo General de la Nación.
1951-53. Ed. Luis Chávez Orozco. 2 vols. Mexico.

Ixtlilxochitl, Fernando de Alva
1965. *Obras Históricas.* 2 vols. Mexico.

Jiménez Moreno, Wigberto
1941. Tula y los Toltecas Según las Fuentes Históricas. *Revista Mexicana de Estudios Antropológicos* 5: 79-83.
1954-55. Síntesis de la Historia Precolonial del Valle de México. *Revista Mexicana de Estudios Antropológicos* 14:219-36.
1959. Síntesis de la Historia Pretolteca de Mesoamérica. In *Esplendor del México Antiguo.* 2 vols. Mexico. 2:1019-1108.
1962. *Vocabulario en Lengua Mixteca por Fray Francisco de Alvarado.* Mexico.
1966. Mesoamerica Before the Toltecs. In *Ancient Oaxaca,* ed. John Paddock. Stanford. Pp. 1-82.

Jiménez Moreno, Wigberto, and Salvador Mateos Higuera
1940. *Códice de Yanhuitlan.* Mexico.

Katz, Friedrich
1966. *Situación Social y Económica de los Aztecas Durante los Siglos XV y XVI.* Mexico.

Kirchhoff, Paul
1954-55. Land Tenure in Ancient Mexico, a Preliminary Sketch. *Revista Mexicana de Estudios Antropológicos* 14: 351-61.

Kubler, G.
1942. Population Movements in Mexico, 1520-1600. *Hispanic American Historical Review* 22: 606-43.

Landa, Diego
1941. *Landa's Relación de las Cosas de Yucatán.* Ed. A. M. Tozzer. Papers of the Peabody Museum 18.

Las Casas, Bartolomé
1966. *Los Indios de México y Nueva España: Antología.* Mexico.

Leander, Brigitta
1967. *Códice de Otlazapan.* INAH Serie Investigaciones 13.

León, N.

1902-1908. Bibliografía Mexicana del Siglo XVIII. *Boletín del Instituto Bibliográfico Mexicano*, nos. 1, 4, 5, 7, 8, 10.

1933. *Códice Sierra*. Mexico.

León Portilla, Miguel

1959. *La Filosofía Nahuatl*. Mexico.

1961. *Los Antiguos Mexicanos a través de Sus Crónicas y Cantares*. Mexico.

1964. *Las Literaturas Precolombinas de México*. Mexico.

1971. *De Teotihuacán a los Aztecas*. Mexico.

Ley Federal de Reforma Agraria.

1971. Mexico.

Ley Orgánica de Ayuntamientos del Estado Libre y Soberano de Oaxaca.

1963. Oaxaca.

Libro de las Tasaciones de Pueblos de la Nueva España, Siglo XVI.

1952. Mexico.

López Austin, Alfredo

1961. *La Constitución Real de México-Tenochtitlan*. Mexico.

López Sarrelangue, Delfina E.

1965. *La Nobleza Indígena de Pátzcuaro en la Epoca Virreinal*. Mexico.

McQuown, N.

1967. History of Studies in Middle American Linguistics. *Handbook of Middle American Indians*. Austin. Vol. 5, *Linguistics*, Pp. 3-7.

Martínez Gracida, M.

1883. *Colección de "Cuadros Sinópticos" de los Pueblos, Haciendas, y Ranchos del Estado Libre y Soberano de Oaxaca*. Oaxaca.

Mendieta, Gerónimo de

1945. *Historia Eclesiástica Indiana*. 4 vols. Mexico.

Mendizabal, Miguel O. de

1946. *Obras Completas*. 6 vols. Mexico.

Millares Carlo, Agustín, and José I. Mantecón

1943. *Ensayo de una Bibliografía de Bibliografías Mexicanas*. Mexico.

1946. *Indice y Extractos de los Protocolos del Archivo de Notarías de México, D.F.* Mexico.

1955. *Album de Paleografía Hispanoamericana de los Siglos XVI y XVII.* 3 vols. Mexico.

Miranda, José

1952. *El Tributo Indígena en la Nueva España Durante el Siglo XVI*. Mexico.

Molina, Alonso de

1966. *Vocabulario Nahuatl-Castellano, Castellano-Nahuatl*. Mexico.

Monzón, Arturo

1946. La Organización Social de los Aztecas. In *México Prehispánico*, ed. J. Vivo. Mexico. Pp. 791-803.

1949. *El Calpulli en la Organización Social de los Tenochca*. Mexico.

Moreno, Daniel
    1970. *Los Partidos Políticos del México Contemporáneo (1926-1970).*
    Mexico.
Moreno, Manuel M.
    1931. *La Organización Política y Social de los Aztecas.* Mexico.
    1946. La Organización Jurídica y de los Tribunales. In *México Prehis-
    pánico,* ed. J. Vivo. Mexico. Pp. 765-776.
Motolinía (Toribio de Benavente)
    1950. *History of the Indians of New Spain.* Ed. and tr. Elizabeth Foster.
    Berkeley.
    1969. *Historia de los Indios de la Nueva España.* Mexico.
Muñoz, Juan B.
    1954. *Catálogo de la Colección de Don Juan Bautista Muñoz.* Madrid.
Muñoz Camargo, Diego
    1947. *Historia de Tlaxcala.* Mexico.
Nicholson, H. B.
    1962. The Mesoamerican Pictorial Manuscripts: Research, Past and Pres-
    ent. In *Proceedings of the 34th International Congress of Americanists.*
    Vienna. Pp. 199-215.
    1967. A "Royal Headband" of the Tlaxcalteca. *Revista Mexicana de Es-
    tudios Antropológicos* 21:71-106.
Nowotny, K.
    1961. *Codices Becker I/II.* Graz, Austria.
Nuttall, Zelia
    1902. *Codex Nuttall.* Cambridge.
Orozco y Berra, Manuel
    1960. *Historia Antigua y de la Conquista de México.* 4 vols. Mexico.
Oviedo y Valdés, Gonzalo Fernández de
    1851-55. *Historia General y Natural de las Indias, Islas y Tierra Firme del
    Mar Océano.* 4 vols. Madrid.
Padden, Robert
    1966. *The Hummingbird and the Hawk.* Columbus.
Paddock, John, ed.
    1966a. *Ancient Oaxaca.* Stanford.
    1966b. Mixtec Ethnohistory and Monte Alban V. In *Ancient Oaxaca,* ed.
    John Paddock. Stanford. Pp. 367-85.
Padgett, L. V.
    1966. *The Mexican Political System.* Boston.
Parra, M. G., and W. Jiménez Moreno
    1954. *Bibliografía Indigenista de México y Centroamérica: 1850-1950.*
    Mexico.
Paso y Troncoso, F. del, ed.
    1905-1906. *Papeles de Nueva España.* 2d ser. Vols. 1, 3-7. Madrid.
    1939-42. *Epistolario de Nueva España, 1505-1818.* 16 vols. Mexico.

Peñafiel, Antonio
1900. *Códice Mixteco: Lienzo de Zacatepec.* Mexico.
Pérez Jiménez
1959. *Las Constituciones del Estado de Oaxaca.* Oaxaca.
Pomar, Juan B.
1941. *Relación de Tezcoco.* Mexico.
Prescott, William H.
1873. *History of the Conquest of Mexico.* 3 vols. Philadelphia.
Proceso Inquisitorial del Cacique de Tetzcoco.
1910. Mexico.
Procesos de Indios Idólatras y Hechiceros.
1912. Mexico.
Puga, V. de
1945. *Provisiones Cédulas Instrucciones para el Gobierno de la Nueva España.* Madrid.
Radin, Paul
1920. *The Sources and Authenticity of the History of the Ancient Mexicans.* University of Calif. Publications in American Archaeology and Ethnology, no. 17.
Ramírez, José F.
1944. *Códice Ramírez.* Mexico.
Recopilación de Leyes de los Reynos de las Indias.
1943. 3 vols. Madrid.
Relación de Michoacán
1913. Morelia.
Revista Mexicana de Estudios Históricos.
1927-28. Vols. 1-2.
Reyes, Antonio
1889. *Arte en Lengua Mixteca.* Mexico.
Robertson, Donald
1959. *Mexican Manuscript Painting of the Early Colonial Period.* New Haven.
1966. The Mixtec Religious Manuscripts. In *Ancient Oaxaca,* ed. John Paddock. Stanford. Pp. 298-312.
Roys, R. L.
1943. *The Indian Background of Colonial Yucatan.* Washington.
Sahagún, Bernardino de
1950-. *General History of the Things of New Spain. Florentine Codex.* Ed. Arthur J. O. Anderson and Charles E. Dibble. 13 pts. Santa Fe.
1956. *Historia General de las Cosas de Nueva España.* 4 vols. Mexico.
Shäfer, Ernst
1946-. *Indice de la Colección de Documentos Inéditos de Indias.* Madrid.
Scholes, F. V.
1952. Franciscan Missionary Scholars in Colonial Central America. *The Americas* 8:391-416.

Scholes, F. V., and E. B. Adams, eds.
1938. *Don Diego Quijada, Alcalde Mayor de Yucatán, 1561-1565.* Mexico. 2 vols.
1955-. *Documentos para la Historia de México Colonial.* Mexico. 7 vols.

Scholes, F. V., and R. L. Roys
1948. *The Maya Chontal Indians of Acalan-Tixchel: A Contribution to the History and Ethnography of the Yucatan Peninsula.* Washington.

Simons, Bente
1968. *Los Mapas de Cuauhtinchan y la Historia Tolteca-Chichimeca.* INAH Serie Investigaciones 15.

Smith, Mary
1963. The Codex Colombino: A Document of the South Coast of Oaxaca. *Tlalocan* 4:276-88.
1972. *Mixtec Place Signs and Maps.* Norman.

Spores, Ronald
1964. The Genealogy of Tlazultepec: A Sixteenth Century Mixtec Manuscript. *Southwestern Journal of Anthropology* 20:15-31.
1967. *The Mixtec Kings and Their People.* Norman.
1969. "Settlement, Farming Technology, and Environment in the Nochixtlan Valley." *Science* 166:557-69.

Swadesh, Morris
1967. Lexicostatistic Classification. *Handbook of Middle American Indians.* Vol. 5, *Linguistics.* Austin. Pp. 79-115.

Testamento de María Alonso, India de Tlatelolco.
1946. *Memorias de la Academia Mexicana de la Historia* 5:198-204.

Torquemada, Juan de
1943. *Monarquía Indiana.* Mexico.

Toscano, Salvador
1946. La Organización Social de los Aztecas. In *México Prehispánico.* Mexico. Pp. 777-90.

Vetancurt, Augustín
1698. *Teatro Mexicano.* 2 vols. Mexico.

Veytia, Mariano
1944. *Historia Antigua de México.* Mexico.

Villa-Señor y Sánchez, Joseph A.
1746-48. *Teatro Americano.* 2 vols. Mexico.

Ximénez, Francisco
1929-31. *Historia de la Provincia de San Vicente de Chiapa y Guatemala.* 3 vols. Guatemala.

Zorita, Alonso de
1941. *Breve Relación de los Señores de la Nueva España.* Mexico.

B. Alternative Views in History: Historical Statistics and Oral History
by James W. Wilkie

Although this section is intended to provide a pragmatic guide to new research techniques developed for the study of Mexico rather than to offer a discussion of theoretical issues, it is important to take the latter into account in order to suggest the nature of inquiry. In several senses, we are dealing with what may be termed alternative views of history. Quantitative analysis (expressed in terms of descriptive time-series data) may differ from oral history's qualitative views as well as provide hypotheses for discussion in interviews. (Oral history here is defined as the scholar's tape recording of his interviews with persons who can shed light on past events, and discussion is developed below at some length because relatively little has been written about methods and intellectual rights in oral history materials.) Further, both techniques treat matters of probability and reliability as well as independent analysis in which scholarly definition influences the outcome of field research.

A basic supposition in the study is that while there is no "truth" to be found, the scholar attempts (as with traditional methods) to approach and to reconstruct historical events by comparing divergence and convergence of his research materials, whether he examines historical statistics and oral history separately or in relation to each other. In any case, perhaps investigators should be as concerned with presenting alternative views as they are with developing consistent themes.[1]

HISTORICAL STATISTICS

Discussion of historical statistics here is limited to the development of time-series data for use as threads which permit historical interpretation or reinterpretation.[2] Essentially this is a descriptive process in which raw data (for example, statistics on personnel employed in industry) are compiled, reorganized, and adjusted to arrive at comparability and/or to explain limitations for yearly or benchmark time periods.[3] Once the series has been completed, it can be related to other historical events or time series in order to confirm or revise standard views of events, especially as they may influence politics. Even if the data do not lead to a new interpretation or raise new questions, they may help to confirm what scholars have suspected but have been unable to prove in their interpretive essays. In this manner time-series data may be of great value in providing themes for the understanding of forces at work over long periods of time.

In the use of historical statistics, one advantage, is that if full statistics are published (as is desirable), other scholars may rework the same data for their own interests and interpretations.[4] The use of historical statistics, however, can lead historians into the problems of social science wherein debates over methodology may well overshadow discussion of content and message unrelated to the data per se. Unfortunately, such debates often center on the question of which method is "right" or "wrong" rather than how alternative views may be developed. In short, as Professor Clark W. Reynolds has noted, debates over the appropriateness of the data and relevant weights can "provide hours of activity for insomniac social scientists."[5]

Much of the latter problem can be overcome, however, by using descriptive rather than inductive statistics which involve analysis of variance, covariance, correlation, regression, and factor analysis.[6] Given the limitations and meaning of the data, the use of such inductive techniques frequently reflects "overkill" with regard to the making and interpretation of hypotheses. Nevertheless, depending upon the particular case, such methods may be very useful; and the interested scholar can keep abreast of general methodological developments, projects, and bibliography throughout the world by subscribing to the *Historical Methods Newsletter: Quantitative Analysis of Social, Economic, and Political Development*, a periodical published by the Department of History at the University of Pittsburgh since 1967.[7] In Mexico, investigators may wish to consult with the Dirección General de Muestreo (Artículo 123 #88, México 1, D.F.) about its research based upon sampling techniques.[8]

Since raw data are generated by almost every Mexican agency, there are nearly limitless opportunities for scholarly development of historical statistics. Usually this can be undertaken by visiting the library of any of the country's numerous centralized and decentralized agencies in order to ascertain the kind of statistics reported in published and unpublished reports. Since in many of these agencies few people use the library, the librarian may be grateful for the attention which is finally given to his long efforts in building a small collection.[9]

Access to unpublished materials may be difficult, since a bureaucrat who does not have a confidential report locked in his desk lacks status and importance. Fortunately, however, the researcher will find most Mexican agencies to be much more open and ready to provide information than any national or international agency in the United States. The main problem may lie in making contacts directly with the agency director or his deputy in order to bypass lower-level functionaries. Once top functionaries agree to help, doors may remain open for many years because, regardless of changes in management, lower-echelon bureaucrats tend to remain in office, continuing routinely to carry out orders to be of assistance.

Some agencies are very careful about the data which they make available; for example, figures on the actual expenditures of the decentralized agencies are available only for the period since 1965. It is notable that in the meantime, detailed data on agricultural credit have become difficult to obtain and reports of the Ejido Bank have not been published since 1962.[10] Because presidents since Adolfo López Mateos have pledged support to poor communal landholders who have received plots under the aegis of the official party, a dearth of recent disaggregated information may mean that the government does not want to reveal how little funding has been made available (or how much has been loaned in the richer and more productive states), the Ejido Bank has been mismanaged, and/or repayment of loans to the bank has not been of the expected magnitude.

One may speculate also about problematic statistics which are available. Time-series figures for questionable data are important in that they offer inherently interesting hypotheses precisely because of their apparent manipulation or inadequacy (as with election and unemployment statistics, respectively). Such data may be analyzed to suggest questions concerning state policy and national development.[11]

Basic historical time-series remain to be constructed for almost all types of government and private activities. Figures may be reorganized for independent analysis from data conveniently provided by Mexico's Dirección General de Estadística (Balderas 71, México 1, D.F.). The best statistical collections are located at the aforementioned agency as well as the libraries of the Banco de México (Calle Condesa 6); Nacional Financiera (Isabel la Católica 51); Secretaría de Hacienda y Crédito Público (El Salvador 47); and Dirección General de Economía Agrícola (Aquiles Serdán 28). In addition, these downtown (postal zone 1) agencies publish innumerable reports and statistical yearbooks.[12]

To keep up with the published data, one should not only receive the yearly *Memorias* of the above agencies but also obtain subscriptions (free) to Nacional Financiera's weekly *El Mercado de Valores* as well as to the Banco Nacional de Comercio Exterior's monthly *Comercio Exterior* (two major publications which have broad social and economic interests not revealed in their titles). Important general and specific guides to available data include the Dirección General de Estadística's *Catálogo General de las Estadísticas Nacionales* (1960), with a separate *Indice* (1960); *Inventario de Estadísticas Nacionales* (1966); and *Anuario Estadístico*, published in alternate years with the *Compendio Estadístico*. Other major guides include the Banco de México's *Informe Anual* and the Inter-American Statistical Institute's *Monthly List of Publications Received*, available (free) from its office in the Pan American Union (Library, IASA, 1725 Eye Street, N.W., Washington, D.C. 20006).[13]

For personal contacts with the Mexican scholarly world, visiting investigators may wish to work through El Colegio de México (Guanajuato 125, Mexico 7, D.F.), which is involved in a broad spectrum of statistical research. El Colegio's *Demografía y Economía*, for example, is a periodical which deals with some statistical materials for recent Mexican history.[14]

Among the above listing of publications which deal with historical statistics, the reader will find Mexican printed documents which deal with the entire range of public and private activity. Though these documents often provide the rationale for change in policy and justify the use of new kinds of data, generally they do not explicitly relate time-series to the historical process. Oral history provides one method for making such a linkage.

ORAL HISTORY

With regard to theoretical aspects of presenting alternative views in Mexico's twentieth-century development, I have attempted at times to link historical statistics to oral history. This has been done by questioning Mexican leaders about patterns in data for periods of their responsibility in public positions. Often these alternative views have not been accepted in my own statistical interpretations, but they stand as participant counterpoint or counterbalance to scholarly investigation; and some tape-recorded interviews have been published in James W. Wilkie and Edna Monzón de Wilkie's *México Visto en el Siglo XX; Entrevistas de Historia Oral: Ramón Beteta, Marte R. Gómez, Manuel Gómez Morín, Vicente Lombardo Toledano, Miguel Palomar y Vizcarra, Emilio Portes Gil, Jesús Silva Herzog* (Mexico: Instituto Mexicano de Investigaciones Económicas, 1969).[15]

Quite apart from historical statistics, because Latin American elites (let alone nonelites) with few exceptions do not have a tradition of writing autobiography or scholarly biography, investigators have found it helpful to interview leaders in order to discuss motivations as well as to establish basic chronologies. In interviewing Mexican public figures of this century, we have found that often they are reluctant to discuss issues which are inextricably involved with their personal history. Thus, where possible our investigation attempts to construct personal history by use of a chronological approach which provides a framework for flashback, flash forward, and spontaneous digression needed to make a point or carry out an idea.

Although oral history interviews can be tape recorded with nonelites, to date historians generally have left the story of the common man within the purview of anthropologists like Oscar Lewis. Given the great need to record the views of national and subnational leaders who can still give us a picture of their role in Mexican history since 1900, perhaps this division of labor is rational. Though the historian asks questions from a different point of view than the anthropologist, in the future investigators may wish to follow the lead of Fernando Horcasitas, who has combined methods from both disciplines.[16]

There are several schools of thought regarding the conduct of oral history interviews with leaders. The original view developed in the United States (principally at Columbia University) seems to stem from the idea that the interviewer should not attempt to guide the discussion since he may introduce bias into the responses. While this view may have varying degrees of validity when the investigator is working with nonelites, oral history allows spontaneous exploration of ideas as well as open-ended questions and answers. As developed for Mexico, the oral history interview is seen as an opportunity to question leaders (who in any case are accustomed to manipulating people for their own ends) in order to cover topics which leaders might not wish to analyze or which they take for granted, discuss public rumors which have never been confirmed or refuted,[17] and provide cues which trigger recall of the past.

Although oral history research presented in *México Visto en el Siglo XX* perhaps offers a convenient guide by providing examples of interviews with seven leaders representing different ideological points of view in the political spectrum, it is important to note here that in creating a synthesis with aspects of both biography and autobiography, the investigator should work with a list of questions which he can check and cancel as they are covered in the course of the conversation. Since one cannot go simply from one question to another in order (as in the yes-or-no type of polling questionnaires) without limiting spontaneity, and since the conversation can develop in any number of ways at any given moment, a checklist is necessary which may be expanded in the course of the conversation or as questions are generated in interviews with other leaders. In this way, questions which are answered before they are asked may be eliminated, and the investigator will have a record of what has or has not been discussed as the interview progresses. The latter aspect is especially important if short interviews are conducted over a long period of time.

In order to stimulate recall, the scholar may wish to confront a leader with speeches or writings of his earlier years as well as to point out apparent contradictions in his thinking. Although some readers might doubt the validity of oral history because persons interviewed discuss the past from the vantage point of the present (thus justifying or shading past events in order to fit into a rational picture which never existed), it is precisely this historical perspective which allows us to assess long-term meaning in history. In short, the leader himself may not have understood what was going on at any given moment in history, and only with time does his interpretation take on meaning. Further, concerning the recall of specific events, it is the position of some psychologists that nothing is ever completely forgotten, but that recall is related to appropriate retrieval cues.[18] In any case, oral history suffers from the same disadvantages as autobiography, yet has the advantage of permitting the scholar to confront his historical figure. In *México Visto en el Siglo XX*, for example, the reader may determine for himself the convergence and divergence of views in order to assess which persons have the most accurate knowledge of different events or leaders commonly discussed.

Publication of oral history interviews involves the editing of verbatim transcripts. Although the tapes stand as recorded, the transcription of oral history interviews may be compared to translation from one language to another because the spoken word may not necessarily carry the same connotation in written form. In addition to problems of emphasis and intonation, which are hard to translate into writing, the written form may be difficult to understand if false starts and repetitious or unnecessary material are included. Furthermore, because the tenor of the conversation may not show in the published version, and because leaders may not be willing to make public the material which they have recorded for posterity, we encourage additions as well as permit deletions in the edited manuscript. Thus, the manuscript may be a second statement which can be compared to the original taped version much as one compares drafts of documents.[19]

Aside from theoretical questions of the type just discussed (some of which may not be taken up in the preface to published oral history without offending the leaders who have offered their cooperation), investigators face a number of technical problems concerning how to record and transcribe oral history interviews. In fact, many oral history ventures fail because of the accidental erasure of tapes and the cost of making transcriptions. And some large oral history projects have had to suspend new recording in order to catch up on the backlog of untranscribed materials. (Needless to say, this latter approach is as self-defeating as the projects which erase the tapes after transcripts have been edited because the project directors assert that it is inconsistent to have two versions of the same interview which are not in exact agreement.)

In addition to a number of technical questions involved in making a tape-recorded interview (including the technical development of the interview;[20] information to be included on each tape;[21] the need for a battery-operated tape recorder because of voltage problems;[22] and the selection of a recorder which can also be used for transcription[23]), a major problem concerns retrieval of information. Regardless of whether or not the scholar intends to publish the entire interview, without transcription the location of specific information may be an overwhelming problem simply because one must listen to the tapes instead of skimming through a manuscript. At an average rate of twenty-five pages per hour of recording time, a five-hour interview (which seemed short in the field) will turn out to be a one-hundred page manuscript involving roughly twenty to thirty hours of transcription time. Thus, scholars can hardly spend their own time in transcription of tapes, and without a research grant they may not have even the equipment to transfer original recordings to seven-inch reels of low-print tape which provide storage copies.[24]

With regard to legal rights in recorded interviews, in Mexican procedure intellectual authorship is held by the interviewer.[25] While this appears to hold true throughout Latin America, such a common-sense position recently has been made explicit in the United States.[26] In the only legal precedent to date, New York State's highest court decided in the case of Mary Hemingway versus Random House, Inc. (publishers in 1966 of A. E. Hotchner's *Papa Hemingway: A Personal Memoir*) that Ernest Hemingway impliedly licensed his rights under common-law copyright when he knowingly permitted Hotchner to interview him. Thus, Mrs. Hemingway lost her contention that her deceased husband's tape-recorded interviews should be considered—as in the case of letters—to be the intellectual property of her husband's estate, even if owned materially by Hotchner.[27] On December 12, 1968, the New York State Court of Appeals (in upholding the decisions of two lower courts) not only denied Mrs. Hemingway's attempt to stop the sale of Hotchner's book, but denied her claims that Hotchner had wrongfully used material imparted in confidence and that the resulting work constituted an invasion of her privacy. In this manner, Mrs. Hemingway's lawsuit for injunctive relief and damages came to naught.[28]

Because the Hemingway decision may not be considered a binding precedent in other states, however, upon conclusion of the oral history interview it is highly desirable to obtain a release permitting publication of the materials or spelling out any limitations on the use of the oral history documents. Sometimes leaders will consent to be interviewed (or will speak freely) only if the scholar agrees not to publish the work for a specified number of years, and they may request that the tapes and transcript must remain completely closed to other investigators for a certain number of years (usually five to ten) or until their death.[29]

Persons recorded in Mexico by the Wilkies include Salvador Abascal, Aurelio R. Acevedo, Juan Andreu Almazán, Silvano Barba González, Clementina Batalla de Bassols, Ramón Beteta, Juan de Dios Borjórquez, Alfonso Caso, Luis Chávez Orozco, Daniel Cosío Villegas, Carlos Fuentes, Francisco Javier Gaxiola, Jr., Marte R. Gómez, Manuel Gómez Morín, Martín Luis Guzmán, Luis L. León, Germán List Arzubide, Vicente Lombardo Toledano, Aurelio Manrique, José Muñoz Cota, Melchor Ortega, Ezequiel Padilla, Miguel Palomar y Vizcarra, Emilio Portes Gil, Manuel J. Sierra, Jesús Silva Herzog, David Alfaro Siqueiros, and Jacinto B. Treviño.[30]

Recordings have also been made recently by other investigators. Thus, John Hart has recorded Celestino Gasca and Rosendo Salazar, and Alan M. Kirshner has recorded Rodulfo Brito Foucher. These interviews and a recent publication of Píndaro Urióstegui Miranda appear to be more topically interested than personally oriented. Professor Urióstegui has recorded Amador Acevedo, Juan Barragán, Nicolás T. Bernal, Nicolás Fernández Carrillo, Luis L. León, Eduardo Neri, Jesús Romero Flores, Aarón Sáenz, and Rosendo Salazar.[31]

With regard to topically oriented oral histories, perhaps the most ambitious Mexican effort dates from 1959, when the Archivo Sonoro de la Revolución Mexicana del Departmento de Investigaciones Históricas del Instituto Nacional de Antropología e Historia began tape recording survivors of the

1910 revolutionary era.[32] Since that time over seventy persons have been tape recorded. Most of these persons played minor roles, but some major figures include Adrián Aguirre Benavides, Gustavo Baz, Federico Cervantes, Roque Estrada, Isidro Fabela Alfaro, Roque González Garza, Martín Luis Guzmán, Raúl Madero, Roberto V. Pesqueira, Alma Reed, Luis Sánchez Pontón, and Luz Corral de Villa. In 1970 the Archivo Sonoro began a publication program, and Professors Alicia Olivera de Bonfil and Eugenia Meyer have published their interviews with Ernest Gruening, Miguel Palomar y Vizcarra, and Jesús Soto Inclán.

Although journalists have also entered the field of oral history (see Elena Poniatowska, *La Noche de Tlatelolco: Testimonios de Historia Oral*[33]), the above listings show that most of Mexico's leaders of the twentieth century remain unrecorded. Clearly, oral history has only barely gotten underway in Mexico.[34]

CONCLUSION

This chapter has touched on only a few of the questions involved in oral history and historical statistics.[35] Various uses of oral history (such as in the development of computer coding to facilitate content analysis and/or investigation in patterns of response, and in personality assessment of aggregate psychological traits found in open-ended interviews) have been excluded as beyond the scope of this study.

In discussing oral and statistical history as used separately or in relation to each other, it is important to note that each is circumscribed by the parameters of definition developed in analysis. In oral history, care must be taken to find a balance between under- and overdirection of the interview. If an oral history is to be successful (and many interviews will not be as successful as one hopes), analysis by the scholar will complement and bring out the leader's views. The result is at once the creation of a document as well as a new type of analytical study.

With historical statistics, as with oral history, it is significant to note that changes in definition (or points of view) will provide alternative views of historical problems. Certainly the problem of definition is no less the case with nonstatistical threads generally used by historians. In sum, perhaps in the future, we need to develop alternative views of historical problems (regardless of the methods used) in order to suggest probabilities as to which method helps us understand different aspects of complex problems. Such an approach would stand in contrast to narrative history, in which we provide neither alternative methods nor alternative interpretations for understanding historical problems. In such a reconstruction of history, the phrase "telling it like it is" becomes less important than attempting to understand complex problems for which we have not worked out appropriate questions, let alone begun to derive a single set of satisfactory "answers."

NOTES

1. Problems of definition in historical statistics and oral history are no less than those encountered in other approaches to historical problems, be they phrased, for example, in the terms of archival studies by the historian or field studies by the anthropologist. Thus, one may note the disparity of methods used for the study of agrarian revolt in Mexico. Whereas John Womack, Jr., wrote a political narrative description of Morelos during the decade 1910-20, Paul Friedrich turned to the study of such items as kinship and diet patterns to explain the course of events in Michoacán during the 1920s. Because the definition of inquiry differs so radically in these two works, the resulting alternative views of the problem of agrarian revolt provide stimulating discussion as pieces are added to work out the puzzle of Mexico's rural history. Compare Womack's *Zapata and the Mexican Revolution* (New York: Knopf, 1969) and Friedrich's *Agrarian Revolt in a Mexican Village* (Englewood Cliffs, N.J.: Prentice-Hall, 1970).

2. Recent examples of works which reorganize official statistics and make new interpretations of Mexican history include Leopoldo Solís, *La Realidad Económica Mexicana: Retrovisión y Perspectivas* (Mexico: Siglo XXI, 1970); and Clark W. Reynolds, *The Mexican Economy: Twentieth-Century Structure and Growth* (New Haven: Yale University Press, 1970).

3. For an example of problems and limitations in adjusting time-series data given in Mexico's industrial censuses, see James W. Wilkie, "La Ciudad de México como Imán de la Población Económicamente Activa, 1930-1965," in *Historia y Sociedad en el Mundo de Habla Española: Homenaje a Jose Miranada*, edited by Bernardo García Martínez et al. (Mexico: El Colegio de México, 1970), pp. 379-95.

4. Thus, for example, in order to develop correlations concerning voter turnout for the official party between 1952 and 1967, Barry Ames ("Bases of Support for Mexico's Dominant Party," *American Political Science Review* 54 [1970]: 153-67), has used historical statistics on urbanization and poverty supplied in James W. Wilkie, *The Mexican Revolution: Federal Expenditure and Social Change since 1910*, 2d ed., rev. (Berkeley: University of California Press, 1970). For use of data on poverty from the same book, see Rodrigo Medellín, "La Dinámica de Distanciamiento Económico Social de Mexico," *Revista Mexicana de Sociología* 31 (1969): 513-46; and for use of data on federal expenditures, see James A. Hanson, "Federal Expenditures and the Political Economy of the Mexican Revolution," *Yale University Economic Growth Center Discussion Paper* 120 (September 1971).

5. Reynolds, *The Mexican Economy*, p. 46.

6. For methodology, see Hubert M. Blalock, *Social Statistics* (New York: McGraw-Hill, 1960). Professor Blalock discusses descriptive statistics (Part II) as compared to inductive statistics (Part III).

7. For example, see Colin B. Burke, "A Note on Self-Teaching, Reference Tools, and New Approaches in Quantitative History," *Historical Methods Newsletter*, March 1971, pp. 35-42. See also Charles M. Dollar and Richard J. Jensen, *Historian's Guide to Statistics: Quantitative Analysis and Historical Research* (New York: Holt, Rinehart and Winston, 1971).

8. The Departamento de Muestreo is an agency of the Secretaría de Industría y Comercio (Cuauhtémoc 80, México 7, D.F.), which sells many statistical publications. The Departamento de Muestreo has published, for example, *La Población Económicamente Activa de México en Junio de 1964*, which is now not only a historical document but contains historical questions on the popularity of such figures as Hernán Cortés and Benito Juárez.

9. For a partial list of agencies, see Secretaría de la Presidencia, *Manuel de Organización del Gobierno Federal, 1969-1970* (Mexico: Comisión de Administración Pública, 1969).

10. Philip Boucher, "Agricultural Credit in Mexico: A Review Article," Department of History, UCLA, 1971.

11. See James W. Wilkie, "New Hypotheses for Statistical Research in Recent Mexican History," *Latin American Research Review* 6, no. 2 (1971): 3-17.

12. Other important libraries with statistical collections include the United Nations Food and Agricultural Organization Library (Hamburgo 63, México 6, D.F.) as well as the United States Embassy Commercial [and Economic] Library (Reforma 305, México 5, D.F.).

13. For background, one should consult two publications by Mexico's Dirección General de Estadística: *Bibliografía Mexicana de Estadística*, 2 vols. (Mexico: Talleres Gráficos de la Nación, 1942); and *Historia de la Estadística Nacional* (1967), reprinted from Rodolfo Flores Talavera's articles in *Sociedad Mexicana de Geografía y Estadística* 86, nos. 1-3 (1958).

14. *El Trimestre Económico* (Avenida de la Universidad 975, México 12, D.F.) and the *Revista Mexicana de Sociología* (Instituto de Investigaciones Sociales, Universidad Nacional Autónoma de México, México 20, D.F.) are among other important periodicals which often publish historical statistics. Recent data are published in the Dirección General de Estadística's monthly *Revista de Estadística*.

15. For example, Ramón Beteta and Vicente Lombardo Toledano have commented extensively on my analysis of federal expenditure and my Poverty Index.

16. See Fernando Horcasitas, *De Porfirio Díaz a Zapata: Memorias Náhuatl de Milpa Alta* (Mexico: Universidad Nacional Autónoma de México, 1968).

17. With regard to discussion of a leader's rumored illegal activities (or of controversial hypotheses about his role), for example, it may be wise to introduce questions with such neutral terms as "it is said" or "they say" in order to avoid pitting the interviewer against the leader, thus encouraging the leader to develop a full account of the matter.

18. See Michael J. A. Howe, *Introduction to Human Memory: A Psychological Approach* (New York: Harper and Row, 1970); and Endel Tulving and Zena Pearlstone, "Availability versus Accessibility of Information in Memory for Words," *Journal of Verbal Learning and Verbal Behavior* 5 (1966): 381-91. Cf. William W. Cutler III, "Accuracy in Oral History Interviewing," *Historical Methods Newsletter*, June 1970, pp. 1-7.

19. This two-version method permits both the retention of the original language and

the sense of the interview as well as revisions. In the editing process, moreover, we discourage changes in sequence of the discussion (so as not to confuse the reader as the interchange of questions and answers develops) or excessive changes which would destroy the informal style inherent in spoken language.

20. The best tape recorder available to date for research purposes is a two-track cassette machine which has automatic volume control so that the investigator is free to concentrate on the interview itself rather than watching to see that the volume is adjusted for distance to the microphone or changes in voice level. Nevertheless, the investigator must glance at his machine now and then to see that the take-up wheel of the cassette is turning and to be sure that he has not run out of tape. It is important not only to listen to the recorded introduction on each side to be sure that the tape is not defective, but to use some sort of timing device as a reminder when the cassette must be changed (see note 23 below). With regard to cassette running time, it is advisable to use the C-60 length (thirty minutes on each side). Although longer-running cassettes are available, they may cause problems because time is gained at the expense of tape thickness.

21. Introductory information recorded (in the presence of the interviewee and as part of the interview) on each side of the cassette should include side sequence, date, city, and names of persons involved in the discussion. Cassettes also should be identified in writing on each side at the moment they are put into the recorder, including such information as name of person interviewed, date, and sequence of each side of the cassette (e.g., 1a, 1b, 2c, 2d, etc.). Once each side is finished, the safety tab at the back of the cassette should be broken to prevent accidental erasure. These precautions are necessary to assure that the interviewee is aware of the fact that he is being recorded, to provide basic interview data for posterity, and to prevent confusion during the interview itself. With regard to the latter point, in the attempt to conduct a spirited discussion while trying to remember where the conversation is headed, some investigators have been known to lose track of which cassette sides are already recorded, thus erasing discussions which are difficult if not impossible to recapture without alienating the leader, who may begin to feel like an actor in rehearsal.

22. Because of voltage (usually 110 or 220) and cycle (50 or 60) variations throughout Latin America, investigators should be prepared to use the kind of battery-operated recorder discussed below (see note 23). The problem is especially serious in Mexico City, Toluca, Pachuca, Cuernavaca, and Taxco as compared to other parts of Mexico. These areas operate on 50-cycle (125-watt) current while the rest of the country uses 60-cycle electric power. Mexico has plans for developing an integrated national system beginning in 1972 *(El Día,* July 23, 1971); but in any case the nominal 110-127-watt system used throughout the country is known to fluctuate widely, thus requiring the use of batteries or a voltage regulator in order to avoid the possibility of recordings with voices which sound like chattering squirrels or mooing cows. For official information (to be used with discretion) on voltage and frequency stability, see the latest issue of *Electric Current Abroad*, published by the U.S. Department of Commerce's Bureau of International Commerce.

23. One of the most convenient machines now on the market, for example, is the Sony TC-110A. The TC-110A is a relatively low-priced machine, yet it offers high voice quality with a built-in microphone which not only has automatic voice control (see note 20 above), but eliminates any tendency to make the interviewee nervous with a standard, visible microphone. In addition, with the use of its accessory foot pedal and earphones, the TC-110A may be used conveniently for transcription because it has an instant replay key. Weighing less than four pounds, it can be operated on four "C" size batteries if

electrical current is unsatisfactory (see note 22 above). This model is equipped with a meter which gauges battery strength and shows the voice level when recording; when used with a Sony cassette, a built-in alarm sounds when the tape is completed. Other automatic volume-control models are listed in the latest *Consumer Reports Buying Guide*; and the reader is advised to check with an electronics dealer with regard to new and more versatile machines which are constantly becoming available.

24. Low-print tape (e.g., Scotch 138-1/4-1200 feet) helps prevent the passing of magnetic signals from one layer of tape to another during long periods of storage. Also, in order to preserve recordings, tapes should be rewound once a year and stored where humidity and heat are not excessive as well as kept away from any magnet or machine with a magnet which could change the pattern of magnetically recorded sound retained by the iron oxide on the tape.

25. Thus, for example, the work cited in note 31 below is copyrighted by Professor Píndaro Urióstegui Miranda.

26. Since most United States oral history programs conduct interviews which are nondirective in nature (in contrast to being a scholarly creation), perhaps this explains their general assignment of legal rights to the program or to the person interviewed rather than to the interviewer, who is only an employee.

27. For a discussion of intellectual rights in authorship of letters, see John C. Hogan and Saul Cohen, *An Author's Guide to Scholarly Publishing and the Law* (Englewood Cliffs, N.J.: Prentice-Hall, 1965), pp. 69-70.

28. For the case history, see 296, N.Y.S.2d 771 (New York Supplement, 2d series, vol. 296 [Saint Paul, Minn.: West, 1969], pp. 771-83).

With regard to legal rights of third parties who might claim defamation of character as the result of an interview, according to Latin American custom, apparently such claims are practically impossible. In the United States, recent court decisions with regard to public figures also have reduced this problem to one of small proportions. (See E. Douglas Hamilton, "Oral History and the Law of Libel," Second National Colloquium on Oral History [New York: Oral History Association, 1968], pp. 47-48).

29. Because the Hemingway case cited above in note 28 suggests that "there should be a presumption that the speaker has not reserved any common-law rights unless the contrary strongly appears" (p. 779), if necessary the scholar might be well advised to draw up a simple agreement stipulating, for example, that he will not open or publish the recorded material within a specified number of years or while the interviewee is alive.

Regardless of the fact that the interviewee may participate in the interview without placing any restrictions on the work, as a simple matter of courtesy the scholar who wishes to publish the entire interview may wish to obtain written permission to publish the materials in order to avoid misunderstandings which could jeopardize the successful development of future interviews.

30. Some of these interviews were foreshortened by such circumstances as death (Ramón Beteta), travel (Carlos Fuentes), and lack of time (David Alfaro Siqueiros).

31. *Testimonios del Proceso Revolucionario de México* (Mexico: Argrin, 1970). Unfortunately, this book of over seven hundred pages lacks an introduction on methodology and indexes.

32. For a useful article on the work of the Archivo Sonoro, see Eugenia Meyer and Alicia Olivera de Bonfil, "La Historia Oral: Origen Metodología, Desarrollo, y Perspectivias," *Historia Mexicana* 21 (1971): pp. 372-87.

33. (Mexico: Ediciones Era, 1971).

34. The Universidad Nacional Autonóma de México's "Voz Viva de México" series

does not involve oral history but the sale of disc recordings in which, for example, Jesús Silva Herzog delivers a brief monologue on the oil expropriation, or an author reads a chapter of his book, in order to make his voice available to the general public.

35. For an elaboration of many of the points discussed here, see Lyle C. Brown, "New Methods and Approaches in Latin American History" (paper presented at the annual meeting of the Southwestern Social Science Association, San Antonio, Texas, March 31, 1972). This paper by Professor Brown of Baylor University discusses both oral history and historical statistics.

Part II

Guide to Field Research

4

Useful Information
for Researchers

by Richard E. Greenleaf

The following comments have grown out of some fifteen years of experience with newly arrived researchers as they settle into their work in Mexico, D.F.

In spite of some disadvantages of bringing an automobile into a new legal and driving environment, I recommend that you do so. (You will need your car title or other proof of ownership to cross the border.) Parking is difficult almost everywhere; many apartments and *pensiones* do not have garage facilities; on-the-street parking overnight may be dangerous; auto *pensiones*, available in most colonias of the city—often one every four or five blocks—are relatively expensive; and the foreigner feels insecure in Mexico City traffic patterns. All of these seeming disadvantages can be overcome by planning and by learning to adjust to the new driving environment. Mexican drivers are excellent, and they drive much more defensively than most North Americans. They rarely have accidents. It is merely a question of your learning to drive within their life style. With a car you can explore Mexico City and its environs and you can make those all-important trips to out-of-the-way archives. You may well improve your feeling for the research topic at hand, and your writing, by visiting the appropriate places on weekends when archives and libraries are closed. Now that the excellent and very reasonable Metro system is open (since 1969), you can park near a subway stop, thus alleviating the time-consuming hassles in getting downtown and parked. Because street names often change from one block to the next, it is desirable to carry a detailed map of the city in the car.

It is not my purpose in this guide to recommend living accommodations.

Instead I wish to indicate principles you should follow as you settle into your research year. Until 1969, most researchers felt the need to live close in to the center of the city. Since that time they have found living near a subway stop in the outer city to be just as convenient and certainly cheaper. Rule One is, Never jump into a leased apartment or house until you have had time to look around. Most researchers with families feel the need to get settled immediately, and they frequently take apartments less desirable and more expensive than those that can be acquired with planned searching for a week or two. If you can, avoid first-floor apartments with a northern exposure because they often are cold and dark. Study the Spanish-language newspapers for apartments available. Get a detailed map of the city and plot your geographical coordinates from archives, libraries, etc. The English-language papers also advertise excellent accommodations, but you may find that a functional conversational knowledge of Spanish will get you a better bargain. Take an electric blanket, a pressure cooker, an electric skillet and toaster, and a radio. Everything else you can buy cheaply in the country.

United States researchers suffer from the fact that they have grown up in a relatively antiseptic environment, and they react with fear to stories of stomach upsets, diarrhea, and other maladies. Some of their problems are related to culture shock as they try to cope with a new language, a new life style, and different water and food. Overworking, overeating, excitement, and exercising—trying to do too much too rapidly—are the major causes of the tourist complaint, not the water or the food. Check a guide to Mexico for comment on health problems, but don't freeze up; enjoy the food and drink of Mexico.

All tourist guides contain more or less the same things, but over the years, for a variety of reasons, I have preferred James Norman's *Terry's Guide to Mexico* (Garden City, N.Y.: Doubleday, 1962, and later editions). Mr. Norman's son, Mexican-born Paul Schmidt (M.A., University of the Americas; Ph.D., Tulane), helped his father with the research and writing of the text and footnotes which especially interest professional historians and anthropologists, information you do not get with clarity and authority in other guides.

I cannot stress too much the validity of remarks made by Professors Cosío Villegas and Scholes, and by other contributors throughout this guide, regarding professional manners of researchers. Dress formally until you see what other researchers are wearing; approach your task with humility, patience, and rectitude. Mexicans expect proper form in professional contacts as well as in social relationships. Observe the amenities as you arrive and as you leave the archive or library each day you are there. Learn as quickly as possible the divisions of authority and responsibility within the staff of the institution where you are researching, and then go to the proper person for advice and resolution of any problem. It is wise to take letters of introduction from your major adviser or from a functionary of your university; the more official they look, the better. Some researchers have also found it useful to prepare beforehand a written statement of intent, outlining in broad terms the objectives of the project. It is also desirable to have cards printed with your name and institutional affiliation. These can be acquired at a reasonable cost in Mexico.

Plan your time. Always keep in mind that there are government holidays the last two weeks in May, in December, and on other national days of observance. Also please remember that archive staff members often leave the building for lunch and for other jobs or professional obligations at closing time. Don't overstay your welcome, and try not to place them in the embarrassing position of telling you that it is closing time. Try to work at a moderate, sustained pace. Mexicans are not particularly impressed by the rapid researcher on the two-week jaunt. Experienced researchers who know the archives from years of working in them can proceed more rapidly, but the fledgling scholar, in order to be thorough and to convey his seriousness to the staff, needs to work at a slower rate. The need for patience and tact is important in all Mexican archives, but it is even more essential when working in small private collections, which are invariably understaffed.

In short, the professional and personal appearance you make in archives and in Mexican scholarly circles is crucial. Often it makes the difference between success and failure of your project.

5

Archives, Libraries, and Newspaper Collections: An Introductory Survey

by Eugenia Meyer and Alicia O. de Bonfil

This introductory survey is intended to serve as a guide to the more detailed descriptions of particular archives in the following chapters. For the purpose of obtaining exact information on archives, libraries, and pertinent newspaper archives for research in the history of Mexico, we believe that the foreign researcher should establish contact with Mexican investigators specializing in his particular field of interest. Only these specialists can provide the most practical lists of places and sources which will be of greatest utility to historians and students. The effort will be amply rewarded because on many occasions the guides which now exist mention collections which are not open to researchers and, even if they are open, often do not provide the services promised in the guide. By seeking out Mexican counterparts the researcher can save himself precious time. In keeping with this sentiment our comments will be brief; they can be amplified by consulting the more specialized chapters in this guide.

Without question the most important archive in Mexico is the Archivo General de la Nación (see chapter 6, section A, and chapter 9, section D) which not only contains primary source material but information from the pre-Columbian period, the colonial period, the era of Independence, the Reform, and the Revolution. Nevertheless, it must be pointed out that not all of the material is cataloged; this often makes the task of the researcher more difficult and drawn out.

The archives of the various ministries of state are also located in the Federal District. These contain information on the unique character and functions of each of these ministries. As examples we cite the archives of the Secretaría de Hacienda y Crédito Público, the Secretaría de Relaciones Exteriores, the Secretaría de Salubridad y Assistencia, and the Secretaría de Defensa National. From the information we have received we should add that generally there are no restrictions in access to these archives; nevertheless, one should prepare a formal request in advance. Certain subjects and certain periods may be closed, especially to foreign investigators, such as some of the documentation in the Foreign Relations and National Defense Archives. [1]

With respect to historical information that can be obtained in the states, there is generally at least one important archive in each state of the republic. In addition to the state archives, there are the local and municipal archives which generally house documentation from parish archives, notarial archives, and judicial archives. It is common practice in the case of municipal archives to seek the permission of the municipal president or the judge in charge. For research in parish archives, although they are considered national property, it is proper to request authorization from the particular parish priest.

In all of these cases it is important to establish in advance a cordial relationship with local authorities. Promptness and efficiency, both in processing the request and in providing the material, depend in great measure upon the cooperation of these officials. Given the characteristic reserve and even mistrust of the Mexican, especially in the more rural areas, it is absolutely essential that foreigners attempt not only to gain confidence but to demonstrate the correctness of their intentions.

Within Mexico one finds an almost endless number of private archives, generally in the hands of the families of the original owners. It would be almost impossible to offer a complete list of them since most are privately maintained and only in special cases are they opened to researchers. It is for this reason that we suggest that foreign investigators establish contact with their Mexican colleagues in the same period of specialization. These specialists can offer information, provide letters of recommendation, and in some cases even establish direct contact with those persons in charge of the private archives.

A comprehensive guide to libraries in the Federal District is included as chapter 8. In addition to these libraries, however, each state of the Republic has at least one important library. It is generally located in the state capital or in the most important city of the area. For example, the main library of the state of Mexico is in Toluca; the main library of Veracruz is in Jalapa, which is also the location of the state university. In addition, the libraries of the state universities often have valuable documentary material.

Concerning private libraries, we must repeat what we indicated for private archives. They are generally not open to the public and it is best to establish initial contact through a Mexican historian who is familiar with them or has access to them.

For newspaper collections, the Hemeroteca Nacional in Mexico City is outstanding both for its organization and its catalog. State newspaper archives (in those states which have them) are also a valuable source for research because on many occasions they hold complete series of state newspapers and magazines which are not held by the Hemeroteca Nacional.

In the list of bibliographies which we include in chapter 12, section A, we have gathered those which are used most often by Mexican researchers in the field of history. Without question new bibliographical publications appear daily. Therefore it is recommended that researchers visiting the country establish contact with the Centro de Investigaciones Bibliográficas of the Biblioteca Nacional de México, which can provide the most up-to-date information.

NOTE

1. The editors would add that it is somewhat more difficult for foreigners to gain access to the National Defense Archives than to the Foreign Relations Archives. (R.E.G., M.C.M.)

6

Major Documentary Collections in Mexico

A. The Archivo General de la Nación

by Richard E. Greenleaf

Most research in Mexican history begins at the Archivo General de la Nación, located on the Zócalo in the south patio of the Palacio Nacional.[1] From around 8:30 in the morning to 2:30 each afternoon (Saturdays 8:30 a.m. to 12:30 p.m.), Mexican investigators, foreign scholars, lawyers, and legal representatives of rural communities probe the vast resources of this archive which grew out of the Archivo de la Secretaría del Virreinato in the early sixteenth century. Because of lack of systematic archive management in the sixteenth century and wide-scale destruction of documentation in the fires and riots of 1624 and 1692, much of the Hapsburg source materials must be consulted in Spain from the Audiencia de México, Justicia, Indiferente General, Escribanía de Cámara, and Contaduría sections of the Archivo General de Indias in Seville. Nevertheless, vast documentation on land, labor, Indian policy, the church, and sixteenth- and seventeenth-century political structure still survive in the Archivo General de la Nación, and the amount of manuscript sources increases in geometrical proportion from the sixteenth century through the nineteenth century.

The Archivo General de la Nación has the largest, most competent, and most helpful staff of any Latin American country. Kindly, courteous, and knowledgeable, these men and women have intimate acquaintance with contents of archival sections (ramos) under their individual supervision. Often they have personal catalogs or "mental catalogs" of ramos which do not have printed guides. Once they are convinced of the sincerity, competence, and willingness to work of the young investigator, they prove to be very productive scholarly associates. The current director of the archive, Lic. Jorge Ignacio Rubio Mañé, is a professional archivist and a recognized historian. Over the twenty years we have been associated he has never failed to be helpful and encouraging to me and to my students. Sr. Rubio's guide to the Archivo General de la Nación, *El Archivo General de la Nación, México, D.F.* (México: Editorial Cultura, 1940), gives the most complete history of the collection as well as lists and descriptions of the holdings in its some 170 ramos.[2]

Every researcher should consult the Rubio guide before arriving in Mexico and he should become familiar with other general data on the Archivo General de la Nación in Manuel Carrera Stampa, Lino Gómez Canedo, and Agustín Millares Carlo.[3] It would also be wise to peruse the complete first and second series of the *Boletín del Archivo General de la Nación* in order to learn about the ongoing publication of indexes to various ramos of the archive. After settling into work at the Archivo General de la Nación, researchers become aware of master lists of indexes and other holdings which are posted on the wall near the book cabinet on the second floor where master copies of each index are kept. Sr. José R. Guzmán will be happy to direct you to these as well as to the cabinets of card files to some of the ramos. The shelf list will indicate to you when guides, indexes, or card files are downstairs and must be used there. Although it is not generally available to individual researchers, the staff may see fit to allow you to consult a handbook typed for its own use when doing reference work for the general public: "El Indice de Guías," a kind of guide to other guides. Here you will learn that at the time the index was typed there were 68,534 volumes, legajos, or cajas of materials in the Archivo General de la Nación arranged in 170 different branches. Data on lost items, restricted items which are kept locked up and must be requested from the director, a list of catalogs of the Archivo General de la Nación, and a tabulation, revised from time to time, of the "Archivo Provisional" are included in the staff handbook.

All researchers should be aware of the ramo known as the Archivo Provisional which now contains some 200 legajos or cajas. In the mid-1950s the archive staff began to sort and classify a mass of loose documentation known variously as "Indiferente," "Papeles no agregados," and "Papeles de la bodega." It was decided to organize an Archivo Provisional under each of the current ramo designations of the existing collection. Hence today there is a ramo entitled Inquisición which is supplemented by an Archivo Provisional de la Inquisición, and this procedure is followed for other important ramos such as Tierras, Civil, Historia, and Temporalidades, among others.

Many selections in this volume (especially chapter 1, section B, and chapters 9, 10, and 11) allude specifically to manuscripts in the Archivo General de la Nación. The archive also has surprisingly strong resources for the study of twentieth-century Mexico. The microfilming service is reasonable and reliable.

NOTES

1. See appendix B, "Map of the Colonial City," for a convenient way to locate the Archivo General de la Nación.

2. If the 1940 Editorial Cultura edition is unavailable, consult the same material in *Revista de la Historia de América* 9 (1940): 63-169.

3. Manuel Carrera Stampa, *Archivalia Mexicana* (Mexico: UNAM, 1952); Lino Gómez Canedo, *Los Archivos de la Historia de América: Período Colonial Español*, 2 vols. (Mexico: PAIGH, 1961); and Agustín Millares Carlo, *Repertorio Bibliográfico de los Archivos Mexicanos* (Mexico: UNAM, 1959).

B. The Archivo Histórico de Hacienda
by James D. Riley

The Archivo Histórico de Hacienda, located in the Palacio Nacional in Mexico City, is the least known and possibly the least used of the major document collections in Mexico. It contains over twenty-two hundred legajos of documents from the archive of Real Hacienda of the Viceroyalty of New Spain and of the Ministry of Hacienda of the early Republic. Over the years many papers were destroyed or lost and apparently some records were weeded out as historically insignificant when the archive was cataloged in 1940. These events have diminished the quantity and completeness of the material available, but the remaining records are still vital for the economic history of the New Spain, especially for the eighteenth and nineteenth centuries, and are of some interest for the financial history of the Republic to 1850.

The collection is located on the second floor of the building housing the Archivo General de la Nación and maintains the same hours (8:30 a.m. to 2:30 p.m. Monday through Friday and 8:30 a.m. to 12:30 p.m. Saturday) and holidays as the Archivo General de la Nación. It is completely independent, however, and the porters of the Archivo General will not bring materials from the Archivo Histórico for you. Researchers must go directly to the room housing the Archivo Histórico and ask the assistants there for the documents that they desire. The archive has no requirements or controls over the use of its documents other than the request that researchers fill out a card giving their name, local address, and university affiliation.

All of the documents are loose and must be asked for by citing legajo and expediente. Information on some of the materials is available in the *Guía al Archivo Histórico de Hacienda, siglos XVI a XIX*, published in 1940 by the Ministry of Hacienda y Crédito Público. This guide is relatively easy to use and in most cases gives adequate descriptions of the material, with one exception. Some of the manuscripts, including many of the Jesuit documents, are contained in expedientes of several hundred pages that are cataloged as correspondence to and from various individuals. The titles of these expedientes can be very misleading and in some instances are not very meaningful for the following reasons. First, *correspondence*, as used in the guide, is a very general term and can include records of all sorts, not just letters. Second, in some

77

instances the documents can be of such a varied nature that the individuals under whose names the expediente is indexed play only a minor role in the records. Moreover, since the catalog description at times does not include positions or titles, you must know beforehand who the individuals are in order to be able to tell whether the documents will be useful to you or not. For these reasons, it is good policy to look carefully at all large expedientes containing correspondence that might have even the remotest chance of being of interest to you. Another failing of the guide is that it does not include information on all of the material that the archive has available. The published catalog includes descriptions of only about four hundred of the twenty-two hundred legajos the archive has. The archive has a catalog of its own which contains details on some of the other legajos, but in order to do a thorough job the researcher must expect to do some personal exploration. The staff in the archive can lend you valuable assistance in this regard.

Information on all aspects of colonial financial administration can be obtained from the archive, but in certain areas the holdings are more complete than in others. The largest sections deal with the Jesuits, the Consulado de Comercio of Mexico City, and the financial history of the intendancies. The Jesuit materials constitute the most complete part of the collection. The coverage runs from 1576 to 1825, with the bulk of the manuscripts concerning events from 1700 to 1780. There are many thousands of manuscript pages detailing the economic activities of the order in the eighteenth century. Most of the material came from the records of the Colegio Máximo de San Pedro y San Pablo, the Jesuit major seminary in Mexico City, and from the archive of the business office of the Mexican Province, also located in Mexico City. The documents provide information on any number of topics dealing with the management of haciendas and business enterprises in the eighteenth century and with the financial affairs of the Jesuit colleges and missions in New Spain. For someone interested in the financial affairs of the Jesuits, this collection is far more important than anything contained in the ramos of the Archivo General de la Nación.

The second large group of documents deals with the financial history of the Consulado de Comercio of Mexico City. Reports and formal correspondence between the viceroys and the consulado, mostly on matters of fees and taxes, make up the bulk of the material. The emphasis in this part of the collection is on the period from 1775 to 1820. This material would be extremely useful to someone interested in the history of colonial trade or of the consulado.

Of similar importance are the manuscripts on the financial administration of the intendants. Formal reports and letters again provide the bulk of the material, with the emphasis on the periods from 1791 to 1795 and from 1810 to 1820. Particularly complete is the correspondence between the intendants of Oaxaca and Mexico and the viceroy in 1791 and between the intendant of Puebla and the viceroy in 1792.

Matters of viceregal finance are the subject of most of the rest of the collection. There is information on government monopolies such as playing cards, gunpowder, minting, and quicksilver. The documents on quicksilver should prove useful to students of eighteenth-century mining. One segment contains sixty-five hundred pages of material on extractions of gold and silver from the mines of New Spain from 1771 to 1791. Documents on the collection of the *alcabala*, consisting mainly of reports and letters, are fairly extensive for the period from 1790 to 1820, and there is also quite a bit of information on the sale of offices.

Within the Archivo Histórico de Hacienda there are many possibilities for major research topics. Some of these possibilities have been mentioned. But the archive also contains an intriguing variety of papers which could be used to supplement work from other sources. For example, the manuscripts include financial statements of Indian villages from the late colonial period that could be very useful for a study of Indian life at that time. From the republican period, there are documents on customs collections, the work of the Junta de Fomento de Minería, and the diplomacy of the Second Empire. These are only some examples of the variety of material contained in the Archivo Histórico de Hacienda. Many more examples can be found by consulting the guide. Any researcher who is considering a project in the colonial or early republican period which has even the remotest economic or financial overtones would be well advised to explore the holdings of this archive.

C. The Archivo de Relaciones Exteriores: Twentieth-Century Holdings
by Berta Ulloa

The Mexican Foreign Relations Ministry has a modern and luxurious twenty-story building located in Tlaltelolco at the Plaza de la Tres Culturas. Tlaltelolco is in the northern part of the city, a few minutes away from the downtown district; it is served by many communication facilities, including the new subway transportation system. The archive, which is both a depository of documents and a place where they can be consulted, is located in the basement of the building. To reach it one uses the elevator located at the back and to the left of the main entrance of the Foreign Relations Ministry.

Dr. Arturo Arnáiz y Freg is the general director of the Library and Archive of the Foreign Relations Ministry. Lic. Eugenia López de Roux is assistant director and Professor Demóstenes Montúfar is the head of the General Archive.

Concentrated in the General Archive are the documents of the various branches of the Foreign Relations Ministry and the holdings of the ministry itself. These were housed in the Archivo General de la Nación until 1923. The material found here treats the entire period of Mexican history since Independence. It has two major catalogs for consultation: a decimal file and a name index. In addition there are several auxiliary catalogs: chronological, geographic, etc. The catalogs refer the user to the documents kept in boxes and packages, as well as to those compiled in bound volumes. For the bound volumes there are, in addition, two guides entitled "Special Indexes . . . Relating to Several Selected Matters of International, Historical, etc., Nature," which were prepared by Mr. Francisco Cabrera. There is a synthesis of this documentation and other holdings in the introduction of my *Revolución Mexicana, 1910-1920* (Mexico: Secretaría de Relaciones Exteriores, 1963).

The majority of the documents filed in boxes and packages are contained in thirty-two general sections which are labeled as follows:

1. Legajos de numeración corrida. Number 1 to 4,177. These are located in forty-four sections of filing cabinets, with each section containing thirty to forty drawers. This is the largest single collection, with documents on a wide array of important topics from the nineteenth and twentieth centuries. The

filing cabinets line the walls of the entire room, with additional sections traversing it.

2. Correspondencia particular del secretario de Relaciones Exteriores. Boxes or packages 1 to 630, from 1920 to 1964.

3. Correspondencia de la subsecretaría de Relaciones Exteriores. Boxes 1 to 288, from 1920 to 1966.

4. Correspondencia de la oficilía major de la secretaría de Relaciones Exteriores. Boxes 1 to 163, from 1931 to 1970.

5. Inventarios de la secretaría de Relaciones Exteriores. Boxes 1 to 495, from 1934 to 1968.

6. Diplomático. Expedientes personales. Boxes 1 to 2,999, from 1932 to 1964.

7. Consular. Expedientes personales. Boxes 1 to 1,175, from 1929 to 1964.

8. Recortes de periódicos remitidos por el servicio exterior de México a la secretaría de Relaciones Exteriores. Approximately 500 boxes, pertaining to the twentieth century.

9. Reclamaciones generales de Gran Bretaña a México. Boxes 1 to 11, from 1928.

10. Reclamaciones generales de Alemania a México. Boxes 1 to 30, from 1928.

11. Reclamaciones generales de Francia a México. Boxes 1 to 4, from 1929.

12. Reclamaciones generales de Italia a México. Boxes 1 to 13, from 1930.

13. Reclamaciones generales de Estados Unidos a México. Boxes 1 to 1,258, from 1925.

14. Reclamaciones especiales de Estados Unidos a México. Boxes 1 to 601, from 1925 to 1930.

15. Comisión general de reclamaciones de México contra Estados Unidos. Boxes 1 to 75, of the twentieth century.

16. Certificados de nacionalidad y cartas de naturalización. Boxes 1 to 1,117, of the twentieth century.

17. Correspondencia: (a) Actas de matrimonio. Boxes 1 to 23, twentieth century. (b) Permisos de importación y extradiciones. Boxes 24 to 101, twentieth century. (c) Permisos para constituir o modificar sociedades comerciales o civiles de conformidad con lo dispuesto en el artículo 27 de la Constitución. Boxes 102 to 775, twentieth century. (d) Minutas de correspondencia

jurídica Various boxes, without numbers, from 1930 to 1968.

18. Permisos a extranjeros para adquirir bienes. Boxes 1 to 419, twentieth century.

19. Asilados españoles en México. Boxes 1 to 132, from 1939.

20. Cartas de naturalización y certificados de nacionalidad a guatemaltecos. Boxes 1 to 248, twentieth century.

21. Comercio exterior de México. Boxes 1 to 33, twentieth century.

22. Organismos internacionales. Boxes 1 to 1,153, twentieth century.

23. Correspondencia particular del licenciado Ignacio Mariscal. Boxes 1 to 8, from 1887 to 1909.

24. Ceremonial de la secretaría de Relaciones Exteriores. Boxes 1 to 118, twentieth century.

25. Servicios culturales de la secretaría de Relaciones Exteriores. Boxes 1 to 118, twentieth century.

26. Decretos y circulares sobre materias de la competencia de la secretaría de Relaciones Exteriores. Boxes 1 to 11, from 1910 to 1964.

27. *Diario de los Debates.* Cámaras de Senadores y de Diputados, bound together but incomplete.

28. *Diario Oficial.* Bound from 1934 to 1964.

29. Documentos de la embajada de España en México. Boxes 1 to 409, twentieth century.

30. Personal de la secretaría de Relaciones Exteriores. Boxes 1 to 55, twentieth century.

31. Personal diplomático de la secretaría de Relaciones Exteriores. Boxes 1 to 215, twentieth century.

32. Indice cronológico de la correspondencia general. Approximately one hundred volumes, bound, covering the nineteenth and twentieth centuries.

The general rules for use of the archive have been defined by the Ministry of Foreign Relations as follows:

PROVISIONAL RULES AND REGULATIONS FOR INVESTIGATORS

1. The documents of the archive of this ministry are divided into two groups, those referring to present affairs and those dealing with historical matters. The historical archive includes, primarily, documents from 1821 to January 1, 1938; the current archive includes documents subsequent to the latter date. The documents of the current archive are not open to the public;

only on the rarest occasions can these documents be used with the express authorization of the secretary, one of the assistant secretaries, or in their absence from the director in charge.

2.. Documents are also classified as accessible, restricted, very restricted, and absolutely prohibited.

3. For convenience of the researcher, two catalogs are available: an ono-mastic one and a systematic one. In addition, he can make use of a collection of volumes entitled *Archivo Histórico Diplomático*, which will provide him with more detailed information.

4. The researcher is required to make a written request specifying the type of material he needs in order to expedite the delivery of the documents.

5. Archive is open from 9:00 a.m. to 2:00 p.m. Monday through Friday, and from 9:00 a.m. to 1:00 p.m. on Saturdays.

6. The documents requested for consultation will be delivered within seventy-two hours of the moment the written application is received. Only under very special conditions can the director or assistant director authorize consultation of documents at different times.

7. In order to obtain permission to use the collection it is necessary for the researcher to be accredited by a cultural institution or research center. It is useful for him to present one or more letters of recommendation from competent persons. He must also demonstrate that he possesses necessary knowledge to make good use of the material he is requesting.

8. Persons who in the judgment of the director or subdirector are well known for their academic work or historical research are exempted from the obligations of the above-mentioned requirement.

9. The researcher should leave his packages, briefcase, and other objects he is carrying with the authorized person when he enters. They will be return-ed upon leaving.

10. The use of fountain pens or other ink pens is absolutely prohibited because any momentary carelessness could stain the documents. The archives will furnish pencils, erasers, or paper to anyone who asks for them.

11. Taking notes while leaning on the packages or bound volumes is strict-ly prohibited. They should be returned in the same way that they are received, without any notes or marks. The pages should not be detached nor mutilated. Failure to observe these rules can result in the expulsion of the researcher without resort to judicial action.

12. The researcher may not take any document from the shelves by him-

self. The administrative officers in charge of helping him are the only persons authorized to place the material at his disposal.

13. When the materials in this archive have been utilized in a substantial way in the production of a work, two copies of the study should be forwarded to the archive when it is published. The corresponding credits should also be mentioned in any publication.

14. Photographic reproduction of the documents can be made only with authorization from the director or assistant director of the library and archive.

D. Archival Collections of the Biblioteca Nacional by Roberto Moreno

The Department of Manuscripts is located in the upper reading room for rare books and manuscripts of the Biblioteca Nacional (on the corner of Isabel la Católica and Uruguay, México, 1, D.F.). It is open to the public from Monday to Saturday, 9:00 a.m. to 9:00 p.m. The department is equipped with microfilm service and photocopying facilities. The present head of the department is Andrea Sánchez Quintanar.

The manuscript holdings of the Biblioteca Nacional were obtained from a number of different sources. The majority were obtained from the nationalization of church properties in 1859; as a result most treat scholastic matters. However, some documents were also obtained from the Real y Pontificia Universidad, the Colegio de Minas, and other institutions. At various times the documentary collection was augmented by the acquisition of small private archives such as the Franciscan Archive, the Benito Juárez Collection, and some of the Francisco I. Madero papers.

The Biblioteca Nacional does not yet have a general catalog of all of the manuscripts but there are guides to some of the resources. These permit easy utilization of the majority. The documentary collections are rich and afford a wealth of primary source material for the researcher in Mexican history.

THE PRE-HISPANIC PERIOD

The documents for the study of pre-Hispanic Mexico are all originally from the colonial period. Some come from the Colección Boturini and a large sampling of convent libraries. These sources have been cataloged.[1] Of the sixty-four registered titles, forty-six are of colonial origin. The remainder are diverse studies, some prepared for the Congress of Americanists (and now published) by Orozco y Berra, Paso y Troncoso, Chimalpopoca Galicia, and others. Most important is the Códice Pérez, a nineteenth-century copy of which the original is now lost.

In the colonial manuscripts, Nahuatl texts on Christian doctrine predominate. Some are by well-known authors such as Sahagún and Olmos. There are a few collections of sermons in other (Indian) languages. The Department of

87

Manuscripts has only three pictographic documents: a codex from the Techialoyan group, a page of a genealogical tree by Felipe Ixtlilxóchitl, and the Apeo y Deslinde de Tierras de Santa María de la Asunción. The pre-Hispanic section also contains Totonac, Nutka, and Opata grammars, and Nahuatl and Otomí vocabularies prepared by Horacio Carochi. Among other documents are a series of wills and testaments collected by Boturini. Finally, the collection contains the beautiful work *Cantares Mexicanos*.

THE COLONIAL PERIOD

The sources for colonial history are the richest in the department. Although not yet cataloged, they are not difficult to use. They can be divided into several groups.

Scholastic Works. This section comprises eight hundred works on general scholastic questions, Aristotelian commentaries, scholastic philosophy, collections of sermons, and other matters. At the present time a partial catalog is available,[2] and a complete catalog of the Latin manuscripts is being prepared under the direction of Jesús Ymhoff.

Franciscan Archive. Coming originally from the Convent of San Francisco, this collection consists of 159 boxes of legajos. Forty-one of the boxes contain documentation on the Provincias Internas, possibly from Jesuit sources acquired at the time of the expulsion. The remainder are Franciscan documents from the sixteenth to the eighteenth century, treating missions, doctrine, and bishoprics not only in Mexico but in the Orient as well. A catalog is now being prepared by Lic. Ignacio del Río, Ch.

Cedulario. The collection of cédulas consists of seventy-six volumes, originally the property of the Cathedral Archive of Mexico. It contains documents on the militia, the royal treasury, income from tobacco, mining, *aguardiente* and other prohibited drinks, pension funds, intendancies, and thirteen miscellaneous volumes on various aspects of viceregal administration. Thirty-three volumes are classified as "Royal Ordinances, Speeches, and Provisions Pertaining to Both Americas." Not all of the material is of an official nature, as private documents of various kinds are also found. The collection has not yet been cataloged.

Scientific Works. The colonial section contains fifty-three manuscripts of a scientific and technical character, including works on mathematics, physics, medicine, biology, astronomy, metallurgy, and geography. They are all from the seventeenth century. A few were acquired from the Colegio de Minería, while others are manuscripts of Alzate, Velásquez de León, and Diego Rodríguez. The collection has been cataloged.[3]

Tierras. Of recent acquisition, this small collection contains documentation on land tenancy in the state of Puebla. It comprises fifty-two boxes (1,362 documents), almost all from the eighteenth century. The documents treat land matters in different villages in the state.

Miscellaneous. In addition to the above-mentioned sections, there is a large number of miscellaneous documents: historical and geographical *relaciones*; reports; original editions; literary works, etc. The large majority of these works are now published.

THE NATIONAL PERIOD

The Biblioteca Nacional has relatively few manuscript collections from the period since Independence. There are only two major archives: the Benito Juárez Archive and the Francisco I. Madero papers.

The Juárez Archive. The collection was donated to the Biblioteca Nacional on July 18, 1926, by Juárez's heirs. It comprises the personal correspondence of the president and includes sundry documents with dates as early as 1849 and as late as 1889. In total there are 14,595 documents. A good portion of these have an onomastic, geographic, and chronological index which is available in the reading room of the Department of Manuscripts. The entire collection will be indexed shortly.

The Madero Papers. The correspondence of President Madero, covering a few months in 1911, consists of 2,431 pieces. The majority are telegrams but some other documents of minor importance are also included. Andrea Sánchez Quintanar is presently in charge of cataloging the collection.

Miscellaneous. A few other sources are available for the study of the nineteenth century. Among them one can mention the compilation of José María Lafragua, the *Documentos para la Historia de México*. In addition there is the *Memorias para la Historia de México Independiente* by José María Bocanegra, the *Crímenes de los Generales Santa Anna y Corona Comprobados por Ellos Mismos*, consisting of two volumes of correspondence between them, the *Estudios Históricos sobre la Guerra de Independencia* by Miguel Martínez, some diplomatic documentation, the private archive of Maximilian (two boxes with only 173 documents), the correspondence of Juan Alvarez (130 letters), and the collection of Agustín Rivera, 3,500 pieces of correspondence of minor importance.

NOTES

1. Roberto Moreno, "Guía de las Obras en Lenguas Indígenas Existentes en la Biblioteca Nacional," *Boletín de la Biblioteca Nacional* 17, nos. 1-2 (January-June 1966): 35-116.

2. Bernabé Navarro, *La Introducción de la Filosofía Moderna en México* (Mexico: El Colegio de México, 1948), pp. 287-307.

3. Roberto Moreno, "Catálogo de los Manuscritos Científicos de la Biblioteca Nacional," *Boletín del Instituto de Investigaciones Bibliográficas* 1, no. 1 (January-June 1969): 61-103.

E. The Hemeroteca Nacional de México
by Charles A. Hale

The Hemeroteca Nacional de México is the central depository for newspapers and serial publications in the capital. From 1912 to 1944 there existed within the Biblioteca Nacional a separate division for newspapers and periodicals, but when the collection grew too large for the inner recesses of the Church of San Agustín, a separate establishment was founded. It was officially inaugurated on March 28, 1944, as the Hemeroteca Nacional de México, a subsidiary of the Biblioteca Nacional, and housed in the former Church of San Pedro y San Pablo, Carmen No. 31, about a five-block walk north from the National Palace. From 1930 to 1961 the director of the Hemeroteca was Rafael Carrasco Puente and since 1961 it has been Dr. Gustavo A. Pérez Trejo.

While the physical conditions for research in Mexico are sometimes frustrating, one of the compensations for the investigator is that the locale of his work is often of great interest. Such is the case with the Hemeroteca Nacional. Since the government has been surfeited with ecclesiastical real estate since 1861, it is only natural that some of these sturdy colonial structures should become libraries and archives. During moments of respite from the tedium of scanning newspapers in the Hemeroteca, the researcher's eyes can wander to the pleasing decor, which includes a large and curious mural in art nouveau style by Roberto Montenegro and several stained-glass windows of "typical" scenes done by his students. An interesting pamphlet by Dr. Pérez Trejo tells us that the edifice served as a public hall for reading and discussion during the regime of José Vasconcelos in the early 1920s. The Church of San Pedro y San Pablo is in the heart of the old Jesuit compound of the city, and on entering the narrow and teeming streets outside, one can identify an adjoining building which was the original sixteenth-century Colegio de San Pedro y San Pablo. Around the corner stands its elegant eighteenth-century successor, the Colegio de San Ildefonso, now the Escuela Nacional Preparatoria. Following the expulsion of the Jesuits, the church building suffered neglect and abandonment, serving at various times as a barracks and a military stable. Its twentieth-century revival as a library is fitting tribute to the Jesuit spirit of learning in New Spain.

The Hemeroteca is certainly not a modernized establishment, but its col-

91

lection of more than 172,594 volumes (including 6,000 periodicals) is generally well organized and the working conditions are satisfactory. The staff is
courteous and helpful, and one tends to see the same faces over a period of
years. All works must be consulted on the premises. There are two principal
reading rooms, one on a raised platform under the dome (for newspapers
since the mid-nineteenth century) and the other a ground-level room below
for periodicals. There is also a windowless inner sanctum known as the *sala de
investigadores* where one is sent to consult eighteenth-century and early nineteenth-century materials. The study tables throughout are supplied with ad-
justable inclined racks that greatly facilitate the reading of newspapers. One is
occasionally distracted by a covey of chattering schoolgirls in off the streets,
but the steady din of street traffic drowns out most disturbing noise. The
hours are among the most accommodating of any Mexican library: 8:00 a.m.
to 9:00 p.m. Monday through Friday; 8:00 a.m. to 8:00 p.m. Saturday; and
9:00 a.m. to 1:00 p.m. Sunday.

The coverage in the collection is good, especially for Mexico City publications. Complete runs of major and minor newspapers of the nineteenth and
twentieth centuries are the special treasure of the Hemeroteca, since these are
simply not available, except in very spotty fashion, elsewhere in Mexico or in
the United States. Provincial newspapers are less well represented. Gaps that
do exist in the Hemeroteca, for example, in mid-nineteenth-century newspapers, can often be filled by the collection in the Hemeroteca de Hacienda
(recently reopened to the public). Perhaps the newly organized Hemeroteca
of the Instituto Nacional de Antropología e Historia, located nearby in the
former Convent of Carmen, can also serve as a supplement to the collection in
the Hemeroteca Nacional. There is an adequate alphabetical catalog, but one
has to rely principally on the memory of long-time employees who can usually find things that are inaccurately cataloged or not cataloged at all. Unfortunately, there are few general reference tools available, though the collection
does include some runs of laws and parliamentary debates. For example, the
Hemeroteca has the entire series of national legislative debates from 1867 to
1910. A special feature of the holdings is a collection of almost 100,000 por-
traits and photographs of important Mexican personages.

One recent addition to the Hemeroteca's service is the institution of photocopying and microfilm copying. The work is done on the premises with
competence, efficiency, and courtesy. Twenty-four-hour service is usually
available for small jobs. Photocopying costs $1.50 (Mexican currency) per
shot, microfilm $.90, payable cash in advance. It is fortunate that system-

atized copying is now increasing in Mexico, because the newspapers are given very hard wear, and they are slowly disintegrating. There should be a concerted effort, in Mexico and abroad, to film complete runs of newspapers, particularly those subsequent to the introduction of low-quality newsprint in the 1890s. Otherwise there is a real danger that parts of a vital corpus of research material for modern and contemporary Mexico will be lost to future scholars.

F. The Centro de Estudios de la Historia de México, Condumex by Ramón Eduardo Ruiz

In 1959 the Anaconda Wire and Cable Company organized a Mexican subsidiary, Condumex, which in 1964 became parent to the Centro de Estudios de Historia de México with the purchase of books and documents collected by Luis Gutiérrez Cañedo. In 1968 the company installed the center on the grounds of its plant on Avenida Poniente 140, number 739, Colonia Vallejo. At present the center ranks among the best-organized and best-managed library-archives in Mexico. Its chief drawback, and an obvious one, is its location in the northern industrial zone of Mexico City, where transportation to and from hotels represents a major problem for the visiting scholar. However, apart from the commuting challenge, the center offers excellent facilities for research, with a courteous and helpful staff of librarians who are in command of their material. The hours are 8:00 a.m. to 6:00 p.m. Monday through Friday.

While the library boasts many collections covering a broad slice of Mexican history, the major holdings fall into four categories. The most important and largest collection covers the era of the Revolution, essentially from 1910 to 1920, though some of the documents antedate the outbreak of the protest against Porfirio Díaz, while others extend beyond 1920. The personal correspondence of Venustiano Carranza, approximately twenty thousand documents and fifty-seven thousand telegrams—about 40 percent of them still in code—form the core of the revolutionary papers. They are arranged chronologically and filed in notebooks, easily accessible for study and note taking. The collection is particularly strong in military affairs relating to the army of the northeast and the politics and squabbles of army chieftains in Guerrero and Oaxaca and, in addition, offers a wealth of fresh information on the Revolution of 1910.

While the Carranza papers account for the bulk of the material, a number of other collections complete the revolutionary section. To the private correspondence of Francisco I. Madero, 1905 to 1908, the library added the papers of Jenaro Amezcua, a Zapatista general, and Manuel González, the Carrancista general whose papers span the years between Díaz and the early 1940s, though the majority lie in the decade 1910-20. On the late Porfiriato, the center has the papers of Francisco León de la Barra and some one hundred letters of Ramón Corral. The complete holdings of the *Diario Oficial* from 1867 to the present, the newspaper *La Convención*, the record of the debates of the Aguascaliente meeting of 1914-15, and a splendid collection of photographs for the years between 1910 and 1920 make the library more valuable on the Revolution.

A second point of strength is the era of the War for Independence, approximately 1810 to 1821. Among the important holdings are the documents and papers of General José Morán, Marqués de Vivanco, which discuss the last years of the colony, the Empire of Iturbide, and the first years of federalist rule. Another important source is the correspondence between Viceroy Francisco Xavier Venegas and Bishop Manuel Ignacio González del Campo, including comments on the nature of the insurgents and on José María Morelos. Also, there are approximately two hundred documents on the Spanish army in the provinces of Guanajuato and Oaxaca in 1821. Other documents, often in substantial collections, and including 167 pamphlets, round out the holdings on the Independence era.

The Reforma and the Empire of Maximilian make up the third concentration. The salient materials are the letters of General Pedro González, Maximilian's minister of war; copies of reports to Napoleon; documents on the leaders of the Liberal party of the Reforma; the correspondence of Ignacio Aguilar y Marocho during the Reforma and the Empire; papers from the archive of Luis G. Cuevas, spanning the years of the wars with Texas and the United States, the Reforma, and the Empire; and the personal library of Rafael García, editor of *La Idea Liberal* and first governor of Puebla after the fall of the Empire, which includes correspondence with Benito Juárez, Porfirio Díaz, Francisco Zarco, and others in the Liberal party. There are also documents on the República Restaurada, though the holdings appear fragmentary.

In the colonial section, the fourth concentration, the center is the repository for documents on Nueva Galicia, the Church in Guadalajara, workers' guilds from the sixteenth through the eighteenth centuries, Mexico City and its cathedral, and about two hundred papers on the Inquisition.

Finally, the center's library has more than twenty-five thousand volumes on the colonial years and the national period, including the *memorias* of the secretaries of state from 1823 to 1959. Many of the volumes are rare first editions.

G. The Archivo Microfílmeco de Geneología y Heráldica

by John C. Super

At times referred to as the Mormon Microfilm Archive, this collection of film represents a major source for the study of social and demographic themes of Mexican history from the sixteenth through the twentieth century. Associated with the Academia Mexicana de Genología y Heráldica and with the Church of Jesus Christ of Latter-Day Saints, the filming program was begun in 1958 and is expected to be completed within the next few years. The goals of the project are to microfilm all parish archives in Mexico until 1930, concentrating on birth, confirmation, marriage, and death entries in the parish registers. It includes documentation from the 1530s to the 1960s, although the most complete coverage is for the seventeenth, eighteenth, and nineteenth centuries. Officials of the archive estimate that 80 percent of the parish registers have now been filmed. The extensiveness of this collection makes it one of the foremost national genealogical archives in the world.

There is not a comprehensive published catalog and, unfortunately, no immediate plan for publishing one. The card file located in the archive contains references to approximately ninety thousand rolls of microfilm, with an uncertain amount still uncataloged. The material located in the catalog is well organized, easy to use, generally accurate, and of fair technical quality. It is organized according to state and within each state according to city and the parishes within that city. For easy reference the sections within each parish are color-keyed to the type of information they contain: red for *matrimonio*, yellow for *informaciones matrimoniales*, green for *bautismos*, and white for *confirmaciones*. Much of the data, especially *bautismos*, are also divided between Indians and Spaniards. Information on *bautismos* is the most complete of all the parish register entries.

To substitute for the parish registers when they were not readily available, approximately 20 percent of the civil registers have been filmed, although most of these are still uncataloged. The majority of the civil registers begin in the 1860s and end in the 1930s, but for some cities filming was continued through the early 1960s. In addition there is a variety of other types of source material, although their chronological continuity and spatial distribution is more uneven than both the parish and civil registers. Although this

97

section forms only a small part of the total volume of film in the archive, it nevertheless contains enough information for serious studies of a variety of different topics. Among the types of documents included are notarial records (mainly for Puebla in the sixteenth century), *testamentos, acuerdos, padrones del sagrario, visitas pastorales, diezmos, amonestaciones*, and *divorcios*. These sources are generally restricted to Mexico City and are found for other areas only in isolated cases, such as *testamentos* for Guadalajara.

At the present time it is impossible to present a complete statistical evaluation in tabulated form of the holdings of the archive; even the figures mentioned on the total number of rolls should be seen as approximations rather than as definitive numbers. The following table, which is meant to serve only as a rough guide to the relative geographic distribution of the holdings of the archive, indicates the number of towns where parish and civil registers have been filmed and cataloged.

STATE	TOWNS (parish registers)	TOWNS (civil registers)
Aguascalientes	42	1
Coahuila	19	0
Chihuahua	36	5
Distrito Federal	43	0
Durango	19	0
Guanajuato	59	0
Hidalgo	56	19
Jalisco	113	23
México	74	0
Michoacán	66	0
Morelos	7	0
Nayarit	14	0
Nuevo León	26	0
Oaxaca	10	0
Puebla	70	0
Querétaro	17	0
San Luis Potosí	11	1
Tamaulipas	13	0
Tlaxcala	23	0
Veracruz	21	0
Yucatán	33	0
Zacatecas	15	0

The sheer physical quantity of the archive, with an estimated eighty-five million pages of filmed documents, constitutes a major addition to the available resources of Mexican history. The holdings of the archive provide an immense amount of material which can serve as the documentary base for a variety of research projects. The completeness of some sections of the parish registers and the civil registers should be especially significant for historical analysis of demographic trends in many regions of Mexico. Detailed studies on the social and ethnic structure of different communities and regions, such as marriage patterns between and among different social, economic, and ethnic groups, can profitably utilize the holdings of the archive. Questions of the general interpretation of Mexican history can be reassessed, for example, the relative strength of the Church in different regions and the impact of the national government on roles traditionally claimed by the church. The chronological depth of the material makes the archive of interest to specialists working on research questions in both the colonial and national period and on topics that transcend this traditional periodization of Mexican history. In short, the availability of such a large body of documentation will provide a firmer foundation for social science research in Mexico.

The archive is located in Mexico City, Colonia Industrial, Norte 26, number 321. The telephone number is 517-59-23 or 517-55-61. For authorization to use the archive, see Lic. Romo Celis, assistant director of the Academia Mexicana de Genología y Heráldica, located on Gante 7, number 402. Nine microfilm readers are available for the use of researchers, eight of which are Recordak Film Readers Model MPE. Copies of all of the film in Mexico are also held by the Genealogical Society of the Church of Jesus Christ of Latter-Day Saints in Salt Lake City.

7

Other Major Documentary Collections

A. Mexican Sources in the Archivo General de Centro América by William L. Sherman

Scholars concerned with some areas of history in southernmost Mexico, during the colonial and early Independence periods will find it necessary to consult the valuable manuscript collections in the Archivo General de Centro América in Guatemala City.[1] For most of the colonial period the Mexican state of Chiapas was attached politically to Central America. First under the Audiencia de los Confines (at Gracias a Dios, Honduras, 1544-49), Chiapas later fell within the jurisdiction of the Audiencia de Guatemala, following transfer to the Guatemalan city of Santiago (now Antigua) in 1549. Consequently, there is a great body of information relating to that province in the AGCA. Included among the richly diverse documents are those treating Church history; originally Chiapas was suffragan to the bishopric of Tlaxcala, but later became part of the bishopric of Guatemala, with which it had better communication.

Other Mexican areas pertained to the Central American government as well. By a royal cédula of January 20, 1553, confirmed in 1556, it was ordered that Soconusco be attached to the authorities of Guatemala, although apparently the formal annexation did not take effect until January, 1569. Moreover, for a short time during the sixteenth century, Yucatán, Tabasco, and Cozumel belonged to the audiencia in Guatemala. The Crown decreed on February 7, 1550, that with the audiencia settled at Santiago those provinces would be transferred from New Spain, whose officials were ordered not to interfere. This arrangement, however, lasted little more than a decade, for in 1560 Yucatán, Tabasco, and Cozumel were returned to the jurisdiction of Mexico.

101

The investigator seeking Mexican materials in Guatemala will find the Archivo General de Centro América one of the best-organized archives anywhere in Latin America. In 1935 the late J. Joaquín Pardo became the director of the archive, and under his supervision documents scattered about in various places were gradually brought together. By 1956, with a new building, the integrated archive greatly facilitated the work of the scholar. In 1968, when Rigoberto Bran Azmitia was interim director, the name was changed from the Archivo General de Guatemala to the Archivo General de Centro América, in recognition of its wider scope, since colonial Guatemala had jurisdictional authority over the other provinces of Central America except for Panama. At this time a concerted effort was also made to conserve the manuscripts and to initiate programs of restoration and preservation.

The archive is conveniently located in the same building as the National Library, near the central plaza, close to hotels, stores, and restaurants. The *sala de investigación* provides ample working space. If its appointments are not so rich as those of the Archivo General de Indias and the Archivo General de la Nación of Mexico, it does provide a table for each individual investigator. The lighting is good and there are drinking and toilet facilities in the building. On the second floor there are a few private research rooms, usually occupied by those working on long projects. The atmosphere in the AGCA is informal and friendly, and the director and staff are courteous and efficient. Arrangements can be made for photocopies of documents at a reasonable rate, and while there are no microfilming facilities offered by the archive, permission can be obtained to photograph manuscripts.

One outstanding feature of the AGCA is the very extensive *fichero,* a monument to the labors of Professor Pardo. Before his death in 1964, Pardo had been indefatigable in his efforts to catalog the great quantity of documents under his care. For thirty years as director of the archive he made cards for the papers, devising his own system of classification. The fruit of his great industry can be found in the many drawers of fichas, with headings under geographical areas, subjects, and personal names. The value of this system can be appreciated by the fact that, according to one estimate, there may be as many as 4,200,000 cards to consult. Some of these references give only a brief description of the documents, such as, "Padrón de los tributarios del pueblo de San Francisco Tonalá, año 1753." But many provide more extensive descriptions, as in the case of the two following citations:

Mueble fichero 8-35   Escuintla   Soconusco

7 de enero de 1707, R.P. — Emplazamiento a Domingo Ramos, José Lópes y Pascual Ramos, indios vecinos del pueblo de Escuintla, Soconusco, para que declaren si vendieron en buena venta, unas tierras al sargento mayor Manuel de Mera Santa Cruz, este emplazamiento fue cometido a Blas García de Amorez, alguacil mayor y teniente de Governador en Soconusco.

Al. 24. Exp. 10220. — Leg. 1576. fol. 1.

Mueble fichero 6.6-31   Proclamación
                                                            Comitán

30 de abril de 1825. — Pedro Celis, quien fuera alcalde 1° Constitucional de la ciudad de Santa María Comitán en 1821, certifica que en agosto de aquel año, Fr. Ignacio Baruoya, proclamó la Independencia del Gobierno de España.

B99.2. Exp. 32998. Leg. 1412. fol. 6.

Helpful as these cards are, however, one should not rely too much on them; there are a few errors in the files, and it sometimes happens that the citation is incorrect and a document cannot be located from the card reference. A researcher interested in eighteenth-century Chiapas cannot assume, for instance, that all pertinent documentation will appear under the Provincia de Chiapas section. Still, the Pardo files make the AGCA one of the easiest of any archive in which to work, and the system saves the investigator many hours of searching. The cataloging project was never completely finished, but the majority of the documents were noted, and very little will escape the assiduous scholar, especially if good use is made of the cross-indexing. While most of the manuscripts can be called from the card files, to be certain one should call the complete legajos.

The address of the Archivo General de Centro América is 4a. Avenida 7a. y 8a. Calles, Zona 1, Ciudad de Guatemala, C.A.; the telephone number is 23-0-37. For further information one may write the AGCA, addressing either Sr. Arturo Valdés Oliva, director, or Srta. Carmen Paláez Olivares, secretaria. Before going to Guatemala for research it would be helpful to consult some of the literature describing the archival holdings and the classification system.

N O T E

1. The writer wishes to thank Christopher Lutz for his generous assistance in this preparation.

B. Resources for Mexican History in the United States National Archives by Kenneth J. Grieb

The National Archives and Records Service of the United States government possesses vast amounts of material useful for the study of Mexican history. These resources shed important light on internal Mexican affairs as well as on Mexican–United States relations, since American representatives kept extensive records during times of turmoil when national officials were fully preoccupied by civil strife.

The records of the Department of State constitute the largest portion of the resources in the National Archives dealing with Mexico. This vast collection is invaluable, and the Mexican files are among the most voluminous. State Department documents, contained in Record Group 59, are located in the legislative, judicial, and diplomatic branches of the archives. Until 1906, the records were divided into four categories: instructions to United States diplomatic and consular representatives, despatches received from these envoys, notes to foreign legations and embassies in the United States, and missives received from these agencies. Using documents from this period is rather cumbersome, since each separate series must be consulted. From 1906 to 1910, a system of subject files was employed. This format is also somewhat cumbersome, as the establishment of files depended upon the foresight of the clerk, resulting in wide variations in length. Since the file numbers were assigned in sequence of creation, they offer no clues to their contents without use of the department's indexes and guides.

In 1910 a new system was adopted, establishing consolidated decimal files organized by nation, with internal subject headings. The two most useful major series are 800 for internal affairs and 700 for international relations. The remaining digits identify the countries involved, with the decimals signifying the subgroupings. The number for Mexico is 12, and that of the United States is 11. Hence the 812.00 file deals with the Internal Affairs of Mexico and contains the bulk of the information, while the 711.12 file encompasses relations between Mexico and the United States. Documents are numbered consecutively as slash numbers, for example, 812.00/8693. There are also subgroupings for special topics, such as 812.51 for financial affairs in Mexico. For certain periods the 711.12 file contains only routine items, while most of the information relating to Mexican-American affairs is in the 812.00 file. Cross-references lead to supplemental files, such as those of the Division of Latin American Affairs, Inter-American Conferences, the various "special agents" detailed to Mexico, and the department's personnel files. The Post Records in Record Group 84 contain the archives of each station, including the consulates and the embassy. They offer insights into local affairs, and contain exchanges between consulates not transmitted to Washington. Since the United States has maintained a large number of consulates in Mexico, these files are quite extensive.

State Department records are theoretically available for study after a twenty-year lapse; but at present only the portions through 1941 constitute the "open period." Records beyond the open period, extending through the year of the most recent volume of *Foreign Relations* constitute the "restricted period," currently 1942 through 1945. These are available to qualified researchers by special permission of the State Department, which is normally extended to recognized scholars, subject to a review of note cards. Documents for years not yet covered in *Foreign Relations* are closed. A fifty-year limit applies to personnel files.

Army Department records housed in the archives also contain vast stores of information regarding Mexico. During the nineteenth century separate topical files were maintained. Records from this period useful to Mexicanists include those relating to the acquisition of Texas and the Mexican War. The files of the Adjutant General's Office, Record Group 94, constitute the most valuable portion of army documents during the twentieth century. Beginning in 1917 they were organized in consolidated decimal files which group information by period, office, and country. These series include such items as reports by military attachés, the archives of the Office of Strategic Services, a section concerning affairs along the Rio Grande frontier, records of army posts located near the border, and files concerning specific campaigns, such as the Veracruz occupation and the Pershing expedition.

Generally, army records are readily open through 1939, although items relating to the intelligence division are partially restricted, necessitating a screening process. Post-1939 materials are available only to bona fide researchers who are United States citizens. Their use requires special clearance and a review of both the notes and the manuscript. Records of the Office of Strategic Services are under the jurisdiction of the State Department and are subject to its regulations.

Navy Department records in Record Group 45 also contain some information regarding Mexico. The daily reports and logbooks of the commanders of United States ships and squadrons operating in Mexican waters constitute a valuable supplement to the consular files, since the United States normally kept ships stationed off the coasts of Mexico, particularly during crisis periods. Nineteenth-century communications were filed in general groups by commanders, alphabetized within each rank, rendering their use difficult. Separate files of reports by squadron commanders are also available. Beginning about 1910, the correspondence was grouped according to station and region. Records concerning Mexico can be found in the Caribbean and Central Pacific sections. Subject files were also instituted, with a series containing the reports of "Naval commanders in Mexican waters during the Revolution," 1913-21.

Other, less voluminous, files containing information about Mexico may be found throughout the records of the various agencies encompassed within the legislative, judicial, and diplomatic branches. For example, a category of General Records contains files dealing with Claims Commissions, Boundary Commissions, and International Conferences. The Department of Justice files contain information regarding investigations of arms smuggling along the Mexican frontier. Records of the Department of the Treasury also deal with this subject, chiefly in the Coast Guard section, and the daily reports of secret service agents stationed along the border. The files of Customs Service posts contain useful data regarding commerce and smuggling. Specialized files concerning joint projects may be found in the appropriate departments. For example, such departments as Agriculture and Commerce receive information on their specialties gathered by their representatives in Mexico.

The military and legislative, judicial, and diplomatic branches of the archives are open from 8:45 a.m. to 5:00 p.m. Monday through Friday. Records from the open period can be transferred to the Central Search Room, which is open from 8:45 a.m. to 10:00 p.m. Monday through Friday, and 8:45 a.m. to 5:00 p.m. on Saturdays. Typewriters are allowed, and photocopy orders are accepted for documents from the open periods. There are ample guides, indexes, and aids available for all records sections, although there are some variations reflecting filing procedures. Archival personnel provide highly competent assistance. Admission to the open-period records is readily obtainable, requiring only completion of a brief form at the archives. It is suggested, however, that researchers write in advance to the director of the appropriate division, giving notice of their intended arrival and details regarding their projects. Dr. Mark G. Eckhoff is director of the Legislative, Judicial, and Diplomatic Records Division, Dr. Robert W. Krauskopf is director of the Old Military Records Division, and Dr. Mabel E. Deutrich is director of Modern Military Records Division. For restricted periods, advance permission from the appropriate agency is necessary. Processing of requests normally requires at least six weeks. The directors of the archival sections will furnish the appropriate information regarding procedures for obtaining such authorizations.

8

Libraries in Mexico, D. F.

by Elsa Barberena

All of the following libraries of special interest to historians are located in Mexico City with the exception of the University of the Americas library, which is in Cholula, Puebla. The researcher will find in these collections much more than the following brief summaries can possibly suggest. Fuller published descriptions exist for all of them, and the researcher interested in a more detailed guide is directed to the *Directory of Mexico City Archives*, 2d ed., rev. and enlarged (1967). The information in this chapter is based upon that work.

List of Abbreviations

Circulation A: Patrons may check out books after meeting registration, membership, or deposit requirements.

Circulation B: Books may be used by the general public only in the library itself.

Film: The collection contains microfilm, motion pictures, slides, microcards, or microfiches.

Inter-1: Interlibrary loan service maintained.

Micro.: Microfilm readers on the premises.

Reprod.: Photographic reproduction of materials is made by the library or is arranged.

ULS: Collaborates with the Union List of Serials available in Mexico. For further information, call 518-20-00, ext. 214.

Academia Mexicana de la Historia
Biblioteca

Plaza Carlos Pacheco 21, Mexico 1, D.F.
Tel. 513-31-15
Established in 1916
Open only on Sat.; call 513-31-15 for hours
8,510 volumes, 30 periodicals (ULS), 10 newspapers
87% Sp., 5% Fr., 5% Eng., 2% Lat., 1% other
Circulation B
Exchange, micro.

The library contains numerous sets of published historical documents; the *Memorias* of the academy (1942-67), and microfilm of the archives of Durango. The *Boletín* of the academy is exchanged for the publications of many learned societies. Although the library is maintained primarily for the members of the academy, it is open to the public on a limited basis. Call 513-31-15 for further information.

Archivo General de la Nación

National Palace, Mexico 1, D.F.
Tel. 512-20-95
Established in 1823
Mon.-Fri. 8:30 a.m.–2:30 p.m.; Sat. 8:30 a.m.–12:30 p.m.
Librarian, Jorge Ignacio Rubio Mañé
16,000 volumes, 150 periodicals (ULS), 6 newspapers
95% Sp., 3% Eng., 2% Fr.
Circulation B
Maps, micro., pamphlet collection, reprod.

This collection is made up of millions of documents which cover all aspects of public administration of the colonial period (lands, finance, tobacco, mines, etc.) and subsequent periods as well. It also contains a reference library for researchers in the history of Mexico. On the main floor there is an exhibition hall where valuable codices and historical documents are on display.

Biblioteca Iberoamericana

Luis González Obregón 18, Mexico 1, D.F.
Tel. 512-76-97
Established in 1924
Mon.-Fri. 8:00 a.m.–2:00 p.m., 4:00 p.m.–1:00 a.m.; Sat. 8:00 a.m.–1:00
   p.m., 4:00 p.m.–7:00 p.m.
Librarian, Margarita Morales; Assistant in Charge, Pascual Avalos
47,883 volumes
95% Sp., 5% other
Circulation B
   Although the collection is general in nature, a large part is dedicated to the
fine arts, literature, education, and Latin American culture. It contains the
former Justo Sierra Library of the Department of Public Education and some
copies of books copyrighted by the department. There are plans for future
expansion.

Biblioteca Isidro Fabela

Plaza San Jacinto #5, Villa Alvaro Obregón, Mexico 20, D.F.
Tel. 548-58-03
Established in 1963
Mon.-Fri. 9:00 a.m.–9:00 p.m.; Sat. 9:00 a.m.–1:00 p.m.
Librarian, Baldomero Segura García
28,000 volumes, 150 periodicals, 100 newspapers
70% Sp., 20% Fr., 5% Eng., 5% Ital.
Circulation B
Exhibitions, films, micro., reprod.
   This is the private library of Mr. Isidro Fabela, specializing in international
law, Mexican and American history, literature, the fine arts, and general
works.

Biblioteca Manuel Orozco y Berra

Castillo de Chapultepec, Mexico 5, D.F.
Tel. 511-40-70, 511-22-23
Established in 1945
Mon.-Fri. 8:30 a.m.–7:00 p.m.; Sat. 8:30 a.m.–1:00 p.m.
In Charge, Dr. Enrique Florescano; Assistant, Iginio Domínguez Barrón

7,025 vols.
90% Sp., 6% Eng., 4% Fr.
Circulation B
Inter-l, maps, pamphlet collection
The collection is rich in Mexican history source material.

Biblioteca Miguel de Cervantes Saavedra

Corner, Héroes and San Fernando, Mexico 1, D.F.
Tel. 513-15-98
Established in 1924
Mon.-Fri. 8:00 a.m.–2:00 p.m., 4:00 p.m.–11:00 p.m.; Sat. 4:00 p.m.–7:00 p.m.
Librarian, Silviano Urzúa Lozano; Assistants, Carmen Cordero and María Sobrereira de Prado
23,400 volumes, 15 periodicals, 6 newspapers
55% Sp., 20% Eng., 15% Fr., 5% Lat., 5% other
Circulation B
Pamphlet collection
This is a general library with major collections in medicine, law, literature, and history.

Biblioteca Nacional de México

Isabel la Católica and República de El Salvador, Mexico 1, D.F.
Tel. 513-56-95, 513-67-97; reading room, 512-56-95
Established in 1867
Mon.-Sat. 9:00 a.m.–11:00 p.m.; Sun. 9:00 a.m.–2:00 p.m.; manuscript collection, Mon.-Sat. 9:00 a.m.–9:00 p.m.
Librarian, Lic. Ernesto de la Torre Villar; Assistants, Javier Campos, Gloria Escamilla González, Guillermo Hernández, and Jorge Inclán Téllez
1,000,000 volumes
50% Sp., 20% Lat., 10% Fr., 8% Eng., 12% other
Circulation B
Inter-l., bibliographies, exhibitions, lectures, reprod.
Now housed in a renovated church, the National Library is rich in old and rare books and manuscripts. In addition, since February, 1958, Mexican publishers have been required to deposit two copies of every book published. Of its many collections the following are especially important: Colección

Lafragua, which is an extensive pamphlet collection dealing with the history of Mexico from the end of the eighteenth century through the first half of the nineteenth; the Colección de la Revolución Mexicana (1910); the rare book collection; and the manuscript collection containing the papers of Benito Juárez and the Archivo Franciscano. The library is also a depository for United Nations and UNESCO publications. It publishes the quarterly *Boletín del Instituto de Investigaciones Bibliográficas*, the monthly *Bibliografía Mexicana*, and the quarterly yearbook of national bibliography. Files of periodicals and newspapers are not maintained here, but in the Hemeroteca Nacional.

Biblioteca Pública de la Dirección General de Derecho del Autor, Secretaría de Educación Pública

Auditorio Nacional, Mexico 5, D.F.
Tel. 520-90-10, ext. 171
Established in 1964
Mon.-Fri. 8:30 a.m.–1:00 p.m., 3:00 p.m.–8:00 p.m.; Sat. 9:00 a.m.–1:00 p.m.
Assistant in Charge, Angel Fuentes
15,631 volumes
100% Sp.
Circulation B
    The collection consists of copies of books that authors must deposit with the Dirección General de Derecho del Autor of the Secretaría de Educación Pública.

Cámara de Diputados Biblioteca del Congreso de la Unión

Tacuba 29, Mexico 1, D.F.
Tel. 521-48-96
Established in 1936
Mon.-Sat. 9:30 a.m.–9:30 p.m.
Librarian, Lic. Alberto Morales Jiménez; Associate Librarian, Lilia Ojeda de Montor
130,000 volumes, 500 periodicals (ULS), 41 newspapers
75% Sp., 15% Eng., 5% Fr., 5% other

Circulation B

Beginning in February, 1958, by presidential decree, Mexican publishers were required to deposit two copies of every Mexican publication in the library. The collection includes up-to-date files of the *Diario Oficial*, the *Semanario Judicial de la Federación*, and state laws.

Capilla Alfonsina
Biblioteca de Alfonso Reyes

Avenida Gral. Benjamín Hill 122, Mexico 11, D.F.
Tel. 515-22-25
Established in 1939
Mon.-Fri. call 515-22-25; closed Sat.
Librarian, Alicia Reyes
40,000 volumes, 50 periodicals, 10 newspapers
55% Sp., 25% Fr., 5% Eng., 2.5% Ital., 2.5% Port., 10% other
Circulation B

The library contains the correspondence of Alfonso Reyes with writers such as Valle Inclán, Valéry Larbaud, Menéndez Pidal, Jules Romains, Jorge Luis Borges, and others, and the historical archive of General Bernardo Reyes. La Capilla Alfonsina publishes a quarterly *Boletín*, edited by the Amigos de Alfonso Reyes. The library serves members of the Amigos only. For further information call 515-22-25.

Casino Español de México
Biblioteca

Isabel la Católica 29 and 31, Mexico 1, D.F.
Tel. 513-18-55
Established in 1863
Mon.-Fri. 11:00 a.m.–1:00 p.m., 4:00 p.m.–7:00 p.m.; closed Sat.
15,000 volumes, 20 periodicals, 10 newspapers
95% Sp., 5% other
Circulation B

This library collection specializes in works on the activities of Spain in Mexico and elsewhere in Latin America.

Centro de Estudios Literarios
Biblioteca Julio Jiménez Rueda

Upper level of the Biblioteca Central, Ciudad Universitaria, Mexico 20, D.F.
Tel. 548-65-00, ext. 440
Established in 1960
Mon.-Fri. 9:00 a.m.–2:00 p.m.
Assistant in Charge, María Isolina Trujillo Maldonado
12,900 volumes, 200 periodicals (ULS), 5 newspapers
80% Sp., 15% Fr., 5% Eng.
Circulation B

This collection includes not only Spanish literature but also Mexican, Latin American, and French literature. It also contains an important collection in Mexican history and literature in general.

El Colegio de México
Biblioteca

Guanajuato 125, Mexico 7, D.F.
Tel. 584-11-22
Established in 1941
Mon.-Fri. 8:00 a.m.–8:00 p.m.; Sat. 9:00 a.m.–1:30 p.m.
Librarian, Lic. Ario Garza Mercado; Assistants, Engracia Sánchez Mejorada, Cecilia Culebra, and Clotilde Tejeda
90,000 volumes, 2,000 periodicals (ULS), 10 newspapers
40% Sp., 30% Eng., 20% Fr., 5% Lat., 5% other
Circulation A
Inter-l., exchange, films, maps, micro., pamphlet collection

This library contains important works in the fields of history, literature, philology, social sciences, and oriental studies. It has microfilm copies of documents concerning international relations between Mexico and the United States and between Mexico and Spain. The library is maintained primarily for students and faculty but is also open to the public on a limited basis.

Colegio Nacional
Biblioteca

Luis González Obregón 23, Mexico 1, D.F.
Tel. 522-07-98
Established in 1963
Mon.-Fri. 4:00 p.m.–9:00 p.m.; closed Sat.
Assistant in Charge, Oscar Camarillo Ramírez
5,000 vols., 150 periodicals, 50 newspapers
80% Sp., 15% Fr., 5% Eng.
Circulation B

Specializing in colonial art and Mexican history, this library serves members only, although in the near future it will be opened to the public. The collection is the personal library of Manuel Toussaint.

Dirección de Servicios Administrativos
Archivo General del ex-Ayuntamiento de la Ciudad de México

Edificio del Ex-Ayuntamiento, Plaza de la Constitución, first floor, Mexico 1, D.F.
Established in the eighteenth century
Mon.-Fri. 9:00 a.m.–2:30 p.m.; Sat. 9:00 a.m.–1:00 p.m.
Librarian, Dionisio Herrera Vieyra; Assistant in Charge, Miguel Mendoza López
8,000 volumes, 2 periodicals
100% Sp.
Circulation B

This archive contains documentation on the development of municipal government in Mexico City since 1523. Its special collections include the *Actas de Cabildo* from the founding of the city until 1928 as well as up-to-date files of the *Diario Oficial* and the *Gaceta Oficial.*

Dirección General de Bibliotecas
Biblioteca Central

Entrepiso, Ciudad Universitaria, Mexico 20, D.F.
Tel. 548-65-00, ext. 168, Director; ext. 360, Public Services
Established in 1924
Mon.-Fri. 8:00 a.m.–8:00 p.m.; Sat. 8:00 a.m.–1:00 p.m.

Librarian, Dra. Alicia Perales de Mercado; Coordinator, Judith Licea Ayala; Assistants, Lic. Angel Martínez, Alejandra Gutiérrez, and Oscar Zambrano
275,000 volumes, 12,451 periodicals (ULS)
60% Sp., 30% Eng., 10% other
Circulation A
Inter-l., bibliographies, exchange, film, maps, micro., pamphlet collection, reprod.

Facultad de Filosofía Letras
Biblioteca Samuel Ramos

Ciudad Universitaria, Mexico 20, D.F.
Tel. 548-65-00, ext. 221
Established in 1910
Mon.-Fri. 9:00 a.m.–9:00 p.m.; Sat. 9:00 a.m.–1:00 p.m.
Assistant in Charge, Lic. Lilia Soberanes
71,500 volumes, 633 periodicals (ULS), 4 newspapers
60% Sp., 20% Eng., 10% Fr., 5% Ger., 5% other
Circulation A
Inter-l., bibliographies, pamphlet collection
   This library is rich in works of world literature, philosophy, and history. It has many of the classics in their original languages as well as in translation, such as the bilingual editions of Didot and Nisara. In addition to the main library there are specialized collections housed in various departments.

Instituto Cultural Hispano-Mexicano
Biblioteca Miguel de Cervantes

Tabasco 68, Mexico 7, D.F.
Tel. 525-82-76
Established in 1961

Mon.-Fri. 11:00 a.m.–2:00 p.m., 5:00 p.m.–7:00 p.m.; closed Sat.
Librarian, Angel Odogherty; Assistant, María Josefa Núñez
7,112 volumes, 20 periodicals, 1 newspaper
100% Sp.
Circulation A
Inter-l, film, micro.
   Among the important collections of this library are those in Spanish literature and the history of Spain.

Instituto de Investigaciones Históricas
Biblioteca Rafael García Granados

Torre de Humanidades, seventh floor, Ciudad Universitaria
Tel. 548-65-60, ext. 200
Mon.-Fri. 10:00 a.m.–2:00 p.m., 4:30 p.m.–8:00 p.m.; Sat. 10:00 a.m.–
  1:00 p.m.
Assistants in Charge, Ana María Rincón and Virginia Limón
6,000 volumes, 20 periodicals
90% Sp., 8% Eng., 1% Fr., 1% other
Circulation B
Micro.

The library contains the holdings of Rafael García Granados on the history of Mexico; reports of government agencies; and works in prehistory and European archeology as well as many important anthropological studies.

Instituto Nacional de Antropología e Historia
Biblioteca Nacional de Antropología e Historia

Paseo de la Reforma and Calzada Gandhi, Mexico 5, D.F.
Tel. 511-07-78, 511-09-93
Established in 1825
Mon.-Fri. 9:00 a.m.–9:00 p.m.; Sat. 9:00 a.m.–2:00 p.m.
Librarian, Antonio Pompa y Pompa; Assistants, Zita Basich-Canessi, M. Carmen Anzures, Bárbara Juárez, Germán Plasencia, Guillermo Sánchez, and Oscar Zembrano
300,000 volumes, 400 periodicals (ULS), 6 newspapers
65% Sp., 20% Eng., 10% Fr., 2% Lat., 3% other
Circulation A
Inter-l., exhibitions, exchange, films, lectures, micro., pamphlet collections, reprod.

The library contains an extensive collection dealing with anthropology and history in general, but especially Mexican history and anthropology. Special collections include the Fondo González Casanova in linguistics, the Fondo Lira in philosophy and theology, and the Fondo Gómez Orozco and González Obregón in Mexican history. It holds a number of sixteenth-century publications as well as some original codices. It receives all United States Library of Congress cards for books in its special subject fields. Manuscripts of theses presented for degrees at the National School of Anthropology and History are deposited here. The microfilm center has 14,000,000 copies, 500 boxes of tapes, and 150 record albums of Indian music.

Instituto Panamericano de Geografía e Historia
Biblioteca

Ex-Arzobispado 29, Mexico 18, D.F.
Tel. 519-19-10, 515-08-20
Established in 1930
Mon.-Fri. 9:00 a.m.–2:30 p.m.; closed Sat.
Assistant in Charge, Agueda Canedo
170,000 volumes, 1,100 periodicals (ULS)
60% Sp., 20% Eng., 10% Fr., 10% other
Circulation A
Inter-l., bibliographies, exchange, maps, micro., pamphlet collections
   In addition to its specialities in history, geography, cartography, science, geophysics, and anthropology, this library is strong in bibliography, literature, and political and social science of the Americas (Salón José Toribio Medina). Much of the basic material came to the library as the gift of Fernando Iglesias Calderón. Through extensive exchange agreements, publications from foreign universities, international organizations, and learned societies are received regularly. The library has a large pamphlet collection and 15,000 Mexican and foreign maps, all cataloged. Because of its affiliation with the Institute, the library specializes in American affairs. It publishes and distributes the *Boletín Aéreo, Boletín Bibliográfico de Antropología Americana, Boletín Bibliográfico de Geografía y Oceanografía Americanas, Revista de Historia de América, Revista Geográfica*, and *Revista Cartográfica*.

Museo de la Ciudad de México
Biblioteca

Pino Suárez 30 and República de El Salvador, Mexico 1, D.F.
Tel. 542-06-71, 542-04-87
Established in 1964
Mon.-Fri. 10:00 a.m.–6:00 p.m.; Sat. 9:00 a.m.–2:00 p.m., 3:00 p.m.–7:00 p.m.
Librarian, Federico Hernández Serrano; Assistant, María Elena Cortés J.
10,000 volumes, 100 periodicals

65% Sp., 30% Eng., 5% other
Circulation B
The library is important for its collection on the history of Mexico City.

Recinto de Homenaje a Don Benito Juárez
Biblioteca

National Palace, Patio Benito Juárez, Mexico 1, D.F.
Tel. 522-56-46
Established in 1957
Mon.-Fri. 10:00 a.m.–2:00 p.m., 3:00 p.m.–7:00 p.m.
Assistant in Charge, María Enriqueta Rojas
4,000 volumes
80% Sp., 12% Fr., 8% Eng.
Circulation B
Bibliographies, exhibitions, film, micro., reprod.

This library is administered by the Departamento de Bibliotecas y Archivos Económicos and contains material treating Benito Juárez and his administration, the Reform, and the Constitutional Congress of 1857. In adjacent halls there is an iconographic collection of the Reform as well as a historical-biographical museum of Juárez and his family.

Secretaría de Educación Pública
Biblioteca de México

Plaza de la Ciudadela No. 6, Mexico 1, D.F.
Tel. 510-25-91, 518-68-93
Established in 1946
Mon.-Fri. 9:00 a.m.–9:00 p.m.; Sat. 9:00 a.m.–8:00 p.m.
Librarian, Dr. María Teresa Chávez; Associate Librarian, Lic. Miguel Palacios
     Beltrán; Assistants, Concepción Alonso Seyec, and Ana María León Perea
111,117 volumes, 174 periodicals, 10 newspapers
65% Sp., 10% Fr., 15% Eng., 8% Lat., 2% other
Circulation A
Inter-l., bibliographies, exhibitions, lectures, micro., pamphlet collections, reprod.

This library is especially strong in science and has such special collections as the Colección Caso, which belonged to Dr. Antonio Caso and comprises 4,500 volumes, largely in philosophy; the Colección Basave, which belonged to Carlos Basave Castillo Negrete and contains a large number of pamphlets

on Mexican history, especially the Revolution; the Vicente Lombardo Toledano Collection, consisting of 11,525 volumes on philosophy and the social
sciences; and the Colección Palafox, which is made up of some 9,000 volumes
on religion, largely in Latin, and originally belonging to various convents. An
important project of the library is the development of a list of subject
headings for use in the catalogs of Spanish-language libraries.

Secretaría de Hacienda y Crédito Público
Biblioteca Miguel Lerdo de Tejada

Avenida República de El Salvador No. 49, Mexico 1, D.F.
Established in 1928
Mon.-Fri. 8:00 a.m.–8:00 p.m.; Sat. 8:00 a.m.–5:00 p.m.
Librarian, Dr. Gustavo A. Pérez Trejo
300,000 volumes, 1,500 periodicals (ULS), 100 newspapers
38% Sp., 28% Fr., 25% Eng., 4% Lat., 5% other
Circulation B
Inter-l., bibliographies, exchange, exhibitions, film, maps, micro., pamphlet
    collections, projectors, reprod., translations made
    For the researcher in Mexican history, economics, and social studies, this
library contains much material. Its collection of nineteenth-century newspapers is exceptionally complete. Special collections include those of Díaz
Dufoo and Martínez Alfaro, as well as the former library of Miguel A. Quin-
tana. The manuscript collection includes the papers of Ignacio Comonfort,
for which there is an annotated index, as well as those of Benito Juárez, Francisco I. Madero, and others. The Secretaría is in the process of microfilming
the documents, and there is a catalog of those completed. The library distributes the *Boletín Bibliográfico* published by the Secretaría. The Sección de
Archivos Económicos of the Departamento de Bibliotecas provides excellent
service.

Secretaría de la Defensa Nacional
Biblioteca del Ejército

Edificio de la Secretaría de la Defensa Nacional, second floor, Lomas de
    Sotelo, Mexico 10, D.F.
Tel. 520-60-00, 520-90-60, ext. 305
Established in 1926
Mon.-Fri. 8:30 a.m.–2:00 p.m.; Sat. 9:00 a.m.–1:00 p.m.

Assistant in Charge, Rudolfo Zapata Hernández; Assistants, Estela Flores López, María del Carmen Flores López, Jorge Alamaraz Arellano, and Juan Velásquez Rodríguez
40,000 volumes, 5 periodicals (ULS), 6 newspapers
60% Sp., 20% Fr., 10% Ital., 10% other
Circulation B
Bibliographies
    This library specializes in military affairs and has complete collections of the military laws of Mexico. It also contains material in the fields of social science and history.

Sociedad Mexicana de Geografía y Estadística
Biblioteca Benemérito Benito Juárez

Justo Sierra 19, Mexico 1, D.F.
Tel. 512-86-55, 522-20-49
Established in 1839
Mon.-Fri. 8:00 a.m.–8:00 p.m.; Sat. 9:00 a.m.–2:00 p.m.
Librarian, Concepción Saavedra; Assistants, Lauro Vite Arenas, Jesús Antonio Rodríguez Valdés, and Ofelia Maldonado Popoca
44,611 volumes, 1,000 periodicals (ULS)
80% Sp., 7% Eng., 5% Fr., 3% Ital., 3% Lat., 2% other
Circulation B
Bibliographies, exchange, maps, pamphlet collections, projectors, reprod.
    This library contains much general material. Special collections include those of Pastor Rouaix on geography and José Castillo y Piña on history. The library is of prime importance for its holdings in Mexican geography and statistics.

Suprema Corte de Justicia de la Nación
Biblioteca

Pino Suárez 2, Mexico 1, D.F.
Tel. 522-15-00, ext. 109
Established in 1917
Mon.-Fri. 9:00 a.m.–1:45 p.m.; Sat. 9:00 a.m.–12:45 p.m.
Librarian, Dr. Luis Dorantes Tamayo
4,633 volumes, 20 periodicals, 2 newspapers
64% Sp., 21% Eng., 7% Ital., 6% Fr., 2% other

Circulation B

Pamphlet collections

Although the collection is primarily in the field of law, there are also works in history and social science. It contains the Corpus Juris, materials for the study of the history of law, and compilations of Spanish laws. A separate office for the compilation of laws maintains an up-to-date file of all Mexican legislation.

Universidad de la Américas
Centro de Fuentes para el Aprendizaje
Biblioteca

Apartado Postal 507, Puebla, Mexico

Tel. 3-10-55, ext. 148, 149, 151

Established in 1940

Mon.-Th. 8:00 a.m.–11:00 p.m.; Fri. 8:00 a.m.–5:00 p.m.; Sat. 10:00 a.m.–
5:00 p.m.; Sun. 3:00 p.m.–9:00 p.m.

Librarian, Dr. Manuel de Ezcurdia; Associate Librarian, Elsa Barberena B.;
Cataloger, Robert L. Abell

80,000 volumes, 1,500 periodicals (ULS), 14 newspapers

50% Eng., 40% Sp., 5% Fr., 5% other

Circulation A

Inter-l., bibliographies, document exchange, maps, micro., pamphlet collections

The collection is general because its primary goal is to serve the needs of the university. The special collections reflect the emphases of the curriculum. It is especially strong in anthropology; fine arts; economics; Mexican, Latin American, and Spanish history; Spanish, Mexican, and Latin American literature; political and social sciences; science; and technology. Its reference collection is up-to-date. Items of special interest are the Robert Barlow Collection of source materials on Mesoamerican anthropology; the General Porfirio Díaz collection of over one million documents; the Lorna Lavery critical and historical texts relating to Spain, Mexico, and Latin America; the Pablo and J. Guadalupe Herrera Carrillo Collection on Mexican history and Mexican and Spanish literature; the economics collection of Dr. Redvers Opie; and the finance collection of Professor James Washington Bell. The library contains an important collection of Mexican periodicals of the nineteenth and twentieth centuries. In addition it maintains an extensive exchange program utilizing studies prepared by the faculty and published in *Mesoamerican Notes, Mexican Quarterly Review*, and *Tlatelolco Economic Monograph*. The book collection of the Museo Frissel de Arte Zapateco (Centro de Estudios Científicos Oaxaqueños) in Mitla, Oaxaca, is affiliated with the library.

A special audiovisual department is maintained under the direction of Charles Buffington. Open from 8:00 a.m. to 5:00 p.m. Monday through Friday, the department serves primarily the teaching faculty of the university and provides collections of films, maps, microfilm readers, projectors, tapes, and reproduction facilities.

Universidad Iberoamericana
Biblioteca

Cerro de las Torres 395, Campestre Churubusco, Mexico 21, D.F.

Tel. 549-35-00, ext. 224, 226

Established in 1962

Mon.-Fri. 8:00 a.m.–9:00 p.m.; Sat. 9:00 a.m.–1:00 p.m.

Librarian, Roberto Cruz; Associate Librarian, Surya Peniche de Sánchez
    McGregor; Assistants, Javier Campos, María Isabel Ader, and Anni Bahnsen

54,000 volumes, 350 periodicals (ULS)

60% Sp., 30% Eng., 10% Fr.

Circulation A

Inter-l., pamphlet collections, reprod.

The library offers service to any person interested in the collection after the presentation of an identification card. Its important collections include business administration, sociology, psychology, art, and history of religion.

9

Research in the Colonial Period

A. Research in Ethnohistory: The Pictorial Codices by Donald Robertson

The pictorial manuscripts, or codices, painted in the native tradition are extremely important sources for the study of the ethnohistory of Mexico in both the pre-Columbian and early colonial periods. Pre-Columbian manuscripts, of which few have survived, use the native system of writing in pictorial forms often called *signs* or *glyphs*. In the early colonial period this native tradition blends with Spanish traditions of writing in the European alphabet and illustrating such written texts. The making of these Indo-European pictorial manuscripts seems to have ceased effectively about 1600, when the style died out. The exception is one group called Techialoyan codices, probably made as late as the eighteenth century.[1]

The information conveyed by the manuscripts includes ethnohistorical information on genealogies, lives of individuals, historical events, chronicle histories, cartographic-chronological histories, cartographic documents, lawsuits, fiscal and economic documents, and ethnological data on acculturation, land tenure, rules governing inheritance patterns, and the evolution of costume, furniture, architecture, and painting.

Appended to this article is a table of major repositories of pictorial manuscripts (codices), significant copies, and related bibliographic aids in Mexico City and other centers in Mexico. In this table we have numbered and listed the names and addresses of the repositories, the librarian or director, telephone number, and hours of opening. These data are accurate, to the best of our knowledge, as of January, 1972, but are subject to change.

In Mexico, more so than in the United States, the first time a young scholar plans to use one of the smaller archives, it is advisable for him to call upon the official in charge (or at least present his card) and to establish a scholarly relationship through conversations, preferably in Spanish, to indicate the legitimacy of the request to use the archive. This is especially true of the small specialized collections marked with an asterisk in the table, since some of these collections are open only by appointment. To use the larger archives this kind of formality is not so necessary, but if asked, one should be prepared to establish the legitimacy of one's request to use the materials. If an introductory visit is to be made, it is good to plan it for one or two hours after the official opening hour of the archive and often the day before use of the collection is to begin. This visit should be courteous and brief and indicate that the visitor has done his or her homework; the visiting scholar should not ask time-consuming, embarrassingly basic and fundamental questions about the use and contents of the library or collection that he should know before arriving on the scene. This is, of course, similar to good practice in the smaller archives of Europe and the United States.

Available catalogs of the collections vary in quality and in accessibility. The collection in the Bodega de los Códices of the Museo Nacional de Antropología (see table, number 4), for instance, has a fine illustrated catalog by John B. Glass.[2] Other collections in the Museo Nacional and the dependencies of the Instituto Nacional de Antropología e Historia (INAH), however, are almost completely without published catalogs, so typescript or manuscript catalogs in the collections must be consulted. Only parts of a catalog of the Archivo General de la Nación (8) have appeared in its *Boletín*, these must be supplemented by unpublished listings in the archive itself.

The reader is here referred to Chapter 3A of this volume and to Howard F. Cline, ed., "Guide to Ethnohistorical Sources," volumes 12 through 15 of *Handbook of Middle American Indians* (Robert Wauchope, gen. ed.), Austin: University of Texas Press, now in press. These four volumes of the *Handbook* amount to an exhaustive summary of ethnohistoric sources and include, among other things, a listing of the known pictorial codices from each repository, their content, place or area of origin, and interrelationships among the manuscripts with bibliographic data. Copies of the *Handbook* should be found in any United States library with even minimal Middle American or Mesoamerican holdings. A convenient copy for continuous use in Mexico will be in the library of the Museo Nacional, the Biblioteca Nacional de Antropología(2).

The major repository of pictorial manuscripts, or codices, in Mexico is the

Biblioteca Nacional de Antropología. Sr. Antonio Pompa y Pompa is the librarian. The pictorial manuscripts are kept in the Bodega de los Códices (4) under the immediate supervision of Sra. Zita B. de Canessi. Sr. Pompa y Pompa is most cooperative with scholars who wish to see the manuscripts under his care. Since there seem to be no set hours when the collection is open, one can make an appointment with Sra. Canessi, usually through Sr. Pompa y Pompa. Sra. Canessi is not only helpful and cooperative with serious scholars who wish to use the codices, but also has a high sense of obligation concerning their use and care; they should be examined carefully, and the scholar should expect a high degree of supervision. After many years of either inaccessibility or disorder, the manuscripts have now been cataloged, placed in folders, and stored so that they are more readily accessible.

The Biblioteca Nacional de Antropología also has a large collection of microfilms, including copies of pictorial manuscripts from other collections (3). These too are in good order and are easily available. In this same library is the Archivo Histórico del INAH (5), under the care of Srta. Carmen Anzures. This collection includes information on the historical background of pictorial manuscripts and some important copies of manuscripts whose originals are kept in other museums or libraries.

The Departamento de Investigaciones Históricas del INAH (7) at the Castillo de Chapultepec is another large repository, especially of microfilm. It is under the care of the historian Dr. Enrique Florescano. Working hours have been somewhat informal and an appointment is strongly recommended, but there is a person on duty from 9:00 a.m. until 2:00 p.m. during the week.

The Archivo General de la Nación (8) has some known pictorial manuscripts, and probably others not yet recorded will be found in such ramos as Indios, Tierras, and Vínculos. The main archive in the Republic, the AGN is well organized, keeps regular hours, and is in a convenient location, the Palacio Nacional (see chapter 6A).

The personal notes of Robert Barlow, a pioneer in the modern study of pictorial manuscripts, are housed in the library of the University of the Americas in Cholula, Puebla. Although the university has no original manuscripts of its own, this collection is important enough to note here.

Several of the other collections listed in the table have only small numbers of codices and one should check their holdings in the relevant articles of the *Handbook of Middle American Indians* before beginning work in them. This is especially advisable in cases where visiting a collection would entail long travel time from one's base of operations. Telephone calls are probably more effective than written requests for information.

Collections with varying numbers of manuscripts exist in some of the Indian villages of Mexico. These are, to all intents and purposes, inaccessible to the scholar who does not have entrée to the "power structure" of the municipal government through personal contact or an introduction from someone who does. Tales of discovery of pictorial manuscripts in native villages circulate commonly among students of the field, but almost invariably, if the tale be true, the discoverer has some connections with members of the community.

Indiscreet sale, and in some cases outright theft, have taken pictorial manuscripts from municipal, pueblo, and other unguarded archives through the years. Some of these have ended up in the hands of dealers in Mexican antiquities; some have subsequently been sold to collectors in the country or abroad. Communication (i.e., gossip) with other students of pictorial manuscripts, librarians or custodians of collections, collectors, and sometimes even dealers, may lead to information on holdings of such pictorial documents in private collections in Mexico and other countries. Microfilm collections sometimes have information on "lost" manuscripts through copies and the present repositories of copies, if they are preserved on film in the collection.

_____

NOTES

1. For a convenient account of early colonial manuscript painting also making reference to pre-Columbian pictorial manuscripts, or codices, see Donald Robertson, *Mexican Manuscript Painting of the Early Colonial Period: The Metropolitan Schools*, Yale Historical Publications, History of Art no. 12 (New Haven: Yale University Press, 1959); chapter 11 discusses the Techialoyan group.

2. John B. Glass, *Catálogo de la Colección de Códices* (Mexico: Museo Nacional de Antropología, Instituto Nacional de Antropología e Historia, 1964).

MAJOR REPOSITORIES OF PICTORIAL MANUSCRIPTS (CODICES), SIGNIFICANT COPIES, AND RELATED BIBLIOGRAPHICAL AIDS IN MEXICO

An asterisk (*) indicates small specialized collections often open by appointment only. Names of officials, telephone numbers, and hours of openings are accurate to the best of our knowledge. See map, Appendix A, for archival locations. I want to thank Dorris Heyden and Fernando Horcasitas for helping to bring this table up to date.

REPOSITORY AND ADDRESS	DIRECTOR OR LIBRARIAN	TELEPHONE	HOURS
México, D.F.			
Instituto Nacional de Antropología e Historia (INAH), Córdoba 43, 45, and 47, México 7, D.F.	Arq. Luis Ortiz Macedo	525-30-89	9:00 a.m.–2:00 p.m.
1. Archivo Fotográfico Museo Nacional de Antropología Calzada Ghandi, México 5, D.F.	Sr. Mario Monterrosa Dr. Ignacio Bernal	533-59-60	9:00 a.m.–2:00 p.m.
2. Biblioteca Nacional de Antropología	Sr. Antonio Pompa y Pompa	511-09-93	9:00 a.m.–2:00 p.m.
3. Microfilm Collection	Sr. Antonio Pompa y Pompa	511-07-78	9:00 a.m.–2:00 p.m.
4. Bodega de los Códices*	Sra. Zita B. de Canessi	533-59-60, ext. 64	9:00 a.m.–2:00 p.m.
5. Archivo Histórico del INAH	Srta. Carmen Anzures	533-59-60, ext. 62	
6. Fototeca*	Sra. Cristina Bonfil		
Castillo de Chapultepec, México 5, D.F.			
7. Departamento de Investigaciones Históricas del INAH	Dr. Enrique Florescano	511-40-70	9:00 a.m.–2:00 p.m.
Palacio Nacional, Zócalo, México 5, D.F.			
8. Archivo General de la Nación	Lic. J. Ignacio Rubio Mañé	512-20-95	
9. Biblioteca Nacional de México, República de El Salvador 70, México 1, D.F.	Lic. Ernesto de la Torre Villar	521-58-98	

Sociedad Mexicana de Geografía, e Estadística

10. Biblioteca,* Justo Sierra 19, México 1, D.F.		522-20-49 512-86-55	
Dirección de Geografía, Meteorología e Hidrología	Sr. Juan Mas Sinta	515-34-91	8:30 a.m.–2:30 p.m.
11. Biblioteca and Mapoteca Orozco y Berra, Observatorio 192, Tacubaya 18, D.F.			

Cholula, Puebla

University of the Americas

12. Library	Dr. Manuel de Ezcurdia	3-10-55, ext. 148, 149, 151	

Guadalajara, Jalisco

13. Museo del Estado (INAH) Avenida Corona	Lic. José Guadalupe Zuno		10:00 a.m.–1:00 p.m.

Jalapa, Veracruz

14. Museo de Antropología de la Universidad Veracruzana, Calle 20 de Noviembre	Prof. Alfonso Medellín Zenil	38-03	8:00 a.m.–2:00 p.m.

Morelia, Michoacán

15. Museo Michoacano	Prof. José Luis Magaña		9:00 a.m.–1:00 p.m. and 4:00 p.m.–6:00 p.m.

Puebla, Puebla

16. Academia de Bellas Artes*
17. Casa del Alfeñique (Museo Regional de Puebla), Avenida 4 Oriente y Calle 6 Norte — Sr. Miguel Sarniento

B. Mexico in the Hapsburg Era: The Sixteenth and Seventeenth Centuries
by William B. Taylor

ARCHIVES IN MEXICO CITY

Mexican archives are rich in documentation for all periods of colonial history.[1] The great national collections housing materials on many topics and geographical areas are located in Mexico City. The Archivo General de la Nación (AGN) is the best-organized and most abundant source of documentation on the sixteenth and seventeenth centuries.

Most of the forty-seven ramos or series in the colonial section of AGN contain some documentation prior to 1700. Hapsburg materials are especially plentiful in the following ramos: Tierras, Civil, Inquisición, Indios, General de Parte, Mercedes, Congregaciones, and Hospital de Jesús.[2] Ramos such as Mercedes (viceregal grants) and Congregaciones (a one-volume listing of Indian towns consolidated in the late sixteenth and early seventeenth centuries) are very specialized, while others, including Tierras, Civil, Hospital de Jesús, and Archivo Histórico de Hacienda, contain records for many subjects. Tierras is a more encompassing section than the title suggests. Any document submitted in a land litigation is likely to appear here, including town and land titles, wills, genealogies, and histories of towns and Indian nobles, as well as boundary measurements and the formal litigation. The Civil series remains one of the great untapped portions of the National Archive, with over three thousand volumes of uncataloged manuscripts, many dealing with land tenure, tribute, and the Indian nobility.

There are manuscript guides to most of the colonial ramos available in the archive. Guides to the Archivo Histórico de Hacienda and the early volumes of Indios have been published.[3] Over the years, the *Boletín del Archivo General de la Nación* has published volume-by-volume lists of expediente titles in Tierras and many smaller ramos of AGN. Since the date of an expediente represents the year or years of litigation it is not always a reliable guide to the contents of the document. Most expedientes contain copies or originals of earlier records related to the dispute. The *Boletín* also publishes important

131

documents and commentaries based on AGN materials and has traditionally favored the colonial and Independence periods.

Other Mexico City archives for the Hapsburg period include the manuscript collection of the Biblioteca Nacional (see chapter 6, section D); the Archivo del Departamento de Asuntos Agrarios y Colonización (Bolívar 145, basement; open Monday through Friday, 9:00 a.m.–2:00 p.m., Saturday, 9:00 a.m.–12:00 p.m.; no duplicating services); the Archivo Histórico del Instituto Nacional de Antropología e Historia (INAH); and the microfilm collection of the Centro de Documentación del Museo Nacional de Historia (both located in the Museum of Anthropology, Chapultepec Park, second floor; open Monday through Saturday mornings; Monday through Friday afternoons).[4]

The Archivo Histórico del INAH has a small but important collection of Hapsburg documents, including the papers of the Convento de San Francisco, and the Colegio Franciscano de Misiones de San Francisco, both of Mexico City. In addition to the Del Paso y Troncoso papers (copies of colonial records found in European archives) the Archivo Histórico has the Ramírez Collection and the Gómez de Orozco Collection (mostly ecclesiastical records). For Mexico City in the early colonial period, the Antiguo Archivo del Ayuntamiento (Palacio Municipal; open Monday through Saturday, 8:30 a.m.–12:30 p.m.) and the Archivo de Notarías del Departamento del Distrito Federal contain actas de cabildo and notarial registers from 1524.[5]

REGIONAL AND LOCAL ARCHIVES

Growing interest in social and economic history for which there are no compact sources has broadened the spectrum of archival research, especially at the local level. Many topics in colonial history can best be attacked at the regional rather than the national level. Colonial society, with such subtopics as land tenure, race mixture, and the development of economic classes, can often be handled convincingly for provinces and cities. What we have in the way of national and viceregal studies of society are supported with isolated examples drawn from a wide variety of geographical settings. The picture that emerges is a composite which may or may not be distorted but which is unlikely to be completely accurate for any one region.

The following paragraphs point to the types of sources which may be found in state and local archives in Mexico. Not all will be found for every region. The vagaries of time, foreign invasion, civil unrest, and revolution have taken their toll in unpredictable ways. A convenient starting point for regional archives is the series of "historia y sus instrumentos" articles for various Mexican states published in *Historia Mexicana*.[6] The microfilm collection of the Museo Nacional de Historia in Mexico City is a good place to begin working with public and private documentation at the local level. The collection includes a large selection of local records from most parts of Mexico.[7]

Regional ecclesiastical, public, and private archives are rich in materials for nearly all social, economic, and institutional topics. Of the ecclesiastical sources, cathedral archives are especially valuable for the management of Church affairs (*actas capitulares*) and tithe records.[8] Parish records from the colonial period will also be found in many parts of Mexico. They often include baptismal registers and *cofradía* (sodality) documentation as well as the financial papers of the local priests. Most state capitals in Mexico have a state archive, a municipal (cabildo) archive, and a notarial archive, which usually house colonial records.[9] Notarial papers record the financial transactions, wills, and legal documents of local citizens. Much miscellaneous information on individuals, valuable for social and economic history, is found in notarial archives.[10]

Municipal archives outside the state capitals and large cities are still very much terra incognita. Nearly every town has a few colonial records relating to community lands and important legal instruments. Copies and some originals of the land records for many communities are to be found in the Archivo del Departamento de Asuntos Agrarios y Colonización which is organized by state, district, and community. As with the ramo of Tierras in AGN, the Asuntos Agrarios documents contain information on many subjects, sometimes only remotely connected with land ownership. Beyond land records and community titles, the former *cabeceras*, or political head towns, of the colonial period may yield valuable court records of the Corregidores de Indios, notarial papers, viceregal orders, and local census data. One very useful archive of this type is located in Tlacolula, Oaxaca. The "archive" amounts to heaps of old papers stored under the Porfirian bandstand. In addition to information on Indian land tenure which is very hard to come by in national archives, the Tlacolula materials include local census records and a variety of civil and criminal records (mostly eighteenth-century), many of which bear upon Indian drunkenness.

Valuable records for the colonial Church, especially the monastic orders, and the great landed estates of rural Mexico are most likely to appear in private collections. Since these privileged groups were stripped of their power after Independence, their legal records were considered worthless and were often confiscated, burned, or thrown away. Some fell into the hands of individuals who value them for their age and history. Personal experience suggests that private collections should be sought out fairly late in a research project in order to make the contact a mutually profitable exchange of documentation rather than a one-sided donation.

NOTES

1. Foreign archives, especially the public and private collections in Spain, also contain much documentation on the colonial history of Mexico. An indispensable guide to Spanish materials is the *Guía de Fuentes para la Historia de Ibero-América en los Archivos de España*, 2 vols. (New York: UNESCO, 1965, 1969). Volume one is devoted to public archives; volume two deals with the little-used private collections.

2. Several of the AGN's most important series, such as Historia and Archivo Histórico de Hacienda contain mostly late colonial documents, with a smattering of Hapsburg records. See Charles Gibson, *The Aztecs Under Spanish Rule* (Stanford: Stanford University Press, 1964), for effective use of AGN Indian materials. Richard E. Greenleaf has demonstrated the varied uses of AGN Inquisición records for social as well as institutional and religious history in his *Zumárraga and the Mexican Inquisition, 1536-1543* (Washington, D.C.: Academy of American Franciscan History, 1962) and *The Mexican Inquisition of the Sixteenth Century* (Albuquerque: University of New Mexico Press, 1969).

3. Luis Chávez Orozco, *Indice del Ramo de Indios del Archivo General de la Nación*, 2 vols. (Mexico: n.p., 1953); *Guía del Archivo Histórico de Hacienda, Siglos XVI a XIX* (Mexico: Secretaría de Hacienda y Crédito Público, 1940).

4. The Asuntos Agrarios archive and the Museo Nacional de Historia microfilm are mentioned under regional and local archives.

5. For information on the Ayuntamiento and notarial archives of Mexico City, see Manuel Carrera Stampa, *Guía del Archivo del Antiguo Ayuntamiento de la Ciudad de México* (Havana: Archivo Nacional de Cuba, 1949) and Agustín Millares Carlo and Ignacio Montecón, "El Archivo de Notarías del Departamento del Distrito Federal," *Revista de Historia de América* 17 (1944): 69-118.

6. Jan Bazant, "Puebla: La Historia y Sus Instrumentos," *Historia Mexicana* 19 (1970): 418-31; Israel Cavazos Garza, "Nuevo León: La Historia y Sus Instrumentos," *Historia Mexicana* 1 (1952): 494-575; Joaquín Fernández de Córdoba, "Michoacán: La Historia y Sus Instrumentos," *Historia Mexicana* 2 (1953): 135-154; Bernardo García Martínez and Andrés Lira González, "Querétaro: La Historia y Sus Instrumentos," *Historia Mexicana* 18 (1968): 286-92; Jorge F. Iturribarría, "Oaxaca: La Historia y Sus Instrumentos," *Historia Mexicana* 2 (1953): 459-76; Miguel de la Mora, "Jalisco: La Historia y Sus Instrumentos," *Historia Mexicana* 1 (1952): 143-63; *Veinticinco Años de*

Investigación Histórica en México (Mexico: El Colegio de México, 1966), pp. 601-13.

7. See Delfina Esmeraldo López Sarrelangue, *La Nobleza Indígena de Pátzcuaro* (Mexico: Universidad Nacional Autónoma de México, 1965) for effective use of the INAH microfilm collection. The collection is described in Berta Ortiz Ulloa, "Catálogo de los Fondos del Centro de Documentación del Museo Nacional de Historia en el Castillo de Chapultepec," *Anales del Instituto Nacional de Antropología e Historia* 7 (1949-50) and 11 (1953); "Centro de Documentación del Museo Nacional de Historia en el Castillo de Chapultepec," *Historia Mexicana* 4 (1954): 275-80; and Silvio Zavala, "Catálogo de los Fondos del Centro de Documentación del Museo Nacional de Historia en el Castillo de Chapultepec," *Memorias de la Academia Mexicana de Historia* 10 (1951): 459-95.

8. An example of how cathedral archives may be used is Woodrow Borah, "Tithe Collection in the Bishopric of Oaxaca, 1601-1867," *Hispanic American Historical Review* 29 (1949): 498-517.

9. An idea of the kinds of materials frequently found in the state capitals can be gleaned from Woodrow Borah, "Notes on Civil Archives in the City of Oaxaca," *Hispanic American Historical Review* 31 (1951): 723-44.

10. James Lockhart has put notarial records to good use in his study of early colonial society in Peru, *Spanish Peru, 1532-1560: A Colonial Society* (Madison, Wisconsin: University of Wisconsin Press, 1968). A provincial notarial archive in Mexico is described in Cayetano Reyes, "Indice y Extractos del Archivo Notarial de Orizaba," *Historia Mexicana* 16 (1967): 588-602.

C. Research on Eighteenth-Century Mexico
by Charles F. Nunn

Eighteenth-century Mexico was a place of vivid colors and pungent smells where Spanish- and Indian-speaking men and women lived out their lives under the flag of Spain. Merchants, missionaries, ranchers, miners, peasants, muleteers, and countless others went about their daily tasks with the feeling that each day would be very little different from the day before. Slowly during the course of the era, the idea of progress planted itself in the minds of the more literate members of the colonial society. The first decades of the following century were to bring revolution and independence, but to see the last hundred years of the colonial experience only as the background for another story is a grave mistake. True, time and events overthrew a way of life, many of its institutions, and its center of authority, but eighteenth-century New Spain was a fabric worth study for itself and not solely for the threads that run through to later times.

Researching a subject drawn from eighteenth-century New Spain is both challenging and potentially rewarding. It is to the records left by Spaniards, both in America and Europe, that the student must turn in order to explore this period of the colonial epoch. In choosing a topic he must have some hope of finding the documentation, lest he have little more than a title to show for his efforts. There are many depositories where collections of papers relating to eighteenth-century Mexico may be found, but two stand head and shoulders above the rest. These are the Archivo General de Indias in Seville and the Archivo General de la Nación in Mexico City.

No student can claim that he has researched his topic completely without having visited both archives in person. Since the following article by Bernard Bobb treats the eighteenth-century holdings of the AGN, I will limit my discussion to the AGI and other depositories in Mexico and Spain. In addition to the rich collection of the AGN, significant holdings survive in many parts of Mexico. Papers relating to municipal and social history may be found in the Archivo Exayuntamiento of Mexico City. The archive of the Museum of Anthropology and Natural History contains many records concerning the Indians, and like the AGN, this depository is cataloged by expediente, or file. In addition, several of the faculties of the National University house the papers of various colonial institutions. An example would be those of the Art Academy of San Carlos which reside in the present-day School of Architecture. Problems have arisen in the past because nonhistorians are often in charge of these collections. Another difficulty presents itself in connection with the ecclesiastical holdings in Mexico. Some of the churchmen in charge virtually hide their old paper for fear that some bureaucrat will confiscate it as a national treasure. And then there are the private archives, reputedly easier for the foreigner to see than for the Mexican because they may contain fugitive documents. The provincial archives found in many of the older state capitals vary in usefulness. Considerable progress has been made in recent years in cataloging these important depositories. Still other papers are in the hands of some of the governmental ministries.

American documents are a little less spread out in Spain, and at first glance it would seem that things would be a bit easier there. Growing out of a 1779 commission appointed to cleanse the historical image of Spain with truth, the Archivo General de Indias is the single most important archive to the history of colonial America anywhere in the world. The AGI has divided its holdings into several sections. Among the more important of these to the history of New Spain are the Audiencia de México, Audiencia de Guadalajara, Audiencia de las Filipinas, and, for Chiapas and Yucatán, Audiencia de Guatemala. In addition there are Indiferente General, Indiferente de Nueva España Contaduría, Contratación, Justicia, and for the second half of the century, the Ministerio de Ultra Mar.

At the Archive of the Indies, the papers are tied in legajos instead of being bound, and these bundles usually contain more closely related records than the volumes of the AGN. Clerks prepared the archival guides as inventories at the time that the documents came into Seville from other depositories in Spain. The unfortunate thing is that only a general description of the bundle as a whole appears in the catalogs. The investigator must call out the interesting-sounding legajos and go through the pile of papers one by one. Since few of the documents are printed, the student must plod slowly through the sometimes treacherous handwriting of the eighteenth-century scribes. Important documents in poorly labeled bundles may slip by unnoticed while others may hide themselves in an uninteresting-looking expediente. One must pick and choose, for there are some forty thousand bundles at Seville, and even a lifetime would be insufficient to do justice to them all. At the end the investigator would still feel that he should go through just one or two more legajos.

Like Mexico, Spain has its provincial, ecclesiastical, private, and ministerial archives. Any of these might prove useful for the specialized topic. In addition to the AGI and the minor archives, there are two other major Spanish depositories containing important eighteenth-century documents. These are the Archivo General of Simancas and the Archivo Histórico Nacional in Madrid. The old castle at Simancas was an archive as early as 1545, and it contains the bulk of the diplomatic papers dealing with colonial problems. In addition, much of the material concerning colonial wars is at Simancas. Some of the records about governmental appointments for the Indies are also there. The Madrid papers, as far as America is concerned, supplement those of Simancas.

The researcher's task is generally easier with eighteenth-century papers than with those of earlier periods. Eighteenth-century paleography is not very difficult, the outstanding differences from modern handwriting being the *Q* that looks something like a *2* and the *ss* that, until mid-century, appears as *ff*. Individual writers have their idiosyncrasies in both penmanship and spelling, but a little common sense usually suffices to untangle the meaning. A word of caution should be offered in regard to vocabulary. The reason is simple enough. Word meanings have changed, and this is especially true of the bureaucratic usage encountered in the eighteenth century. As in the case of paleography, judgment tempered with experience will be the final arbiter.

D. The Eighteenth Century in the Archivo General de la Nación

by Bernard E. Bobb

It is difficult to imagine a subject concerning New Spain in the eighteenth century which could be effectively investigated without using materials from the Archivo General de la Nación. Indeed, actual work in the archive itself would seem to be a necessity. To be sure, there are rather extensive collections of films of a good many AGN documents in various places such as Berkeley and Austin, for example, which may be profitably utilized. Nevertheless, the nature of the sources in Mexico City is such that the researcher who does not consult them before calling his task completed should feel at least some small sense of unease.

The eighteenth century is particularly well represented in the AGN. The perils of earlier times, climaxed by the burning of the palace in the 1692 upheaval, certainly did little to help preserve the record. Fortunately, no disaster of that magnitude has occurred since then, although occasional documents, for example, some viceregal correspondence, show serious water damage. (Not incidentally, the originals of these damaged documents may frequently be found in the AGI in Seville.) But the more efficient Bourbon administrators, particularly those of the latter half of the century, instituted improvements in archival management which continue to bear fruit for the historian. As a consequence, the scholar whose focus is the Bourbon era enjoys distinct advantages and should, by and large, find his work in the AGN most profitable.

The great mass of material in the archive is divided into ramos, that is, subdivisions along subject-matter lines. The lists available at the AGN in the summer of 1971 revealed a total count of 170 ramos. To be sure, a few of them consist merely of a single volume. Most, however, contain an encouraging number of volumes (or legajos, or cajas), and a number of them are of formidable size. A few examples may serve to clarify what kinds of subjects comprise ramos and how large some of them are. Thus: Acordada (31); Aduanas (2,368); Alcabalas (657); Archivo de Guerra (1,469); Californias (89); Casa de Moneda (470); Civil (2,601); Clero Regular y Secular (217); Criminal (746); Historia (583); Indiferente de Guerra (970); Inquisición (1,556); Justicia, Epoca Colonial (679); Matrimonios (127); Minería (234);

Oficios Vendibles (40); Provincias Internas (266); Real Hacienda (240); Temporalidades (247); and Universidad (566). According to these same lists, the total number of volumes, legajos, and cajas reached 68,534. Of course, certain large blocs have no connection with the eighteenth century, for example, 4,376 volumes of the correspondence of Cárdenas, Avila Camacho, Alemán, and Ruiz Cortines. Nevertheless, a very large proportion of the ramos do contain Bourbon material.

Regarding the availability of indexes or catalogs for these ramos, fifty-four had at least partial catalogs in 1971. However, several qualifying comments seem appropriate. First, not all of them are complete, but the process of indexing continues regularly. Second, they are not all of equal utility. For example, the index for Reales Cédulas offers a brief description of each document, such as "Vol.[umen]14, Exp.[ediente]19, F.[oja]34. Patente de Corso. Da poder a los virreyes y gobernadores de los puertos de Indias para dar patente de corso a las personas que lo pidieren. (Cédula impresa) Madrid, febrero 22 de 1674." In contrast, the catalog for Correspondencia de los Virreyes is not particularly useful because it offers simply a one-word listing of the subject of each document, with no further description.

Third, it is important to note that the AGN has been publishing these indexes in their *Boletín* for many years. For example, the index for the ramo of Tierras (which contains 3,832 volumes) begins in volume 2 of the *Boletín* and continues until it is completed. A thoughtful perusal of this journal can reveal a very great deal about the contents and system of the archive.

For purposes of general orientation the researcher should consult, in addition to Rubio Mañé's indispensable *El Archivo General de la Nación*, the *Reseña Histórica del Archivo General de la Nación, 1550-1946*, by Mario Mariscal, and the *Guía del Archivo Histórico de Hacienda, Siglos XVI a XIX*, published by the Secretaría de Hacienda y Crédito Público.

It seems safe to assert that virtually any eighteenth-century subject one can think of, be it in the realm of social, political, economic, or religious history, or a combination of these, can be profitably pursued in the AGN. There are, of course, a variety of procedures that one may follow, depending in part on one's topic. Certain basic sources, however, would seem to have some bearing on almost any topic and probably ought to be looked at.

In view of the all-pervasive presence of the agencies of the Crown, executive documents touch on nearly everything. Thus, Reales Cédulas, Bandos, and Ordenanzas are ramos which could be useful. Note that there are two distinct sets of Reales Cédulas, and although one is labeled Duplicadas, this is merely for purposes of identification, and the contents are totally different. Also of potential general use is viceregal correspondence; inasmuch as in most cases the covering letters between Mexico City and Madrid are accompanied by all related papers, such documents are usually to be found in the latter part of the same volume or in the succeeding volume. A word of caution, however, with respect to this ramo. It does not begin until 1755, and even the first few years of that viceregency are rather thinly documented. Prior to that time, each viceroy took his papers with him when he returned to Spain. By the 1760s, however, the files become fairly complete, and since the viceroy was compelled to be concerned with everything, these volumes are usually more revealing.

Another obvious move would be to investigate ramos directly related to one's subject. Any economic topic would demand attention to a variety of ramos—Real Hacienda, Real Caja, Alcabalas, Propios y Arbitrios, Consulado, and so on. A religious subject, an administrative study, a regional inquiry— each would require at least a sampling of a variety of ramos. Also, the investigator should bear in mind that categorization of documents has not been precise or consistent over the many years and that there are great quantities of material waiting to be gathered and bound. Some documents which are out of place may well be located in another ramo, or in several other ramos.

All this is merely suggestive of one of the great joys of the profession—the search for interesting and significant information, a search that is so often rewarded. But anyone who has worked at the AGN knows that pursuing a topic there has a hazardous side, too, which derives from the tantalizing nature of the material one constantly runs across but which may be totally irrelevant to the subject one is investigating. The index to the Historia ramo (583 volumes) offers a case in point. As one browses through it, searching, perhaps, for information on the militia, he notes three entire volumes devoted to documents concerning "Temores de trastornos en el orden público," or, a bit farther on, a document on a case, "Contra Pedro Castillo por haber siseada a la bailarina 'La Nueva Italiana,'" or another, "Sobre palcos para el Ayuntamiento y el Corregidor y sobre que los regidores no debían usar sillas de brazos."

Now, these are pretty hard to resist. Were the fears of public disorder realized, or were the authorities merely paranoid? Was "La Nueva Italiana" really that bad, or did Pedro Castillo have some hidden personal motive for his deplorable behavior? And what *regidor* of any character is going to stand still for such discrimination? The answers to these and many other fascinating questions are to be found in the documents in the AGN. Good hunting.

10

Research on Nineteenth-Century Topics

A. Independence and Early National History
by Jaime E. Rodríguez

The Latin American Collection of the University of Texas at Austin is a logical starting point for research on many aspects of the Independence and the early national periods. Inasmuch as it is one of the best research libraries on Mexico, the investigator will find most of the printed sources, including government reports, scholarly journals, and books, that he might need to begin his inquiry. The collection also houses more than a million pages of manuscripts pertaining to Mexico, the majority dealing with the period covered by this chapter. The manuscript collection contains the papers of some of Mexico's leading statesmen: Lucas Alamán, José Mariano Michelena, Francisco García, Valentín Gómez Farías, and Mariano and Vicente Riva Palacio, to mention only a few. There are also papers important for social and economic history, such as the records of the vast Sánchez Navarro haciendas. These materials have been described in two comprehensive guides: Carlos E. Castañeda and Jack A. Dabbs, *Guide to the Latin American Collection at the University of Texas Library* (Cambridge: Harvard University Press, 1939) and Lota M. Spell, *Research Material for the Study of Latin America at the University of Texas* (Austin: University of Texas Press, 1954). Complete and detailed calendars of four collections are now available, thanks to the dedication of three scholars: Pablo Max Ynsfran, "Catálogo del Archivo de Don Lucas Alamán que se Conserve en la Universidad de Texas, Austin," *Historia Mexicana* 4 (October-December 1954): 281-316; ibid., 4 (January-March 1955): 431-53; Carlos Castañeda and Jack Dabbs, *A Calendar to the Juan E. Hernández y Dávalos Manuscript Collection* (Mexico: Editorial Jus, 1954); Pablo Max

Ynsfran, *Catálogo de los Manuscritos del Archivo de Don Valentín Gómez Farías* (Mexico: n.p., 1968); and Jack A. Dabbs, *The Mariano Riva Palacio Archives*, 3 vols. (Mexico: Editorial Jus, 1968-69).

One of the most important sources for the history of the early Republic, but one little used, is Carlos María de Bustamante's massive forty-four-volume "Diario de lo Especialmente Ocurrido en México." The diario remains in manuscript form with the exception of a volume on 1822 published by Elías Amador as *Diario Histórico de México* (Zacatecas: J. Ortega, 1896). Bustamante was an active participant in almost every Congress from Independence to his death in 1848. Consequently, he knew figures from all phases of Mexican society—political, social, economic, clerical, military, and intellectual. He daily recorded the principal events he witnessed, heard, or read about, and often included pamphlets and newspaper clippings. For certain topics, his diary is the only remaining source. Bustamante evolved from a radical to a liberal, then to a moderate, finally ending as a conservative. Since most of his later published works were conservative, that is how he is generally classified. However, unlike his published works, Bustamante's diary reflects what he saw and believed rather than what he later claimed to have seen and to have believed. Since other writers of the time did the same thing, the diario can be used as a "primary control" for a critical analysis of contemporary printed sources. The manuscript is located in the Elías Amador Library of the state of Zacatecas and microfilm copies are found in the library of the Anthropological Museum in Mexico City and at the Latin American Collection of the University of Texas.

Although nearly all aspects of the history of the early national period remain to be studied, it is not because archival material is lacking. Unfortunately, all too often those in charge of archives in Mexico have other duties as well; some archives do not have adequate personnel and others have untrained staffs. As a result they do not know their archives well, and the researcher is often told that the sources do not exist, that they were destroyed by fire or some other disaster, or that no one knows anything about them. While these stories are valid in a few instances, they are generally not true. An investigator armed with tact, patience, perseverance, and good recommendations will, more often than not, succeed in finding and using materials not previously exploited. The congressional archives provide a good example. It is widely believed that the early records were destroyed by fire. Nevertheless, they are there; both the Senate and the Chamber of Deputies have archives dating to the First Congress. The materials have remained virtually untouched to this day. Similarly, state legislatures have archives which have never been studied. After being told that they did not exist, a scholar recently discovered the legislative records of the state of Mexico in the legislature's own chambers. Having located them, he was given unlimited access to the materials. Other states also have legislative archives that have remained untouched.

Most of the important cities have municipal archives. Mexico City has the Archivo del Antiguo Ayuntamiento de la Ciudad de México and its successor, the Archivo del Gobierno del Distrito Federal. Other cities have repositories often called Archivo General de la Secretaría del Ayuntamiento de [Puebla or Guadalajara], for example.

Notarial archives are excellent sources for social and economic history. In Mexico City these records are housed in the Archivo General de Notarías del Distrito Federal. Although some states such as Puebla have placed the notarial archives in the state palace, most archives are still in the hands of the notaries. Since virtually all important cities had but one notary until the twentieth century, the problem is locating the oldest notary office. In most cases, the records are piled up all around the office and in adjoining rooms, and the notary is only too pleased to allow the researcher to work there. Notarial archives are not difficult to use unless one is looking for a specific fact. They are generally organized chronologically and include different ledgers for marriage contracts, wills, inventories, etc. Marriage contracts lend themselves to the study of family structure and the imaginative student will find these records a gold mine for social history.

Church records are also plentiful. As a result of the Reform, some of these records were turned over to the Archivo General, but most remain in the hands of cathedral chapters, local churches, nunneries, monasteries, and other Church institutions. Michael Costeloe has described one such archive in "Guide to the Chapter Archives of the Archbishopric of Mexico," *Hispanic American Historical Review* 45 (February 1965): 53-63.

The National University has several important collections. For example, the Archivo Histórico de la Escuela de Medicina has the archive of the *proto-medicato.* Other institutions with important collections for the early Republic are the Archivo Histórico del Museo Nacional de Antropología and the newly organized Centro de Estudios de Historia de México, Condumex. The latter has some important papers, such as the Luis G. Cuevas documents pertaining to the Pastry War and the War with the United States. Its collections are briefly described in *Centro de Estudios de Historia de México* (Mexico: Fundación Cultural de Condumex, 1969). The Cuevas Collection of the Jesuit

Colegio Máximo also contains important materials gathered by the late Father Mariano Cuevas.

Private manuscript collections exist, but they are harder to use. The researcher should try to learn if there are any living descendants of the persons being studied who might have papers, and then attempt to obtain permission to use those materials. Many papers remain in the same family, while other collections have changed possession many times.

There are countless federal, state, and local archives which have materials pertaining to the early Republic. Depending on his topic, the researcher must look for these little-used archives which often contain priceless materials. Although slightly outdated, Manuel Carrera Stampa's *Archivalia Mexicana* is still the best general description of Mexican archives.

Since the early Republic was a time of great political debate, pamphlets are some of the most important sources for the period. These publications treat all manner of topics, from politics and religion to economics and society. Often they reproduce documents not found elsewhere. Although the researcher should use them with care because of their partisan nature, pamphlets are indispensable sources. The most important repositories of early national pamphlets are the Lafragua Collection of the Biblioteca Nacional de México, the Basave Collection of the Biblioteca de México, and the Archivo General de la Nación in Mexico. The Latin American Collection of the University of Texas and the Sutro Branch of the California State Library in San Francisco contain the largest holdings of Mexican pamphlets in the United States. The latter has conveniently published a *Catalogue of Mexican Pamphlets in the Sutro Collection*, 14 vols. (San Francisco: California State Library, 1939-40).

B. Research Collections on the Early Republic
by C. Alan Hutchinson

Archivo General de la Nación (AGN). Professor Herbert E. Bolton's famous *Guide to Materials for the History of the United States in the Principal Archives of Mexico* can unfortunately no longer be entirely depended upon either for the AGN or for other Mexican archives. Bolton prepared most of it in Mexico between June, 1907, and October, 1908, and many of the documents whose description and location he discusses have in the intervening years been lost, reshuffled, or moved. However, certain important ramos, such as Californias, Justicia, Misiones, or Provincias Internas, which he indexed for references to the borderlands of the United States are in the AGN so that his guide may still prove useful. On the other hand, documents from the Old Records of the Secretaría de Gobernación or from the Secretaría de Guerra y Marina, now moved to the AGN, can no longer be located from his indexes. The staff of AGN has prepared a number of new indexes since Bolton's day (there is an excellent published index for Provincias Internas), and these are valuable even though some of them give no more than the number on the legajo or bundle with the approximate corresponding dates of the enclosed papers. In a few cases (such as Gobernación and Indiferente de Guerra) a reverse index is available which provides a list of legajo numbers after each succeeding date. It should be added that the dates for each package do not always correspond exactly with the actual dates on the manuscripts in the legajos.

The AGN is extremely rich in material on the early republican period. There are many series of documents, both bound and unbound, running sometimes into the thousands of volumes or bundles. A convenient list of these long series is given on pages 43 to 46 of Manuel Carrera Stampa's *Archivalia Mexicana*, which is still the most useful general work on Mexican archives. Carrera Stampa also indicates which series had indexes at the time he prepared his book. In deciding which series he wishes to examine, the investigator should bear in mind how each succeeding Mexican administration organized its affairs so that he will be better able to trace the correspondence or reports that he requires. The titles of certain ramos are self-explanatory— Instrucción Pública, Padrones (censuses), Expulsión de Españoles, and Pasaportes, for instance. Others, such as Justicia Eclesiástica (correspondence on ecclesiastical matters coming to the Minister of Justice and Ecclesiastical Affairs) or Bienes Nacionales (property nationalized at the time of the Reform), require more explanation. Still others defy any attempt to label them; Gobernación, for example, seems to be a general catchall for a wide variety of documents.

The Casa Amarilla. This overflow storehouse for the AGN is situated in a former chapel in Tacubaya close to a Metro station. With the permission of the director of the AGN, investigators have been allowed to consult documents in this archive when custodians can be present. No catalog of the contents of the Casa Amarilla seems to be available, but a cursory examination of its shelves revealed that the material in it for the early republican period is mostly from the Secretaría de Hacienda. Many of the bundles are piled up in such a way that it is impossible to consult them.

Archivo Histórico de Hacienda. This archive is located in a room adjacent to the main reading room of the AGN. Besides its obvious importance for research in economic history, it also provides material on social and religious matters. It is well indexed in the *Guía del Archivo Histórico de Hacienda* (Mexico, 1940) and in additional index cards in the archive.

Archivo Histórico del Instituto Nacional de Antropología e Historia. This important collection is in the library of the National Museum of Anthropology in a room for rare books and manuscripts. The collection is well indexed on cards. Carrera Stampa's *Archivalia Mexicana* describes some of its holdings, which include much of value for the early nineteenth century. Also in the library is a large collection of documents on microfilm from the former Centro de Documentación at Chapultepec Castle. These are mainly from documents in state archives such as Durango, Monterrey, San Luis Potosí, Zacatecas, etc. Catalogs of the contents of these reels are available at the microfilm reading center in the library. A microfilm copy of Carlos María de Bustamante's diary (1822-41) is in the collection.

Archivo Histórico Militar. This is an immensely rich archive for the period under review. It is well indexed, for the early years of the Republic only, in the *Guía del Archivo Histórico Militar de México* (Mexico: n.p., 1949), but permission to work in it may be difficult to obtain. It has microfilm facilities.

Archivo de la Secretaría de Relaciones. Again, this is a major source of early nineteenth-century material. Many of the documents in it are indexed on cards available at the archive. Berta Ulloa has described its organization in "La Revolución en Relaciones," *Historia Mexicana* 10 (January-March 1961): 526-32. Professor Martín Quirarte has provided a useful new typescript index for it. It lacks microfilm facilities.

Archivo de Notarías del Departamento del Distrito Federal. This archive is a little-used but potentially invaluable source for wills, deeds, contracts, and other legal instruments for the period. Its contents are discussed in an article by Agustín Millares Carlo and José Ignacio Mantecón in *Revista de Historia de América* 17 (June 1944): 69-118. The article provides a chronological and alphabetical list of the notaries whose legal instruments are preserved in the archive.

Archivo del Ayuntamiento. There is much in this archive on the early Republic in addition to Actas de Cabildo. A catalog of its contents is available at the archive and it is discussed in Carrera Stampa's article "El Archivo del ex-Ayuntamiento de México," in *Historia Mexicana* 12 (April-June 1963): 621-32, and in the same author's *Guía del Archivo del Antiguo Ayuntamiento de la Ciudad de México* (Havana: Archivo Nacional de Cuba, 1949).

Other Mexico City Archives. There are a number of smaller but nonetheless valuable archives for the early national period in Mexico City which should be considered. The archives of the Department of Health and Welfare, which have been found useful for religious and architectural history in the colonial period, also contain some four hundred unclassified volumes on the period from 1801 to 1860. Donald B. Cooper's article "A Selective List of Colonial Manuscripts in the Archives of the Department of Health and Welfare," *Hispanic American Historical Review* 42 (August 1962): 385-414, provides specific information on the collection. The chapter archives of the Archbishopric of Mexico have recently been described as of "particular interest and value," although the minutes of the meetings of the chapter are not generally open to scholars. For further information on this archive the reader may consult Michael P. Costeloe, "Guide to the Chapter Archives of the Archbishopric of Mexico," *Hispanic American Historical Review* 45 (February 1965): 53-63. The historical archive of the Condumex Corporation has a fine library of rare books on Mexican history and a rapidly growing, admirably indexed, and well-preserved collection of manuscripts. They include the papers of Luis Gonzaga Cuevas, Luis Chávez Orozco, Alamán correspondence, and much more. The collection of Mariano Cuevas, the Church historian, is in the Jesuit Colegio Máximo de la Provincia at San Angel. The fine rare-book collection and archive at the Biblioteca Nacional has the valuable Lafragua pamphlet collection, for which an index will soon be published. The archive also holds collections of Franciscan papers from Sonora and Sinaloa covering the period under review up to 1847, Benito Juárez papers from 1849 through 1872, and documents on Jalisco collected by J. E. Hernández Dávalos. The archive at the Chamber of Deputies, reportedly destroyed by fire in 1872 and

1909, still possesses sufficient *actas* to make a visit worthwhile. The Senate was said to have no remaining archive, but nevertheless some scholars have apparently used it to advantage. These are among the archives in Mexico City which are important for the early national period.

C. The Period of La Reforma
by Robert Knowlton[1]

To term Mexico's political history unsettled is to understate the case. Before and after the Reform, as well as during the years of that nineteenth-century movement, the country suffered frequent upheavals. Accounts abound of the ransacking of offices, the destruction and loss of documents, the disregard for preserving the country's historical records. Sad stories circulate of the conspiracy of man and nature seemingly designed to obliterate the written record of the past. These occurrences were not confined, however, to the heat of political turmoil in the distant past but may be documented for recent years as well. In view of the undeniable losses, the investigator may well wonder whether anything remains from which to reconstruct the Reform. In fact, the resources are extensive and diverse, though they are not always readily accessible to the researcher, nor are the documents always in good condition or well organized.

Materials on the Reform are widely scattered and diverse in nature. They may be found in the national capital and at state and municipal centers, located in official archives and libraries and in private collections. The holdings include personal and official correspondence and documents on church-related questions, military and foreign affairs, and a wide range of social, political, and economic aspects of the period. The treatment here focuses on only a few of the Mexican depositories; of course, major resources are housed elsewhere, for example in the outstanding Latin American Collection of the University of Texas Library. Some reference will be made, as well, to journal articles that deal with particular archives which the student of the Reform will find worth consulting.

The Archivo General de la Nación (AGN), located on two floors in the south end of the National Palace in Mexico City, is an important source of information on the Reform. The director, Jorge Ignacio Rubio Mañé, is very helpful and a knowledgeable, publishing scholar as well. The materials in the archives are divided topically into some ninety different ramos (sections) containing widely varying numbers of bound volumes and unbound legajos (bundles); each legajo contains numerous expedientes (files). Although the bulk of the ramos are devoted to colonial affairs, there are significant materials on the

153

Reform period, especially those confiscated from religious organizations. The ramo of Bienes Nacionales has 1,933 legajos dealing with a whole range of ecclesiastical property affairs; it includes information on the financial condition of religious corporations and property transfers and in general reveals the impact of and response to liberal legislation on clerical property. There is a card index file for this ramo listing the title and number of the expedientes in each legajo. Consultation of the index, useful as it is, should not replace actual reference to the manuscripts, because while legajo numbers are accurate, expediente numbers often are not.

Justicia Eclesiástica, a ramo of 188 volumes, contains correspondence, reports of religious orders, material on the suppression of monasteries, and other information for the period from 1821 to 1861 when ecclesiastical affairs were under the jurisdiction of the Ministry of Justice and Ecclesiastical Affairs. Both Bienes Nacionales and Justicia Eclesiástica contain detailed documentation and statistics on the finances of individual clerical corporations and individual clergy as well. This documentation includes specific properties owned, their location and value, mortgages held, the names of tenants and debtors, and transfers or disposal of corporate wealth as a result of liberal laws and clerical response to these measures. The records reveal, however, not just the cold financial and economic details, but the human aspects of the cataclysm through the turbulent early years of Reform and civil war. The 217 volumes in the ramo of Justicia Imperio have manuscripts dealing with the Empire of Maximilian; Ayuntamientos (246 volumes) relates to town administration; and Templos y Conventos (32 volumes) concerns churches and convents, including their loss of property during the Reform. The researcher should consult the *Boletín* of the AGN, issues of which often contain guides and lists of materials in various ramos.

Also located in the National Palace with the AGN is the Archivo Histórico de Hacienda which merits reference for financial topics, for example, on the Second Empire. Other important depositories in the capital would include the Biblioteca Nacional de México. Among the pertinent materials housed there are the Archivo de D. Benito Juárez and documents on the controversy between the national government of Ignacio Comonfort and the caudillo of Nuevo León, Santiago Vidaurri.

If the AGN is especially noteworthy for study of church-state relations in the Reform, the Archivo de Notarías is important for social and economic history. Indeed, the notarial registers throughout the Republic are increasingly being recognized as significant historical sources. Access to these archives is often difficult to obtain. Also, they are not easy to use because usually one must be able to identify the document desired by name of the notary and exact date of the transaction; the investigator may not simply browse at his leisure. The offices are also seldom prepared for researchers, so space, work tables and chairs, and even lighting may be inadequate. On the other hand, the notarial records are generally well organized and quite complete for the Reform period; at least this is true for those cited here. A very special recommendation, difficult to obtain, is necessary to use the Mexico City Archivo de Notarías (Donceles 104, open 9:00 a.m. to 2:00 p.m.; director, Sánchez de la Barquera); doubtless the aid of the director of the AGN, Sr. Rubio Mañé, will be indispensable in this, as in so many other ways. In any event, the time and energy expended on access and the frustrations of use restrictions will be well worthwhile. The registers contain contracts, deeds, property transfers, mortgages, wills—all manner of notarized documents. These archives thus are valuable for, among other things, genealogy and the economic and social effects of Reform legislation on corporate property, both generally and specifically. The history of particular properties and their owners, for example, may be traced through the years of political change; by examining the records from notarial archives in different localities, comparisons may be made of the Reform's impact.

In contrast to the Archivo de Notarías in Mexico City, those in Guadalajara, Morelia, Puebla, San Luis Potosí Jalapa, and Oaxaca are relatively accessible. The addresses are easily ascertained locally; customarily the records are located in public buildings. For example, in Morelia and Oaxaca the archives are in the government palace; in Guanajuato, in the Archivo Histórico de Guanajuato, University of Guanajuato; and in Jalapa, in the Biblioteca de la Universidad Veracruzana.

Municipal archives are another rich source for examination. One defect of the traditional emphasis on national events and actions, as necessary as that may be, is that such an approach obscures or disregards local differences and developments. Subnational analysis may reveal quite a different picture from that apparent from national events, laws, and decisions. Local records will at least clarify and amplify our knowledge of what took place during the Reform; they may corroborate impressions from the national scene or rectify our judgments of the course of the movement. Increasingly, students of Mexican history are turning to examination of subnational history. The Archivo Municipal de Guadalajara, located in the new Civil Registry Building (Alcalde 964), is a well-organized, well-maintained, and accessible depository. Permission to enter the archive must be obtained from the secretary of the Ayuntamiento of Guadalajara, whose office is in the Municipal Palace. This is a memorable experience in itself—standing in line, waiting with other petitioners to present one's request to the august secretary, a politician in the grand style, but nevertheless a pleasant and cooperative individual.

The archivist (in 1967), Salvador Gómez García, is friendly, professional, and, like his staff, ever ready to be of assistance. The materials in the second-floor archive (open daily from 9:00 a.m. to 3:00 p.m.) are indexed by year caja (or box, usually two for each year), expediente with short title of contents, and often by general topic as well. The index should be used with care; though it is usually accurate, there were some mistakes in recording contents. The archives contain documentation on every aspect of municipal activities, including minutes of ayuntamiento sessions, acts of the cabildo (Libro Capitular de [year] and Actas de [year]), records on municipal property (grouped by year under Ejidos y Agua), education (under Instrucción), justice (Juzgados), and treasury and finance (Hacienda). In addition, there are statistics, state laws and circulars, communications, and other records of relations between the state authorities and Guadalajara. There is information not only on the state capital city but on the other towns in the municipality. While the archives do not provide a complete historical record for the Reform, they do illuminate the day-to-day administration of Mexico's second city during this period when control alternated repeatedly among different political factions. The meaning of these changes is revealed in the sessions and actions of the ayuntamiento. Other documents help fill out the local picture—the meager financial resources of the city; the condition of the schools, streets, markets, and jails; the disposal of lands; the problems posed by the oath to the 1857 constitution. These records and others get at the fundamentals of the Reform—how it affected the lives of the people; what it meant for municipal officials and employees, from important council members to lowly jailors; what it signified for teachers and renters of municipal lots.

The treasure available in the Guadalajara municipal archives may be anticipated for other localities, though perhaps without the good organization and maintenance. For example, the Archivo Municipal de la Ciudad de Oaxaca (located on the second floor of the ayuntamiento building; permission for its use is easily obtained from the president of the ayuntamiento) is largely unorganized; but the Borradores de Actas are organized and fairly complete.

A valuable project was initiated by the Instituto Tecnológico y de Estudios Superiores de Monterrey in the early 1960s to microfilm municipal archives in the state of Nuevo León. By mid-1967 some 2,145,000 pages of manuscripts had been microfilmed, covering seven of the thirty-seven municipalities in Nuevo León. The long-range plans envision microfilming the municipal records in the neighboring states of Tamaulipas and Coahuila as well. Not only municipal records but also parish church records and other public documents are included in the microfilming. Parish records include the expected baptismal, matrimonial, and burial documents, and often information on affairs pertinent to parish governance and life. The municipal archives include, as for Guadalajara, diverse materials on the administration of municipalities, cabildo session minutes, judicial and financial records, and other items.

State archives are yet another source, though not always usable because of the deplorable physical condition of documents, the lack of organization and indexing, and poor housing facilities. These conditions help explain the reluctance of officials to permit access to the materials. The Jalisco state archives are an example, but for the colonial documents, at least, a cooperative microfilming project is under way. The records in the Oaxaca state archives are also disorganized except for civil registry records (from the 1860s on) and a small section of miscellaneous documents (called *carpetas negras*) covering all time periods. Other state archives are apparently in a better state of repair and may be of value for local, state, or regional history of the period. The Correspondencia Particular de Santiago Vidaurri, consisting of some twenty thousand letters to and from prominent individuals of the Reform era (located in the Archivo de Nuevo León in Monterrey), are obviously also valuable for national political history.

This brief survey can do no more than suggest a few of the possibilities from among a large number and variety of archives that might be consulted by the researcher in mid-nineteenth-century Mexican history. The particular topic under study will partially determine the most useful depositories. Nothing can really replace the generosity and cooperation of colleagues who have preceded the researcher in the field, although the heavy demands on their energies and time will be greatly reduced by the growing number of guides to archives, of which the current publication is an important one. Although such guides are generally broad, surveying an entire archive or several archives, they contain valuable data for the student of the Reform.[2]

NOTES

1. In the preparation of this chapter I have been aided directly or indirectly, knowingly or unknowingly, by several colleagues whose assistance I gratefully acknowledge: Jan Bazant, Charles Berry, Charles Hale, Donald Cooper, and Michael Costeloe.

2. A useful bibliography of guides to archival collections in the Mexican states has been prepared by Professor C. Alan Hutchinson and is included as chapter 12, section C, pp. 193-96.

D. Research Materials
for the Porfiriato
by Paul Vanderwood
and Anthony T. Bryan

Recent trends in Mexican historiography reveal renewed scholarly interest in the Porfiriato (1876-1910). The multiple volumes on this period, *Historia Moderna de México*, researched under the direction of Daniel Cosío Villegas, best exemplify this trend. Original manuscript collections have not often been utilized, and most older accounts have relied mainly on published documents, memoirs, and newspapers. We have selected several important, available private and public collections which in the future should assist scholars in their research of this period.

The single richest source of material for a general study of Porfirian Mexico has only recently become available. It is the Colección General Porfirio Díaz the private papers of Porfirio Díaz from 1876 to 1916, now on "permanent loan" from the Díaz family to the University of the Americas in Puebla. The collection contains 663,843 items consisting of letters, telegrams (many of them coded), pamphlets, newspapers, maps, and reports. Among the materials are those which the late Dr. Alberto María Carreño edited in preparing the printed volumes of the *Archivo del General Porfirio Díaz: Memorias y Documentos*, 30 vols. (México: Editorial Elede, 1947-61). Documents in the archive are arranged chronologically, by month, in boxes and legajos. The entire collection has been microfilmed (on 374 rolls of 16mm film) and researchers work from the film, although the original documents are available.

The majority of the material consists of incoming, handwritten letters to Díaz, with a political emphasis. Many are from state governors. Only rarely are the president's full letter responses found in the collection. Instead one encounters handwritten, penciled notes that contain many abbreviations which Díaz apparently dictated to a secretary. Many are illegible, even when using the original document.

A perusal of the material suggests areas for important research. For example, it appears that the structure of the Porfirian political system rested upon the relationship of the president to his territorial and state governors. An apparent paucity of economic data in the papers might indicate the degree of the president's dependence on Limantour.

159

A general guide to the collection by Laurens B. Perry, *Inventario y Guía de la Colección General Porfirio Díaz* (Mexico: University of the Americas Press, 1969) is available. A name, place, and subject catalog is also planned. Permission to use the collection must be obtained beforehand from Dr. Steven Niblo at the University of the Americas.

A second valuable source for the Porfiriato is the Archivo Particular de Bernardo Reyes. General Reyes himself started this excellent private archive and it was inherited by his son, Alfonso Reyes, who died in 1958. The collection is part of the forty-thousand-volume library left by Don Alfonso and known as the Capilla Alfonsina. It is located at his family's home, Avenida Benjamín Hill, No. 122, in Mexico City and is under the supervision of Alicia Reyes Mota.

The Bernardo Reyes archive contains more than seventy legajos consisting of bound volumes, boxes, and loosely tied packages of letters to, and copies of letters from, Reyes that date from 1889 to 1913. Photographs, newspaper clippings, and rare books are also in the collection. The documents are well preserved, but their lack of proper organization poses some problem for the researcher. The archive is not cataloged in any systematic manner, although the majority of boxes and *libros copiadores* are arranged chronologically and some attempt was made to keep Reyes's correspondence with Díaz and members of the cabinet separate. There is no guide to the material, and one must be careful to leave the documents in their original order simply to provide others with some consistent basis for citing the papers.

The collection abounds with information on local and state politics in northern Mexico, as well as on policy making at those levels, during the Díaz era. Furthermore, since Reyes was probably Mexico's most prominent military figure during that time, his papers contain extensive correspondence with military personnel concerning the conduct and strategy of various military campaigns. Particularly important are those waged against the Yaqui Indians in the north and the Maya in Yucatán at the turn of the century. Because of Reyes's service as minister of war (from 1900 to 1902) and his subsequent "military mission" to Europe (from 1909 to 1910), the archive also contains lengthy analyses of the state of the military under Díaz and suggestions for its reform. From this perspective the Reyes papers lend insight into the Díaz military machine and point to reasons for its collapse.

Generally, the documents are strongest in research potential from 1897 through 1910; they are somewhat frustrating for the period from 1911 to the general's death in 1913. Though the archive has long been available to scholars, few have consulted it.

The Archivo Espinosa de los Monteros is of prime interest for Mexican politics from 1908 to 1911. Samuel Espinosa de los Monteros, one of Reyes's most faithful adherents, personally owned the archive, and it is one of the major collections of this type presently held by an agency of the Mexican government. It is housed in the rather rustic facilities of the historical annex to Chapultepec Castle, a division of the Departamento de Investigaciones Históricas.

The archive consists of seven large bound volumes of original manuscripts and newspaper clippings. The minutes of all the major pro-Reyes political organizations in the federal district and in some other parts of the nation are included. Original handwritten drafts and printed copies of the party manifestos, as well as extensive lists of names of the Reyista faithful, are carefully preserved. The documents can provide the researcher with some insight into the internal machinations of a prerevolutionary political movement led by individuals who desired to reform the Porfirian structure from within. As such they complement the documents contained in the Archivo de Francisco I. Madero (twenty-two reels of microfilm) at the Instituto Nacional de Antropología e Historia. The curator of the Samuel Espinosa de los Monteros collection, Josefina González de Arellano, has prepared an excellent mimeographed guide which briefly indicates the contents of every document in each of the legajos.

Within the Archivo General de la Nación, the Ramo de Gobernación remains the most important sector to be studied for the history of Mexico from Independence to the Revolution. It contains more than three thousand unbound legajos that pertain to the nation's domestic affairs, elections, public security, presidential decrees, and official correspondence with the states. Fewer in number but equally important documents treat matters dealing with church-state relations, colonization, industrialization, lotteries, and education.

Some 65 percent of all the material in the ramo deals with Mexico's rural police force (the rurales). It includes detailed logistical records, personnel folders, complaints of illegalities committed by corpsmen, and regular reports from unit commanders outlining field conditions. Although mainly concerned with military details, the documents provide scholars with valuable insight into the ambiance of rural Mexico from the Reform to the Revolution. The ramo also contains a considerable group of materials dealing with the French intervention as well as documents concerning Mexico's financial problems and search for internal tranquillity. Although limited in scope, it should prove especially valuable to scholars of the early Independence period.

A rough guide to the ramo exists, although it is not entirely accurate. Titles which are given too often refer only to the first document rather than the entire content of the material. Most of the legajos have been labeled with a short title designation, but while helpful, this does not adequately indicate the contents of the legajo.

The availability of the above materials should further encourage scholars to consider the Porfiriato as an area worthy of study in itself.

11

Research on
Revolutionary Mexico, 1910-72

A. The Military Revolution, 1910-20
by William H. Beezley
and Michael C. Meyer

The number and accessibility of archival collections for the revolutionary decade from 1910 to 1920 have increased substantially in the past several years. The improved research situation results from the passage of mandatory time limitations and the decline of personal and governmental sensitivity. With the termination of the fifty-year restriction, public records of national agencies are now available for the entire decade, with the notable exception of the virtually impregnable Archivo Histórico de la Defensa Nacional. Major public repositories now open include the Archivo General de Relaciones Exteriores de México and the Archivo General de la Nación.

In the Foreign Relations archive, in addition to a number of small collections of documents, there are two massive collections. (a) The Flores Magón section contains abundant manuscripts on this precursory movement—reports from government agents, consuls, and private detectives, as well as a substantial amount of material seized from the Mexican Liberal party as evidence against them. Copies of this ramo are also available in the library of the Secretaría de Hacienda, which has longer working hours and is located nearer the center of the city. (b) The Ramo de la Revolución Mexicana constitutes the most important single holding of the archive. Consisting of 259 volumes numbered L-E 610 to L-E 868, the collection contains reports from bureaucrats and consuls, spies and legal counsels, and private agencies, plus a massive amount of material seized or telegraphically intercepted from various rebel movements. It is strongest on those movements that emanated from the United States or that had agents recruiting, working for recognition, or acquiring arms and supplies north of the boundary line. As a result it is less useful for the Zapatistas than for the Maderistas, Orozquistas, Villistas, or Constitucionalistas.

The researcher is fortunate to have a general guide to the revolutionary collection of Foreign Relations, replete with notation on each expediente, in Berta Ulloa's *Revolución Mexicana, 1910-1920* (Mexico: Secretaría de Relaciones Exteriores, 1963).

In addition to the two major collections, the researcher in the Foreign Relations archive should also consult the various personal and topical expedientes for the role of public officials and the negotiation of specific international incidents. The topical items are not always available and, as in the case of the Zimmerman Telegram, may no longer exist. On the other hand, the section entitled Mensajes Relativos a la Evacuación del Puerto de Veracruz por los Americanos is actually somewhat broader than the title would seem to indicate. The personal files may consist of no more than appointment and dismissal papers, but in some cases there is substantial documentation on the official's public and confidential life. Personal files are available for virtually every important office holder who served the ministry in any capacity.

The second major public depository for the period from 1910 to 1920 is the Archivo General de la Nación, especially the Ramo de Gobernación and the Ramo de la Revolución. The former contains information on various topics such as reports of the federal police and the rurales, elections and interventions, and the other affairs of the government's interior agencies. The latter section does not include the scope of material which the title suggests, but rather is primarily a collection on the presidency of Venustiano Carranza. Also preserved in the AGN are scattered personal papers such as four letterbooks (outgoing correspondence) of Francisco I. Madero, numbered 1, 2, 3, and 12, and the papers of Zapatista General Francisco Leyva.

The personal papers of major figures during the first revolutionary decade are more readily available than ever before. The major collection of Madero manuscripts, the Archivo de Madero, is found in the Secretaría de Hacienda and also is available on microfilm in the library of the new Museo Nacional de Antropología e Historia. The film consists of twenty-two reels, including correspondence and letterbooks, some of which remain in stenographer's shorthand. The early years of Madero's political activity (from 1908 to 1911) are well represented until the time he reentered Mexico in February, 1911; after that date the collection is uneven, although there is ample material on the situation in Morelos and the Orozquista rebellion. There is also a collection of photographs and momentos and the original text of Madero's famous *La Sucesión Presidencial en 1910*. Complementary documents are the letter-books in the AGN and a small but important file of four boxes in the Biblioteca Nacional for the period from February to May, 1911, containing records on the imminent break between Madero and Orozco, the Battle of Ciudad Juárez, and efforts to establish rebel civil government.

A more extensive personal collection is the Archivo de Zapata, thirty-one boxes in the archives of the National University. Originally belonging to Gildardo Magaña, it includes twenty-three boxes of records from the interim presidency of Francisco León de la Barra, a few boxes on the 1914-15 Convention period, and four boxes and scattered documents devoted exclusively to the Zapata movement.

A third major personal archive for the decade is the Archivo de Venustiano Carranza, which is the primary source for the Constitutionist campaign and its leader. Some twenty thousand manuscripts and an additional fifty-seven thousand telegrams, many still in code, provide documentation for Carranza's role in revolutionary developments from 1913 to 1919. The materials are readily available in the pleasant surroundings of the Centro de Estudios de Historia de México, an appendage of Condumex. Condumex also possesses two other collections of value for the decade. The Archivo de Jenaro Amezecua is a useful source on the Zapata movement from 1911 to 1920, especially for the men and officers of his forces. Another supplementary collection is the Correspondencia Personal y Oficial de Francisco León de la Barra, covering his tenure as ambassador to the United States, as provisional president of the Republic, and his activities subsequent to the Huerta presidency.

Also for the Maderista rebellion, several other collections are noteworthy. The Archivo Espinosa de los Monteros in the historical annex to Chapultepec Castle provides some documentation on the governmental perspective and response to the Revolution from 1910 to 1914, especially the National Defense Leagues created at the time of the Veracruz invasion. The Archivo Particular de Bernardo Reyes in the Capilla Alfonsina, although devoted largely to the Díaz period, contains some material to 1913. Finally, for the official view there is the tremendous Archivo de Porfirio Díaz now being cataloged by the University of the Americas, Puebla, and available in a disorganized state on microfilm in Mexico City. The university can provide authorization for its use and further information. Also for the early revolutionary movement, the Archivo de Alfredo Robles Domínguez has hundreds of manuscripts and documents on insurrection in regional perspective. It is housed in the Instituto

Nacional de Estudios Históricos de la Revolución Mexicana in Mexico City. Several collections of unusual value remain in private hands or have been removed from Mexico. The voluminous Archivo de Pablo González remains the property of Pablo González, Jr., in Saltillo, Coahuila, although the University of Texas obtained microfilm copies of the material which spans the first two decades of the twentieth century; it is particularly useful on the progress of the Carranza campaigns. The University of Texas has also added a group of Pancho Villa papers, mainly of an economic nature, to its Latin American Collection. These are now being cataloged and will soon be available to researchers. Other privately owned documents include the Archivo Isidro Fabela, held by Josefina E. de Fabela; Archivo de Jesús Sotelo Inclán, held by the family in Mexico City; the personal papers of Antonio Díaz Soto y Gama; the collection of Marte R. Gómez; the Ethel Duffy Turner Archive in Cuernavaca; and the Archivo Particular del General Roque González Garza, with records of the Convention government and correspondence with leading revolutionaries associated with that faction, also in Mexico City. Sources outside Mexico of particular interest are the correspondence of Francisco Vázquez Gómez, held in the university library, University of Southern Illinois, Carbondale; the Emilio Rabasa papers and William F. Buckley papers at the University of Texas; the O'Shaughnessy collection at the New York Public Library; the Papers of Senator Albert B. Fall Relating to Mexican Affairs at the Huntington Library; and the Papers and Correspondence of Silvestre Terrazas in the Bancroft Library, University of California, Berkeley. The latter includes two very useful sections, a Flores Magón file of four boxes and a great deal of material on Villista civil government in Chihuahua.

Finally, the vast holdings of the Hemeroteca Nacional must be mentioned. These include complete serials of government and agency reports and official publications of the various states, as well as capital and state newspapers. The importance of the newspapers is enhanced because of the many historical articles and edited documentary collections published in these journals. Many of the edited documents are now otherwise inaccessible. Published archives include materials for Madero, Corral, Creel, and Zapata, among others. The scope of this historical material can best be appreciated and approached by using the masterful guide compiled by Stanley Ross et al., *Fuentes de la Historia Contemporánea de México: Periódicos y Revistas* (Mexico: El Colegio de México, 1965), volume 1 for the period of the military revolution.

One can anticipate that as the Revolution fades into the past an increasing number of private collections will be opened and that as scholars investigate the regional aspects of the Revolution, local materials will be more readily available.

B. Two Decades of Social Revolution, 1920-40 by Lyle C. Brown and Albert L. Michaels[1]

The two decades between 1920 and 1940 span an era of increasing social change in Mexico. During this period the 1917 Constitution's expressions of nationalism, secularism, anticlericalism, agrarianism, and social consciousness were implemented through legislative acts, judicial rulings, executive orders, and military force. As a result, these twenty years featured sharp conflicts between Church and state, labor unions and employers, peasant organizations and hacendados, nationalists and representatives of foreign interests.

All researchers working in the period bracketed by the downfall of Carranza and the beginning of the Avila Camacho administration will encounter something of value in the Papeles Presidenciales section of the Archivo General de la Nación.[2] Permission to consult this collection must be obtained from the AGN director, but the bodega containing twentieth-century presidential papers is under the care of Sr. Luis Cortes Huerta. Documents for the Calles and Obregón administrations (most of which concern the Obregón era) are indexed in a card file as Cajas de Tarjetas de Obregón-Calles. Cards are filed in boxes according to name and subject matter. Each card cites one or more expedientes; and the expedientes are located through use of a bound reference guide (generally referred to by AGN personnel as "La Biblia") which indicates the paquete in which each expediente should be found. The guide lists 216 paquetes, but some are missing and occasionally Sr. Huerta finds an unnumbered paquete. Expedientes supposedly found in paquetes 8 to 14 have been collected separately under Período Obregón-Calles, Diversos Años, 1921-1928. Neither card files nor guides are available for the papers of later presidents, but the volume of this unorganized material is suggested by the following approximate numbers of paquetes: Portes Gil, twenty-five paquetes; Ortiz Rubio, ten paquetes; Rodríguez, only a few scattered papers; Cárdenas, nine hundred paquetes. Consisting mainly of letters and telegrams, this mountain of official papers includes communications ranging in subject matter from congressional elections to oil expropriation, from Masonic organizations to labor unions, and from military operations to garbanzo production. Although many politically sensitive documents are not included, this ar-

chive constitutes the largest national collection of available, and largely un-
exploited, research material for the 1920-40 period.

Researchers investigating Mexican church-state relations during these
twenty years will encounter an important archival collection housed on the
eighth floor of the Biblioteca de la Universidad Nacional Autónoma de México. Under the care of Srta. Ana Rosa Carreon, this material is organized in
three parts: Archivo de la Liga Nacional Defensora de la Libertad Religiosa
(LNDLR), the personal papers of Lic. Miguel Palomar y Vizcarra, and documents from the Archivo de VITA México (commonly used abbreviation for
Union Internacional de Todos los Amigos de la Liga Nacional Defensora de la
Libertad Religiosa de México). The importance of this archival collection is
suggested by the following facts: the Catholic LNDLR served as the coordinating body for the Cristero Rebellion of 1926-29; Palomar y Vizcarra was a
member of the directing committee of the LNDLR; and VITA México functioned as the European arm of the LNDLR for the purpose of seeking economic and moral support for the Cristero movement. Microfilm copy of this
archival material can be consulted at the Biblioteca de Antropología
of the Instituto Nacional de Antropología e Historia. No catalog is
generally available to the public, but researchers using this microfilm may
consult with Mtra. Alicia Olivera Sedano de Bonfil, who has prepared a type-
written guide for her personal use.[3]

Also available in the Departamento de Investigaciones Históricas are
twenty-six rolls of microfilmed documents relating to the first administration
of Ing. Adalberto Tejeda as governor of Veracruz (1920-34). The original
documents from which this microfilm was made form part of three hundred
crudely bound and totally unorganized expedientes belonging to the Instituto
de Historia Contemporánea, which is located at the Universidad Veracruzana
in Xalapa, Veracruz. Other portions of the Xalapa archive cover Tejeda's
years as Secretario de Gobernación (1925-28) and his second administration
as governor of Veracruz (1928-32). Although much of the Tejeda archive consists of papers concerning routine administrative matters, there is a substantial
amount of significant material relating to the petroleum industry, church-
state relations, and agrarian reform. Hacienda records for some of the more
important municipalities in Veracruz have been collected and deposited with
the Facultad de Economía of the Universidad Veracruzana. Also, the
Facultad de Antropología of that university has microfilm copies of documents concerning land and other subjects that are found in the municipal archive of Zongolica and which date from 1592 to 1944.[4]

Researchers interested in Mexico's agrarian problems during the 1920-40 period will wish to consult the archive of the Departamento de Asuntos Agrarios y Colonización in Mexico City. This archive is an important source of information concerning *ejidos*, agricultural colonies, and private properties which are classified according to location in states and municipalities. Its documents concern such matters as land seizures, petitions for land, and distribution of land. Also included in these files is information regarding the functioning of *ejidos* since their formation, for example, election of *ejido* officials, censuses, distribution of land, and applications for extension of *ejido* holdings. Another source of information concerning agrarian matters is the archive of the Confederación Nacional Campesina (CNC), which is also located in the national capital. This archive contains files on *ejidos*, agricultural colonies, and small land owners who have filed petitions for assistance by the CNC in obtaining land. Permission to use the CNC archive must be obtained from the organization's Secretario de Acción Agrario. Systematic cataloging facilitates research.

In addition to the CNC, over 3,000 other associations have been identified in Mexico. These range from national organizations with well-staffed headquarters in Mexico City to local groups with very small memberships. No attempt has been made to determine the archival holdings of these associations, but many have been in existence since 1920 and some undoubtedly maintain archives that can be exploited with profit by scholars. For example, of the 621 associations which have cooperated with recent information-gathering activities of the Instituto de Investigaciones Sociales of the Universidad Nacional Autónoma de México, 171 were founded in 1940 or earlier.[5] Although Mexico's labor unions generally do not open their archives to researchers, archival materials of the Confederación Regional Obrera Mexicana (CROM) for the period from 1920 to 1940 may be consulted at union headquarters located in Mexico City at Cuba 60.

Researchers concerned with people and events that have been the subject of newspaper articles during the past forty years will find much valuable material in the approximately ten million clippings in the Archivos Económicos of the Secretaría de Hacienda y Crédito Público. Files of clippings are cataloged according to subject matter, and each clipping is identified with the date of publication and the newspaper from which it is taken. Also found in Mexico City is the unique Casasola photograph collection, which represents the work of two generations of the Casasola family. Prints of photographs may be purchased.[6]

Located in the Biblioteca Nacional is the Fichero Bio-Bibliográfico Mexicano, which was compiled over a period of forty years by Lieutenant Colonel Silvino Macedonio González Sánchez. Composed of over 250,000 cards bearing notes and newspaper clippings concerning a great variety of people and events that have figured in Mexico's history, the fichero contains much useful information concerning the 1920-40 period. One section of the fichero is arranged chronologically according to each day in the year; the other part is organized alphabetically according to the names of persons, subjects, and events.[7]

Many important private archives are to be found in Mexico, some of which contain valuable documents for the 1920-40 period. Occasionally a researcher with the right contacts and good luck may obtain access to these sources. For example, shortly before his death Dr. Rodolfo Brito Foucher made available to a graduate student his extensive personal archive consisting of correspondence, telegrams, photographs, newspaper clippings, and pamphlets. Included were materials relating to the De la Huerta Rebellion of 1923, Dr. Brito's service as law school dean and rector of the Universidad Nacional Autónoma de México, and his opposition to Tomás Garrido Canabal in Tabasco.[8]

Without doubt there exists in Mexico a staggering amount of archival material that should be exploited by scholars seeking to write the history of that country's social revolution during the 1920-40 period. To date, however, only a relatively small portion of this treasure has been made available to researchers. Nevertheless, as powerful political figures leave the scene, each passing year increases the possibility of access to both public and private archive collections.

NOTES

1. Appreciation is expressed for valuable information supplied by David C. Bailey, Eduardo Blanquel, James C. Brown, Nick Buford, Israel Cavazos Garza, Heather Fowler, Ignacio González-Polo y Acosta, Timothy C. Hanley, James Horn, Alan Kirshner, John B. Williman, and James W. Wilkie.

2. For an example of a book which is based in part on Papeles Presidenciales, see Edwin Leiuwen, *Mexican Militarism: The Political Rise and Fall of the Revolutionary Army, 1910-1940* (Albuquerque: University of New Mexico Press, 1968).

3. For an example of masterful use of this archival material, see Alicia Olivera Sedano, *Aspectos del Conflicto Religioso de 1926 a 1929: Sus Antecedentes y Consecuencias* (Mexico, D.F.: Instituto Nacional de Antropología e Historia, 1966). Additional

materials concerning the church-state conflict are found in Miguel Polomar y Vizcarra, *El Caso Ejemplar Mexicano*, 2d ed. (Mexico, D.F.: Editorial Jus, 1966); and in Polomar y Vizcarra's oral history interview in James W. Wilkie and Edna Monzón de Wilkie, *México Visto en el Siglo XX: Entrevistas de Historia Oral* (Mexico, D.F.: Instituto Mexicano de Investigaciones Económicas, 1969), chapter 5. For an account of the work of VITA México, see Dr. J. Antonio López Ortega, *Las Naciones Extranjeras y las Persecución Religiosa* (Mexico, D.F., 1944). The most complete inventory of archival and other unpublished sources relating to this church-state conflict is found in Jean A. Meyer, "La Christiade: Société et Idéologie dans le Mexique Contemporain," (Ph.D. diss., Paris, 1971), chap. 1, pp. xiii-xxxviii.

4. See Luis Reyes García, "El Archivo Municipal de Zongolica, Veracruz," *Historia Mexicana* 77 (July-September 1970): 119-42.

5. See Pablo Velázquez and Pedro Zamora, *Guía de Associaciones de la República Mexicana* (Mexico, D.F.: Universidad Nacional Autónoma de México, 1970).

6. For a large number of photographs from the Casasola collection, see Gustavo Casasola, *Histórica Gráfica de la Revolución Mexicana, 1900-1960*, 4 vols. (Mexico, D.F.: Editorial F. Trillas, 1962).

7. See Huberto Serralde Nieto, "Silviano Macedonio González Sánchez (1884-1967)," *Boletín del Instituto de Investigaciones Bibliográficas* 1 (January-June 1969): 117-40.

8. See Alan M. Kirshner, "Tomas Garrido Canabal and the Mexican Red Shirt Movement" (Ph.D. diss., New York University, 1970).

C. Scholarly Investigation of the Institutional Revolution, 1940-72 by Robert J. Shafer

Historians have made little use of archival materials dealing with Mexico since 1940. This omission is mostly due to inaccessibility, although the sheer bulk of the published record made available by the government, the press, and private organizations, together with the fact that there are relatively few historians dealing with the post-1940 years, are contributing factors. Inaccessibility is a compound of restrictions—legal, personal, social, political, and traditional—on studies of certain types of recent events, poor indexing of recent materials, and a simple lack of knowledge of the existence or content of many archives. Even with these difficulties, considerable research of value can now be done in some government archives, on many subjects; much research is possible on business, charitable, social, and interest-group activity in notarial and property registers in various places; and some research can be carried on in the archives of private organizations. Much preliminary scholarly work must be done to describe properly the archival resources of Mexico for investigation of the immensely important developments of recent years.

FEDERAL GOVERNMENT AND FEDERAL DISTRICT ARCHIVES

The Archivo General de la Nación. The Archivo General de la Nación, by law, is to receive the papers of extinguished federal agencies and the documentation of extant agencies when no longer needed for business purposes. The result is that federal agencies decide when to pass materials to the national archive, and most of the post-1940 records are retained in various ministerial and other archives, mostly in the Federal District. There are no published descriptions of the post-1940 documentation in the Archivo General.

Executive Agencies of the Federal Government. There is virtually no published material on post-1940 documentation in the archives of the executive agencies of the federal government. The putative content of such archives can, of course, be inferred from what the government is known to be collecting and from what it has published; that is, certain types of material have at least at one time existed in great profusion in certain federal government repositories. It is also well known that certain investigations and controversies since 1940 have involved prolonged study and information gathering, many committees, much application to interest groups, and much bargaining and compromise. In describing most of such cases scholars have been forced to rely heavily upon what they could find in the press or in the spotty published record of the government, or what they could dredge up in interviews. This is not satisfactory, and many well-known developments of recent years have been inadequately analyzed. It is to be hoped that eventually the archives of such agencies as the Secretariás of Hacienda and of Industria y Comercio (earlier Economía Nacional) will prove to be the gold mines of typescript, mimeograph, and holograph materials that the known character of their activities suggests that they might be. The amount of such material must be immense, distributed among the several hundred *secretarías* and *departamentos, organismos descentralizados,* and *empresas de participación estatal,* to say nothing of the records of the legislative and judicial branches of the federal government. It would at least be a great step forward to know what has and what has not been preserved, and what the policies for retention and for access in the future are likely to be.

Federal District Archives. In the Federal District, the Archivo de Notarías has many types of records on property, business, testaments, and other matters; and the Registro Público de la Propiedad y del Comercio includes records on buildings, real estate, and registration of business companies and of *sociedades civiles* (nonprofit organizations, some of which are educational, some charitable, and some representing interest groups). These two archives are of great value for the study of the economic and social history both of the Federal District and of Mexico generally (for example, some of the companies and associations registered have country-wide connections, interests, or operations). The Archivo del Distrito Federal is important not only for the governmental aspects of the history of the capital city during the period of its recent and almost unbelievable growth, but also for many other areas, including business and social history. At the National University the archives of the rectory and of the faculties should be useful in examination of recent intellectual trends and the groupings and social-action goals of faculty and students, as well as the pedagogical and research aims and attainments of the institution.

STATE AND MUNICIPAL ARCHIVES

State Archives. Each Mexican state has state archives. There is variation in their names, organization, and quality.[1] Some of them were only "organized" at the beginning of the period under discussion. The literature on them is poor. With the years, the activity of the state governments has increased in magnitude, variety, and importance. Without abandoning centralized control of government and party, the ruling group in Mexico has found it necessary to permit and even encourage social, and especially economic, development activity by state governments. Despite the provision to the states of planning studies and of decisions of various sorts from Mexico City, it is clear that the activity of state bureaucracies—especially in some of the wealthier states, such as Nuevo León, Sonora, and Jalisco—has been growing. For many social, economic, and political studies, access to state government records of recent years must be of value. Some of the new state public-private economic and planning study groups—as in Jalisco—are of interest not only for growth patterns, but in relation to interest-group interactions and to regional pressures in politics. There should be in the coming years a trend in Mexican historiography—repeating what happened earlier in the United Kingdom and the United States—toward new state, local, or regional studies, much more sophisticated than the rather simplistic state histories published in the past (which in any event scarcely deal with the post-1940 years). These would seem especially appropriate for the recent decades of rapid demographic and economic growth and social change.

Municipal Records. Most Mexican municipal records are little known to historians,[2] and this is especially the case for the documentation of recent developments. It is in the rapidly growing cities of recent years that one finds most of the larger socioeconomic effects of growth and modernization, the effects of new transportation, communications, and education, the proliferation of service occupations, and the effects of the social security systems. As noted above in connection with state government, for all the continuing predominance of the federal government, the new municipalities have had to develop broader functions and more specialized knowledge and instruments. The records of legislation, taxation, policing, sanitation, even a bit of zoning, and many other matters, should increasingly be pursued by historians of recent times in the records of the municipal governments. In addition, many municipalities—including all the larger ones—have notarial archives and civil registers similar to those in the Federal District. Another set of records that should be used is that of the *juntas de mejoras materiales*, dedicated to local civic improvements. Although some of these juntas have done little, others have accomplished quite a lot, and in any event they are interesting for the interaction of the public and private sectors in the face of new urban problems.

NONGOVERNMENT ARCHIVES

Political Parties. In Mexico, as in other countries, political parties do not organize or manage their records for the convenience of scholars. The extent of the archives of the Partido Revolucionario Institucional's national headquarters is not known; they have not been open to scholars. One scholar recently obtained access to PRI working papers at the municipal level in the provinces simply on the basis of personal relationships. His experience suggests that record keeping will be found less than comprehensive and rather untidy. Another scholar recently had some access to the Partido de Acción Nacional's Mexico City office files, and found them scanty and patchy; he found other PAN papers in the personal files of party officers. Yet another scholar recently obtained access to the Partido Popular Socialista records in the private papers of Vicente Lombardo Toledano. It would thus appear that manuscript materials bearing on political parties are going to be found in important measure in private collections.

Business Organizations. The chambers of commerce and of industry, their respective confederations, and other business organizations have paid little attention to the retention or organization of records. This is partly on the supposition that their published material constituted a sufficient record, partly because they are "business" rather than "historically" oriented. Few of them have many working materials for the earlier part of the post-1940 period, to say nothing of the years before 1940. Coparmex has done more than the others to bring together some historical materials; but even in this case they are scant. There is, however, as the present author has discovered, one class of important working papers that exists for all the period since 1940 (and for at least a decade before then). These are the packets of typed or mimeographed material put together by the staffs of business organizations for the use of delegates to regular annual or extraordinary assemblies. Most often they are simply titled, for example, XL Asamblea Ordinaria de la Confederación de Cámaras de Comercio de México. The packets often run well over two hundred pages, and include an agenda, *iniciativas* (proposals) by delegations to the assembly, papers prepared by the national staffs of the organizations, and comments on *iniciativas* by the national staffs. These materials reveal a great deal about business conditions and opinions in Mexico, about differences between regions and between segments of the business community, and about the relations between business and government. Only very rarely was much of this material printed in the public, published reports (sometimes titled Informes) of the organizations. Chronological runs of these packets are not complete in the headquarters of any business organization I visited.

Business Firms. It appears that the records of firms in Mexico are both scantier and less accessible to scholars than those in the United States. I have been permitted to see some records and reports as the result of personal relationships with individual executives. It does not appear, however, that more massive or regular access is likely to be afforded many researchers.

Others. Little is known about the possible archival materials for the years since 1940 of church and church-related groups, nonsectarian charitable groups, or artistic or intellectual groups. Such contemporary organizations remain to be analyzed in depth in historical literature. Almost the same may be said of the papers of prominent individuals (see discussion of political parties, above), which are widely scattered and almost never open to the ordinary scholar. The lack of available collections of working papers for Mexico's presidents since 1940 is most serious.

NOTES

1. Agustín Millares Carlo, *Repertorio Bibliógrafico de los Archivos Mexicanos y de los Europeos y Norteamericanos de Interés para la Historia de México* (México: UNAM, 1959), gives the names and locations of many state and municipal archives, but the listings in this bibliography hold out little hope that the content of the archives for the years from 1940 on can be ascertained without a visit or correspondence with each archive. Many states have *archivos del gobierno del estado*; some have historical archives, and there are other arrangements; e.g., Coahuila has an Archivo General del Estado, an Archivo del Congreso del Estado, and an Archivo de la Tesorería. The program of microfilming state historical archives for the Museo Nacional de Historia (Chapultepec) has not included post-1940 materials.

2. Felix F. Palavicini, "Archivos de México," in *México: Historia de Su Evolución Constructiva* (Mexico: Edit. S de R. L., 1945), vol. 4, pp. 99-119, claimed there were more than 2,220 municipal archives in Mexico, although about 230 had been partially or completely destroyed.

12

A Scholar's Bibliography for Research

A. A Bibliography of Bibliographies and Other Guides

by Eugenia Meyer and Alicia O. de Bonfil

Andrade, Vicente de P. *Bibliografía del Siglo XVII*. Mexico: n.p., 1902.

Anuario Bibliográfico Mexicano. Mexico: Imprenta de la Secretaría de Relaciones Exteriores, 1932-.

Bassols Batalla, Angel. *Bibliografía Geográfica Mexicana*. Mexico: Secretaría de Agricultura y Ganadería, 1955.

Berroa, Josefina. *México Bibliográfico, 1957-1960*. Mexico: Gráfica Cervantina, 1960.

Biblioteca Nacional de México. *Catálogos de la Biblioteca Nacional de México*. 9 vols. Mexico: Oficina Tipográfica de la Secretaría de Fomento, 1889-1908.

Blair, Calvin P.; Schaedel, Richard P.; and Street, James H. *Responsibilities of the Foreign Scholar to the Local Scholarly Community: Studies of U.S. Research in Guatemala, Chile and Paraguay*. Washington: Latin American Studies Association, 1969.

Bobb, Bernard E., and Ross, Stanley R. "Historiografía Mexicanista: Estados Unidos, 1959-1960." *Historia Mexicana* 19 (1960): 286-313.

Boggs, Ralph Steele. *Bibliografía del Folklore Mexicano*. Mexico: Instituto Panamericano de Geografía e Historia, 1939.

Boletín [de la biblioteca nacional]. Mexico: Universidad Nacional Autónoma de México, 1950-.

Boletín Bibliográfico Mexicano. Mexico: Porrua Hermanos y Compañía, 1939-.

Borah, Woodrow. "Notes on Civil Archives in the City of Oaxaca." *Hispanic*

American Historical Review 31 (1951): 723-44.

Bullejas, José. *La Bibliografía Económica de México en 1954-1955.* Mexico: Departamento de Estudios Económicos del Banco de México, 1956.

———. *Diez Años de Literatura Económica: Bibliografía Básica de la Economía de México, 1943-1953.* Mexico: Instituto de Investigaciones Económicas, 1954.

Carrera Stampa, Manuel. "El Archivo del ex-Ayuntamento de México." *Historia Mexicana* 12 (1963): 621-32.

———. *Archivalia Mexicana.* Mexico: UNAM, Instituto de Historia, 1952.

———. *Guía del Archivo del Antiguo Ayuntamiento de la Ciudad de México.* Havana: Archivo Nacional de Cuba, 1949.

Castañeda, Carlos E. *Guide to the Latin American Manuscripts in the University of Texas Library.* Cambridge: Harvard University Press, 1939.

Castañeda, Carlos, and Dabbs, Jack A. *A Calendar to the Juan E. Hernández y Dávalos Manuscript Collection.* Mexico: Editorial Jus, 1945.

Castillo, Ignacio B. del. *Bibliografía de la Imprenta de la Cámara de Diputados.* Mexico: n.p., 1918.

———. *Bibliografía de la Revolución Mexicana de 1910 a 1916.* Mexico: Talleres de la Secretaría de Comunicaciones y Obras Públicas, 1918.

Catálogo Especial de Obras Mexicanas o Sobre México en la Biblioteca Nacional. Mexico: n.p., 1911.

Chamberlain, Robert S. "A Report on Colonial Materials in the Government Archives of Guatemala City." *Handbook of Latin American Studies* 2 (1937): 387-432.

Chávez Orozco, Luis. *Indice del Ramo de Indios del Archivo General de la Nación.* 2 vols. Mexico: n.p., 1953.

Chinchilla Aguilar, Ernesto. "Documentos Existentes en el Archivo General de la Nación: La Clasificación del Archivo Nacional de Guatemala, Obra del Profesor J. Joaquín Pardo." *Anales de la Sociedad de Geografía e Historia de Guatemala* 39 (1966): 443-49.

Colegio de México, El. *Veinticinco Años de Investigación Histórica en México.* Mexico: El Colegio de México, 1966.

Cooper, Donald B. "A Selective List of Colonial Manuscripts in the Archives of the Department of Health and Welfare." *Hispanic American Historical Review* 42 (1962): 385-414.

Cosío Villegas, Daniel. *Cuestiones Internacionales de México. Bibliografía Mexicana.* Mexico: Secretaría de Relaciones Exteriores, 1966.

———. *La Historiografía Política del México Moderno.* Mexico: El Colegio Nacional, 1953.

————. *Nueva Historiografía Política del México Moderno.* Mexico: El Colegio Nacional, 1965.

Costeloe, Michael. "Guide to the Chapter Archives of the Archbishopric of Mexico." *Hispanic American Historical Review* 45 (1965): 53-63.

Cruzado, Manuel. *Bibliografía Jurídica Mexicana.* Mexico: Tipografía de la Oficina Impresora de Estampillas, 1905.

Cumberland, Charles C. "The United States–Mexican Border: A Selective Guide to the Literature of the Region." Supplement to *Rural Sociology* 25 (1960).

Dabbs, Jack A. *The Mariano Riva Palacio Archives.* 3 vols. Mexico: Editorial Jus, 1968-69.

Esquenazi-Mayo, Roberto. *Historiografía de la Guerra Entre México y los Estados Unidos.* Pittsburgh, Pa.: Duquesne Hispanic Review, 1962.

Estrada, Genaro. *200 Notas de Bibliografía.* Mexico: Imprenta de la Secretaría de Relaciones Exteriores, 1935.

Foster, Merlin H. *An Index to Mexican Literary Periodicals.* New York and London: Scarecrow Press, 1966.

Galindo y Villa, Jesús. *La Clasificación de los Conocimientos Humanos y la Bibliografía Mexicana.* Mexico: Imprenta del Gobierno Federal, 1901.

Gall, Francis. "Soconusco (Hasta la Epoca de la Independencia)." *Anales de la Sociedad de Geografía e Historia de Guatemala* 35 (1962): 155-68.

Gans, A. L., ed. *Catalogue of the Mexican Pamphlets in the Sutro Collection, 1623-1888: Supplements, 1605-1628.* San Francisco: California State Library, 1941.

García Icazbalceta, Joaquín. *Bibliografía Mexicana del Siglo XVI.* Mexico: Andrade y Morales, 1886. New ed. by Agustín Millares Carlo. Mexico: Fondo de Cultura Económica, 1954.

García y García J., Jesús. *Los Archivos de México.* Mexico, in press.

Glass, John B. *Catálogo de la Colección de Códices.* Mexico: Museo Nacional de Antropología, 1964.

Gómez Canedo, Lino. *Los Archivos de la Historia de América: Período Colonial Español.* 2 vols. Mexico: PAIGH, 1961.

González, Luis; Monroy, Guadalupe; and Uribe, Susana. *Fuentes de la Historia Contemporánea de México: Libros y Folletos.* 3 vols. Mexico: El Colegio de México, 1961-62.

González de Cossio, Francisco. *Libros Mexicanos: Contribución a la Bibliografía Tipográfica de la Ciudad de México en el Siglo XVI y Principios del XVII.* Mexico: n.p., 1949.

Griffin, Charles C., ed., and Warren, J. Benedict, asst. ed. *Latin America: A Guide to the Historical Literature*. Austin: University of Texas Press, 1971.

Guía al Archivo Histórico de Hacienda: Siglos XVI a XIX. Mexico: Secretaría de Hacienda y Crédito Público, 1940.

Guía de Fuentes para la Historia de Ibero-América en los Archivos de España. 2 vols. New York: UNESCO, 1965-69.

Guía del Archivo Histórico Militar de México. Mexico: n.p., 1949.

Guzmán y Raz Guzmán, Jesús. *Bibliografía de la Independencia de México*. 3 vols. Mexico: Secretaría de Relaciones Exteriores, 1937-39.

―――. *Bibliografía de la Reforma, la Intervención y el Imperio*. 2 vols. Mexico: Secretaría de Relaciones Exteriores, 1930-31.

Hale, Charles A., and Meyer, Michael C. "Mexico: The National Period." in *Latin American Scholarship since World War II*, edited by Roberto Esquenazi-Mayo and Michael C. Meyer. Lincoln: University of Nebraska Press, 1971. Pp. 115-38.

Handbook of Latin American Studies. Cambridge, Mass.: Harvard University Press; Gainesville, Fla.: University of Florida Press, 1936-.

Herrera Gómez, Nestor, and González, Silvino M. J. *Apuntes para una Bibliografía Militar de México, 1536-1936*. Mexico: Talleres Gráficos de la Nación, 1939.

Hill, Roscoe R. *The National Archives of Latin America*. Cambridge, Mass.: Harvard University Press, 1945.

Johnson, Charles W. *México en el Siglo XX: Bibliografía Política y Social de Publicaciones Extranjeras*. Mexico: Universidad Nacional Autónoma de México, 1969.

Jones, Cecil Knight. *Bibliography of the Mexican Revolution*. Baltimore: n.p., 1919.

León, Nicolás. *Bibliografía Mexicana del Siglo XVIII*. 6 vols. Mexico: Díaz de León, 1902-1908.

Martínez Ríos, Jorge. *Tenencia de la Tierra y Desarrollo Agrario en México: Bibliografía Selectiva y Comentada*. Mexico: Instituto de Investigaciones Sociales, 1970.

Medina, José Toribio. *La Imprenta en México (1539-1821)*. 8 vols. Santiago de Chile: n.p., 1907.

México. Dirección General de Estadísticas. *Bibliografía Mexicana de Estadísticas*. 2 vols. Mexico: Talleres Gráficos de la Nación, 1941-42.

―――. Secretaría de Comunicaciones y Obras Públicas. *Bibliografía, 1891-1943*. Mexico: Tipográfica La Nacional Impresora, 1943.

———. Secretaría de Hacienda y Crédito Público. *Bibliografía de la Secretaría de Hacienda y Crédito Público, 1821-1942.* Mexico: n.p., 1943.

Meyer, Eugenia. *Conciencia Histórica Norteamericana de la Revolución de 1910.* Mexico: Instituto Nacional de Antropología e Historia, 1970.

———. "Indice Bibliográfico de Libros Norteamericanos sobre la Revolución Mexicana." *Anales del INAH* 19 (1966): 265-78.

Millares Carlo, Agustín. *Repertorio Bibliográfico de los Archivos Mexicanos y de los Europeos y Norteamericanos para la Historia de México.* Mexico: Biblioteca Nacional, 1959.

Millares Carlo, Agustín, and Mantecón, José Ignacio. *Ensayo de una Bibliografía de Bibliografías Mexicanas.* Mexico: Secretaría de Educación Pública, 1943.

———. *Repertorio Bibliográfico de los Archivos Mexicanos y de las Colecciones Diplomáticas Fundamentales para la Historia de México.* Mexico: n.p., 1948.

Moore, Ernest Richard. *Bibliografía de la Revolución Mexicana.* Mexico: El Colegio de México, 1941.

Moreno, Roberto. "Catálogo de los Manuscritos Científicos de la Biblioteca Nacional." *Boletín del Instituto de Investigaciones Bibliográficas* 1 (1969): 61-103.

———. "Guía de la Obras en Lenguas Indígenas en la Biblioteca Nacional." *Boletín de la Biblioteca Nacional* 17, nos. 1-2 (1966): 35-116.

Navarro, Bernabe. *La Introducción de la Filosofía Moderna en México.* Mexico: El Colegio de México, 1948.

Noguera, Eduardo. "Bibliografía de Códices Precolombinos y Documentos Indígenas Posteriores a la Conquista." *Anales del Museo Nacional de Antropología e Historia* 8 (1933): 583-603.

Okinshevich, Leon. *Latin America in Soviet Writings: A Bibliography.* Baltimore: Johns Hopkins Press, 1966.

Orozco Farías, Rogelio. *Fuentes Históricas de la Independencia de México, 1808-1821.* Mexico: Editorial Jus, 1967.

Ortega y Medina, Juan. *México en la Conciencia Anglosajona.* Mexico: Antigua Librería Robredo, 1955.

Pardo, J. Joaquín. "Indice de los Documentos Existentes en el Archivo General del Gobierno." *Boletín* del Archivo General del Gobierno 1-10 (1935-45).

Parra, Manuel Germán, and Jiménez Moreno, Wigberto. *Bibliografía Independiente de México y Centroamérica, 1850-1950.* Mexico: Instituto Nacional Indigenista, 1954.

Partido de la Revolución Mexicana. *Selección Bibliográfica Revolucionaria.* Mexico: La Impresora, 1943.

Perales Ojeda, Alicia. *La Obras de Consulta: Reseña Histórica Crítica.* Mexico: Facultad de Filosofía y Letras, Seminario de Consulta Bibliográfica, 1962.

Perry, Laurens B. *Inventario y Guía de la Colección General Porfirio Díaz.* Mexico: University of the Americas Press, 1969.

Potash, Robert A. "Historiography of Mexico since 1821." *Hispanic American Historical Review* 11 (1961): 362-412.

Quirarte, Martín. *Historiografía sobre el Imperio Mexicano.* Mexico: Universidad Nacional Autónoma de México, 1970.

Radin, Paul, ed. *Catalogue of Mexican Pamphlets in the Sutro Collection, 1623-1888.* 14 vols. San Francisco: California State Library, 1939-40.

Ramos, Roberto. *Bibliografía de la Historia de México.* Mexico: Talleres de Impresora de Estampillas y Valores, 1956.

———. *Bibliografía de la Revolución Mexicana.* 3 vols. Mexico: Talleres Gráficos de la Nación, 1959.

Robertson, Donald. *Mexican Manuscript Painting of the Early Colonial Period: The Metropolitan Schools.* New Haven: Yale University Press, 1959.

Ross, Stanley R. "Aportación Norteamericana de la Revolución Mexicana." *Historia Mexicana* 10 (1961): 282-308.

———. "Bibliography of Sources for Contemporary Mexican History." *Hispanic American Historical Review* 39 (1959): 234-38.

———. *Fuentes de la Historia Contemporánea de México: Periódicos y Revistas.* 2 vols. Mexico: El Colegio de México, 1967.

Rubio Mañé, J. Ignacio. *El Archivo General de la Nación, México, D.F.* Mexico: Editorial Cultura, 1940.

Simpson, Lesley B. "The Colonial Archives of Guatemala." *Handbook of Latin American Studies* 1 (1936): 232-34.

Spell, Lota M. *Research Materials for the Study of Latin America at the University of Texas.* Austin: University of Texas Press, 1954.

Stein, Stanley. "Historiografía Latinoamericanista: Balance y Perspectivas." *Historia Mexicana* 14 (1964): 1-41.

Trask, David; Meyer, Michael; and Trask, Roger, comps. and eds. *A Bibliography of United States–Latin American Relations since 1810: A Selected*

List of Eleven Thousand Published References. Lincoln: University of Nebraska Press, 1968.

Ulloa, Berta. *Revolución Mexicana, 1910-1920.* Mexico: Secretaría de Relaciones Exteriores, 1963.

———. "Centro de Documentación del Museo Nacional de Historia en el Castillo de Chapultepec." *Historia Mexicana* 4 (1954): 275-80.

Uribe de Fernández de Córdova, Susana, comp. *Bibliografía Histórica Mexicana.* 4 vols. Mexico: El Colegio de México, 1967-70.

Valton, Emilio. *Impresos Mexicanos del Siglo XVI.* Mexico: Biblioteca Nacional 1935.

Valverde Téllez, Emeterio. *Bibliografía Eclesiástica Mexicana, 1821-1943.* 3 vols. Mexico: Editorial Jus, 1949.

Vivó, Jorge A. "Catálogo de la Biblioteca del Instituto Panamericano de Geografía e Historia. Mexico: Instituto Panamericano de Geografía e Historia, 1940.

Ynsfran, Pablo Max. "Catálogo del Archivo de Don Lucas Alamán Que Se Conserva en la Universidad de Texas, Austin." *Historia Mexicana* 4 (1954): 281-316.

———. *Catálogo de los Manuscritos del Archivo de Don Valentín Gómez Farías.* Mexico: n.p., 1968.

Wagner, Henry Raup. *The Spanish Southwest, 1542-1794: An Annotated Bibliography.* Berkeley: J. J. Gillick and Co., 1924.

Zavala, Silvio. "Catálogo de los Fondos del Centro de Documentación del Museo Nacional de Historia en el Castillo de Chapultepec." *Memorias de la Academia Mexicana de Historia* 10 (1951): 459-95.

B. Bibliographical Essay on Mexican Independence by Romeo Flores Caballero

The period of Independence has commanded the close attention of researchers in Mexican history. The abundance of material makes it imperative that the student interested in the subject be familiar with the most important guides and collections as well as the primary sources and basic secondary works before beginning his investigation.

The student should initiate his project by consulting the following guides to archives: Herbert E. Bolton, *Guide to Materials for the History of the United States in the Principle Archives of Mexico* (Washington, 1913); Manuel Carrera Stampa, *Archivalia Mexicana* (Mexico, 1952); and Agustín Millares Carlo and José Ignacio Mantecón, *Repertorio Bibliográfico de los Archivos Mexicanos y de las Colecciones Diplomáticas Fundamentales para la Historia de México* (Mexico, 1948). For guides to Mexican libraries, the following are useful: Elsa Barbarena, comp., *Directorio de Bibliotecas de la Ciudad de México* (Mexico, 1967) and *Directorio de Bibliotecas de la República Mexicana* (Mexico, 1968).

For the compilation of raw data, the resources of the Archivo General de la Nación are truly fundamental. In addition to the invaluable manuscripts contained in the sections of Bienes Nacionales, Consolidación, Historia, Infidencia, Inquisición, Operaciones de Guerra, and Viceroys (catalogs for which are available in the archive) the sources include a rich collecion of contemporary pamphlets. Equally important is the Colección Lafragua in the Biblioteca Nacional, which contains the most important collection of cataloged pamphlets from the period. Also important are the materials from the Hemeroteca Nacional, especially the *Gazeta de México, Gaceta del Gobierno de México, Diario de México, Despertador Americano, Jornal Económico Mercantil de Veracruz, Noticioso General de Méjico* and *Seminario Económico de Noticias Curiosas y Eruditas sobre Agricultura y Demás Artes y Oficios*. Of interest as well are the collections in the library of the Museo Nacional de Antropología e Historia and the Centro de Estudios de Historia at Comdumex which has been able to pull together important collections previously in private hands. In the United States the Latin American Collection of the University of Texas, the Sutro Collection at the University of California, the

189

Henry R. Wagner Collection at Yale, and the vast holdings of the Library of Congress are indispensable.

A large portion of the material in these centers has been listed and annotated in a number of bibliographical studies. Oustanding as guides to the materials in Mexico are Jesús Guzmán y Raz Guzmán, *Bibliografía de la Independencia de México*, 3 vols. (México, 1937-39); Genaro Estrada, *200 Notas de Bibliografía Mexicana* (México, 1935); and Juan B. Iguiñiz, *Bibliografía Bibliográfica Mexicana* (Mexico, 1930). Lucina Moreno Valle has finished a new index to the Lafragua Collection, and the classification of the pamphlet collection of the Archivo General de la Nación is nearing completion. For guides to other archival sources one should consult the *Boletines* published by the Archivo General de la Nación and the Biblioteca Nacional.

For guides to Mexican collections in the United States, the following are basic: Carlos E. Castañeda and Jack A. Dabbs, eds., *Guide to the Latin American Manuscripts in the University of Texas Library* (Cambridge, 1939); Lota M. Spell, *Research Material for the Study of Latin America at the University of Texas* (Austin, 1954); A. L. Gans, ed., *Catalogue of the Mexican Pamphlets in the Sutro Collection, 1623-1888: Supplements, 1605-1828* (San Francisco, 1941); and P. Radin, ed., *Catalogue of the Mexican Pamphlets in the Sutro Collection, 1623-1888*, 14 vols. (San Francisco, 1939-40).

Among the most important collections of published documents for research in the Independence of Mexico, the following stand out: J. Hernández y Dávalos, *Colección de Documentos para la Historia de la Guerra de Independencia de México de 1808 a 1821*, 6 vols. (Mexico, 1877-82) and Genaro García, ed., *Documentos Históricos Mexicanos*, 7 vols. (Mexico, 1910-12). For the economic and social aspects of the period one can consult Luis Chávez Orozco, ed., *Documentos para la Historia Económica de México* (Mexico, 1933-39), and the series directed by Luis Chávez Orozco under the title *Colección de Documentos para la Historia del Comercio Exterior de México*, sponsored by the Banco Nacional de Comercio Exterior de México.

For the Mexicans who left impressions of their experiences in the period of Independence, the following works are essential: Lucas Alamán, *Historia de Méjico desde los Primeros Movimientos Que Prepararon Su Independencia...*, 5 vols. (Mexico, 1849-52); Carlos María Bustamante, *Diario Histórico de México* (Mexico, 1896) and *Continuación del Cuadro Histórico de la Revolución Mexicana* (Mexico, 1953); Agustín de Iturbide, *Correspondencia y Diario Militar* (Mexico, 1930) and *Carrera Militar y Política de D. Agustín de Iturbide o Sea Memoria Que Escribió en Liorna...*, (Ximeno, Mexico, 1827);

Servando Teresa de Mier Noriega y Guerra, *Historia de la Revolución de Nueva España, Antiguamente Anáhuac* (London, 1813); José María Luis Mora, *México y Sus Revoluciones*, 3 vols. (Paris, 1950) and *Obras Sueltas* (Mexico, 1963); and Lorenzo de Zavala, *Ensayo Histórico de la Revoluciones de Méjico*, 2 vols. (Paris, 1831-32).

Among the observations of foreigners the accounts of Alexander von Humboldt are basic: *Ensayo Político de la Nueva España*, 5 vols. (Mexico, 1941), including his *Tablas Geográfico-Políticas del Reyno de Nueva España*. One should also consult Mariano Torrente, *Historia de la Independencia de México* (Madrid, 1918) and the French interpretation contained in Ernesto de la Torre Villar, ed., *Correspondencia Diplomática Franco-Mexicana, 1809-39* (Mexico, 1957).

It is difficult to select the principal secondary works from the enormous body of excellent literature on the Independence period. Nevertheless, the following are especially recommended: Nettie Lee Benson, ed., *Mexico and the Spanish Cortes, 1810-1822* (Austin, 1966); Francisco Bulnes, *La Guerra de Independencia, Hidalgo—Iturbide* (Mexico, 1910); Michael Costeloe, *Church Wealth in Mexico* (Cambridge, 1967); Luis Chávez Orozco, *Historia de México: 1808-1836* (Mexico, 1947); Nancy M. Farris, *Crown and Clergy in Colonial Mexico* (London, 1968); Romeo Flores Caballero, *La Contrarrevolución en la Independencia* (Mexico, 1969); Gastón García Cantú, *El Pensamiento de la Reacción Mexicana* (Mexico, 1965); Luis González Obregón, *La Vida en México en 1810* (Mexico, 1911); Luis González y González, comp., *El Congreso de Anáhuac, 1813* (Mexico, 1963); Charles Hale, *Mexican Liberalism in the Age of Mora* (New Haven, 1968); Hugh Hamill, *The Hidalgo Revolt* (Gainesville, 1966); Enrique Lafuente Ferrari, *El Virrey Iturrigaray y los Orígenes de la Independencia de México* (Madrid, 1941); Miguel Lerdo de Tejada, *Comercio Exterior de México . . .* (México, 1853); Francisco López Cámara, *La Génesis de la Conciencia Liberal en México* (Mexico, 1954); J. M. Miguel y Verges, *La Independencia Mexicana y la Prensa Insurgente* (Mexico, 1941); José Miranda, *Las Ideas y las Instituciones Políticas Mexicanas . . .* (Mexico, 1952); and Alejandro Villaseñor, *Biografías de Héroes y Caudillos de la Independencia* (Mexico, 1967).

C. Bibliographical Guide to Archival Collections in the Mexican States by C. Alan Hutchinson

Historians are becoming increasingly interested in Mexican state archives, some of which are remarkably rich and well preserved, although most of them are still woefully neglected by the authorities. In fact state authorities sometimes think of local documentary collections as good material for selling to paper mills or to American universities or dealers to raise some money. In addition to this danger of loss there are the more general ones of damage from insects, dampness, flood, fire, and loss in moving to other buildings. Indeed, some state archives listed in guides have actually disappeared without leaving a trace. The hazardous existence of these archives has made all the guides more or less out of date so that the best way to learn about a particular state archive is to talk with someone who has just returned from working in it. It is not yet possible to prepare an authoritative guide to these invaluable repositories, but perhaps a listing of some of the available descriptions of their contents (at the time the list was made) will be useful.

Still the most satisfactory general guide to the state archives is Manuel Carrera Stampa, *Archivalia Mexicana* (Mexico, 1952). Most compilers of guides since the appearance of this book have relied rather heavily on it for part of their information. A more recent general survey which can be highly recommended is Lino Gómez Canedo, *Los Archivos de la Historia de América: Período Colonial Español*, 2 vols. (Mexico, 1961). Volume 1 has a valuable section on Mexican regional and local archives and libraries (pp. 306-53). Also very useful is Agustín Millares Carlo, *Los Archivos Municipales de Latinoamérica* (Maracaibo, 1961), which discusses municipal archives in Mexico City and the Mexican states on pp. 108-61. Among the other guides is the famous work by Professor Herbert E. Bolton, *Guide to Materials for the History of the United States in the Principal Archives of Mexico* (Washington, D.C., 1913), which despite its age is still useful. It describes archives in the cities of Guadalajara, Querétaro, Zacatecas, San Luis Potosí Durango, Saltillo, and Monclova. It also has general discussions of archives in the states of Nuevo León, Tamaulipas, Chihuahua, and Sonora. Vito Alessio Robles, *Bosquejos Históricos* (Mexico, 1937) includes discussions of the archives of Guadalajara, Querétaro, Durango, Parral, Saltillo, Monterrey, Parras, Monclova, Yucatán, and Campeche. Another older treatment which mentions some archives not touched upon in the above is Antonio Pompa y Pompa, "Contribución del Instituto Nacional de Antropología e Historia para la Conservación de los Archivos Mexicanos fuera de la Capital," in *Memoria del Primer Congreso de Historiadores de México y los Estados Unidos* (Mexico, 1950), pp. 71-81. Consideration is given here to archives in Querétaro, Guanajuato, San Luis Potosí, Monterrey, Saltillo, Toluca, Morelia, Guadalajara, Tepic, Culiacán, and Hermosillo. A discussion of Franciscan missionary college archives in the Mexican Franciscan provinces of San Diego, Michoacán; Santa Cruz of Querétaro; Jalisco; and Zacatecas is provided in Lino Gómez Canedo, "Some Franciscan Sources in the Archives and Libraries of America," *The Americas* 13 (October 1956): 141-74.

In addition to the general guides discussing Mexican state archives noted above there is a growing periodical literature on the archives of individual states. The following list is arranged alphabetically by states:

Chihuahua

West, Robert C. "The Municipal Archive of Parral, Chihuahua, Mexico." *Handbook of Latin American Studies.* Washington, D.C., 1940. Pp. 523-29.

Colima

Berthe, Jean-Pierre. "El Archivo Municipal de Colima." *Historia Mexicana* 8 (1958): 222-25.

Durango

Gallegos C., José Ignacio. "Durango: La Historia y Sus Instrumentos." *Historia Mexicana* 11 (1961): 314-20.

"Inventario General de los Libros y Papeles del Excelentísimo Ayuntamiento de Durango [up to 1833]." Supplement to *Memorias de la Academia Mexicana de la Historia* 7 (1948): 7-74.

Guanajuato

Vicente González del Castillo is publishing an index of the Archivo Histórico Municipal of León in *El Boletín: Organo del Archivo Histórico Municipal.* The only one I have seen is in number 60 (May, 1970).

Jalisco

Kroeber, Clifton B. "La Biblioteca Pública del Estado de Jalisco, Guadalajara," *Hispanic American Historical Review* 44 (1964): 377-81.

Mora L., Miguel de la, and González Navarro, Moisés. "Jalisco: La Historia y Sus Instrumentos." *Historia Mexicana* 1 (1951): 143-63.

Páez Brotchie, Luis. *La Nueva Galicia a través de Su Viejo Archivo Judicial.* Mexico, 1940.

Michoacán

Fernández de Córdoba, Joaquín. "Michoacán: La Historia y Sus Instrumentos." *Historia Mexicana* 2 (1952): 135-54.

———. "Sumaria Relación de las Bibliotecas de Michoacán." *Historia Mexicana* 3 (1953): 134-56.

Nuevo León

Cavazos Garza, Israel. "Nuevo León: La Historia y Sus Instrumentos." *Historia Mexicana* 1 (1952): 494-514.

Hoyo, Eugenio del. *Indice del Ramo de Causas Criminales del Archivo Municipal de Monterrey.* Monterrey, 1963.

Oaxaca

Borah, Woodrow. "The Cathedral Archives of Oaxaca." *Hispanic American Historical Review* 28 (1948): 640-45.

———. "Notes on Civil Archives in the City of Oaxaca." *Hispanic American Historical Review* 31 (1951): 723-49.

Iturribarría, Jorge Fernando. "Oaxaca: La Historia y Sus Instrumentos." *Historia Mexicana* 2 (1953): 459-76.

Puebla

Bazant, Jan. "Puebla: La Historia y Sus Instrumentos." *Historia Mexicana* 19 (1970): 432-37.

Borah, Woodrow. "Archivo de la Secretaría Municipal de Puebla: Guía para la Consulta de Sus Materiales." *Boletín del Archivo General de la Nación* 13 (1942): 211-39, 423-64.

Querétaro

García Martínez, Bernardo. "Querétaro: La Historia y Sus Instrumentos." *Historia Mexicana* 18 (1968): 286-92.

San Luis Potosí

Meade, Joaquín. "San Luis Potosí La Historia y Sus Instrumentos." *Estilo: Revista de Cultura* 39 (1956): 155-78.

Pompa y Pompa, Antonio. "Archivalia Histórica." *Fichas de Bibliografía Potosina* 2 (1955): 90-93.

———. "Relación de Documentos Microfilmados en los Archivos." *Fichas de Bibliografía Potosina* 2 (1955): 11-21.

Veracruz

González, Juan José. *Documentos Coloniales de la Nueva Veracruz.* Veracruz, 1943.

Reyes García, Luis. "El Archivo Municipal de Zongolica, Veracruz." *Historia Mexicana* 20 (1970): 119-42.

D. Two Decades of Unpublished Doctoral Dissertations on Mexico, 1950-70

by William D. Raat

The following compilation of unpublished dissertation topics in the field of Mexican history (broadly defined to include colonial New Spain as well as the modern epoch) is primarily the result of surveys conducted under the auspices of the Conference on Latin American History and the American Historical Association. For the titles between 1967 and 1969 I am especially indebted to my colleagues Michael Meyer and Charles Hale, whose listing of dissertations on Mexican history was published in the October, 1969, CLAH *Newsletter*. Those individuals needing more information are encouraged to consult the several listings of dissertations from 1958 to 1970 published by the American Historical Association. For titles prior to 1958 see Warren F. Kuehl's *Dissertations in History* (Lexington, Ky., 1965).

The topics have been arranged in chronological order under the following headings: General, Colonial, Independence (1800-1824), the early Republic and the Reform (1824-76), the Porfiriato (1876-1911), the Revolution (1911-40), and the Contemporary Era (1940–the present). Obviously some titles did not fit nicely into this scheme and had to be either classified as general or placed in an overlapping category. The dates included indicate the year in which the project was completed. In those cases where no termination date has been verified, the dissertations are listed as in progress. When conflicting termination dates have been found, a question mark is added. Further information should be obtained from the graduate school of the university in question.

GENERAL

Cornelius, Wayne A., Jr. "Political Correlates of Urban Migrant Assimilation in Mexican Metropolitan Areas." Stanford University, 1970.

Duncan, W. Raymond. "Education and Ideology: An Approach to Mexican Political Development." Fletcher, 1964.

Ewing, Morgan R. "A History of Archaeological Activity at Chichen-Itza from the Discovery to the Present." Kent State University, in progress.

Flores, Louis Joseph. "The Evolution of the Role of Government in the Economic Development of Mexico." University of Southern California, 1968.

Fuller, Clarissa P. "A Reexamination of Bandelier's Studies of Ancient Mexico." University of New Mexico, 1950.

Helms, James E. "Origins and Growth of Protestantism in Mexico to 1920." University of Texas, 1955.

Kennedy, Anneliese. "The United States Private Foundations and Mexico." University of North Carolina, in progress.

Krause, Corinne. "The Jews in Mexico: A History with Special Emphasis on the Period from 1857 to 1930." University of Pittsburgh, 1970.

McNeely, John H. "The Politics and Development of the Mexican Land Programs." University of Texas, 1958.

Meier, Matthias S. "History of the Tehuantepec Railroad." University of Southern California, 1954.

Penton, Marvin James. "Mexico's Reformation: A History of Mexican Protestantism from Its Inception to the Present." University of Iowa, 1964.

Pratt, Lucile. "Immigration to Mexico." Columbia University, 1961.

Priestley, Samuel. "The Agrarian Problem in Mexico." New York University, 1950.

Randall, Robert William. "The Real del Monte Mining Company." Harvard University, 1964.

Ronan, Charles E. "Francisco Javier Mariano Clavigero: A Study in Mexican Historiography." University of Texas, 1958.

Schmidt, Henry Conrad. "The Meaning of Mexico: A Study in National Consciousness." University of Texas, in progress.

Vanderwood, Paul J. "The Rurales: Mexico's Rural Police Force, 1861-1914." University of Texas, 1970.

Williman, John B. "Church and State in (the State of) Veracruz, 1840-1940: The Concord and Conflicts of a Century." Saint Louis University, 1971.

COLONIAL

Adams, David B. "The Tlaxcalan Colonies of Spanish Coahuila: An Aspect of the Development of Northern Mexico." University of Texas, in progress.

Archer, Christon I. "The Defense of New Spain, 1789-1810." State University of New York, Stony Brook, in progress.

Benedict, Harold B. "The Distribution of the Expropriated Jesuit Properties in Mexico with Special Reference to Chihuahua (1767-1790)." University of Washington, 1970.

Boyd, Maurice. "Don Gaspar de Quiroga: A Study of His Ecclesiastical and Inquisitorial Policies in Spain, 1592-1594." University of Michigan, 1951.

Boyer, Richard E. "Urban Crisis: The Flood of 1629 in Mexico City." University of Connecticut, in progress.

Breedlove, James M. "The Growth of a Mexican Colonial City: Guadalajara, 1750-1800." University of Texas, 1968.

Brooks, Francis J. "The Alienation of the Parochial Clergy from the Colonial Regime in the Last Years of Spanish Rule." Princeton University, in progress.

Brown, Thomas A. "The Academy of San Carlos in Mexican Colonial History." Duke University, 1967.

Carter, Constance Crowder. "The Visita of Tello de Sandoval in New Spain (1543-1547)." Columbia University, in progress.

Cook, Warren. "Spain in the Pacific Northwest, 1774-1795." Yale University, 1961.

Daniel, James M. "The Advance of the Spanish Frontier and the Despoblado." University of Texas, 1955.

De Laix, Edwin M. "Juan Vicente de Guemez Pacheco, the Second Conde de Revilla Gigedo of New Spain." University of Southern California, in progress.

Evans, Dudley Gordon. "Introduction of Agricultural Crops into the American Southwest from Spain." University of Southern California, 1964 (?).

Fireman, Janet. "The Royal Corps of Engineers of New Spain: Institution of the Bourbon Reforms." University of New Mexico, in progress.

Garner, Richard L. "Zacatecas: The Study of a Late Colonial Mexican City, 1750-1821." University of Michigan, 1970.

Georgiadis, Alex. "The Development of the República de los Indios in New Spain, 1520-1620." University of California, Berkeley, in progress.

Gillaspie, William R. "Juan de Ayala y Escobar, Sargeant Major of Florida: A Case Study of Spanish Colonial Administration, 1685-1720." University of Florida, 1964 (?).

Gschaedler, Andre. "Mexico and the Pacific, 1540-1565: The Voyages of Villalobos and Legazpi and the Preparations Made for Them." Columbia University, 1954.

Guest, Florian Francis. "The Pueblo as a Municipal Institution in Spanish California, 1769-1821." University of Southern California, 1961 (?).

Hallett, William H. "The Criollo in the Cabildo of Mexico City, 1595-1543." University of Washington (St. Louis), in progress.

Harris, Charles H. III. "A Mexican Latifundio: The Economic Empire of the Sánchez-Navarro Family, 1765-1821." University of Texas, 1968.

Hewitt, Harry P. "The Military Defense Structure and System of Nueva Vizcaya during the Seventeenth Century." University of Utah, in progress.

Howard, David A. "The Royal Indian Hospital of Mexico City." Duke University, in progress.

Kramer, V. Paul. "Arms and Armor in New Spain, 1519-1821." Texas Christian University, 1969 (?).

Larréy, Martin F. "A Viceroy and his Challengers: Supremacy Struggles during the Viceregency of Martín Enríquez (1568-1580)." University of California, Santa Barbara, 1967 (?).

Lavrín, Asunción. "Religious Life of Mexican Women in the 18th Century." Radcliffe, 1961.

Lundy, Jack E. "Don Gastón de Peralta, Marqués de Falces, Third Viceroy of New Spain." University of California, Santa Barbara, in progress.

McCarty, Fr. Kieran "The Spanish Missions of Sonora after the Jesuit Expulsion, 1767-1853." Catholic University of America, 1964.

Maclachlan, Colin M. "The Tribunal of the Acordada: A Study of Criminal Justice in Eighteenth Century Mexico." University of California, Los Angeles, 1969.

Marín, Miguel. "Neo-Colonial Puebla: A Social History of New Spain's Second City, 1780-1830." Columbia University, 1969.

Martin-Vegue, George B. "The Silversmiths in Mexico: A Study in Colonial Trade Guilds." University of Texas, 1951.

Maughan, Scott Jarvis. "The Life and Contributions of Francisco Tomás Hermenegildo Garcés." University of Utah, 1961 (?).

Miller, Wilbert J. "The Commandant System of Spanish Louisiana." Louisiana State University, 1967 (?).

Mitchell, Frederick C. "Spanish Manipulation of the Cacique in Sixteenth Century New Spain." University of California, Berkeley, 1964 (?).

Montgomery, Barbara. "The Acordada: An Instrument of the King's Justice in New Spain." Loyola, 1967.

Morales Valerio, Francisco, O.F.M. "Antecedentes Sociales de los Franciscanos en México: Siglo XVII." Catholic University of America, 1971.

Morton, Charles J. "Martín de Mayorga, Viceroy of New Spain, 1779-1783." Duke University, in progress.

Mulvihill, Daniel J. "Juan de Zumárraga, First Bishop of Mexico." University of Michigan, 1954.

Myres, Sandra L. "The Development of Cattle Ranching in Spanish Texas." Texas Christian University, 1967 (?).

Nieser, Albert B. "The Dominican Mission Foundation in Baja California, 1769-1822." Loyola University, 1960.

Nunn, Charles F. "The Foreigner in New Spain." Duke University, in progress.

Nuttall, Donald A. "Pedro Fages and the Northern Frontier of New Spain." University of Southern California, 1961 (?).

Nwasike, Dominic Aziliwe. "The Socio-Economic Composition of Mexico City Cabildo Members, 1590-1650." University of Wisconsin, in progress.

Osborn, Wayne S. "A Community Study of Metztitlan, New Spain, 1520-1810." University of Iowa, 1970.

Padden, Robert C. "The Colonial Church in New Spain: Era of Establishment." University of California, 1959.

Padelford, Victor W. "Mexican Society during the Vice Regency of Conde Revilla Gigedo II, 1789-1794." Washington State University, in progress.

Poole, R. Stafford. "The Indian Problem in the Third Provincial Council of Mexico (1585)." Saint Louis University, 1961.

Reynolds, Judith. "The Mixton War, Nueva Galicia, 1540-1541." University of Michigan, in progress.

Riley, G. Michael. "The Cortes Estate in the Cuernavaca Valley (Mexico) to 1547." University of New Mexico, 1965.

Riley, James Denson. "The Management of the Estates of the Colegio Máximo de San Pedro y San Pablo of Mexico City in the Eighteenth Century." Tulane University, in progress.

Ross, Oliver D. "Studies of Selected Mexican Communal Institutions: Colonial Period." Ohio University, 1953.

Sherman, William L. "Indian Slavery in Spanish Guatemala, 1524-1550." University of New Mexico, 1967.

Steck, Larry James. "Val de Cristo: A History of the Atlixco Valley, 1520-1650." University of Michigan, in progress.

Stowe, Noel J. "The Tumulto of 1624: Turmoil at Mexico City." University of Southern California, 1971.

Williams, Lyle W. "Struggle for Survival: The Northern Frontier of New Spain, 1751-1800." University of Texas, in progress.

Wilson, Iris. "Spanish Scientific Exploration in North America in the Late Eighteenth Century." University of Southern California, 1961 (?).

INDEPENDENCE

Anna, Timothy E. "Mexico in the War of Independence, 1810-1821." Duke University, 1969 (?).

Flaccus, Elmer W. "Guadalupe Victoria: Mexican Revolutionary Patriot and First President, 1786-1843." University of Texas, 1951.

Hadley, Bedford K. "The Enigmatic Padre Mier." University of Texas, 1955.

Korn, Peggy A. "Miguel Hidalgo y Costilla and the Ideology of Mexican Nationalism." University of Pennsylvania, 1964.

McElhannon, Joseph C. "Foreign Relations of Imperial Mexico, 1821-1823." University of Texas, 1951.

Macias, Anna. "The Apatzingán Constitution of 1914." Columbia University, 1961 (?).

Morgan, William A. "Sea Power in the Gulf of Mexico and Caribbean during the Mexican and Colombian Wars of Independence, 1818-1830." University of Southern California, 1969 (?).

Parrish, Leonard D. "The Life of Nicolás Bravo, Mexican Patriot (1786-1854." University of Texas, 1951.

Resnick, Enoch F. "The Cortes of Cádiz and the Movements for Independence in Spanish America: With Special Reference to the Viceroyalties of New Spain and Peru." American University, 1967.

Robertson, Frank D. "The Military and Political Career of Mariano Paredes y Arrillaga, 1797-1849." University of Texas, 1955.

Rodríguez, Jaime. "Vicente Rocafuerte and Mexico, 1820-1830." University of Texas, 1970.

Speck, Doris Ladd. "The Mexican Aristocracy at Independence: An Introduction." Stanford University, 1969.

THE EARLY REPUBLIC AND THE REFORM

Acuña, Rudolf. "The Times of Don Ignacio Pesqueira, Sonora Mexico, 1856-1876." University of Southern California, 1967 (?).

Adams, Paul L. "The American Struggle for a Pre-eminent Position in Mexico, 1822-1876." Ohio University, 1950.

Amos, Virginia Court. "A Mexican Positivist: Gabino Barreda, His Life and Work." Texas Christian University, 1969.

Baker, George T. III. "Mexico City during the Mexican War." Duke University, 1967 (?).

Bauer, Karl J. "United States Naval Operations during the Mexican War." Indiana University, 1953.

Berninger, Dieter. "Immigration as a Social and Political Issue in Mexico, 1821-1857." University of Wisconsin, 1971 (?).

Berry, Charles R. "The Reform in the Central District of Oaxaca, 1856-67: A Case Study." University of Texas, 1967.

Betts, John L. "The United States Navy and the Mexican War." University of Chicago, 1954.

Bidwell, Robert L. "The First Mexican Navy, 1821-1830." University of Virginia, 1960.

Bloom, John P. "With the American Army into Mexico, 1846-1848." Emory University, 1956.

Bodson, Robert Louis. "A Description of the United States Occupation of Mexico as Reported by American Newspapers Published in Veracruz, Puebla and Mexico City, September 14, 1847, to July 31, 1848." Ball State University, 1971.

Brack, Gene Martin. "Imperious Neighbor: The Mexican View of the United States, 1821-1846." University of Texas, 1967.

Brennan, Mary Holroyd. "American and British Travellers in Mexico, 1821-1876." University of Texas, in progress.

Brent, Robert A. "Nicholas Philip Trist: Biography of a Disobedient Diplomat." University of Virginia, 1950.

Broussard, Ray F. "Ignacio Comonfort: His Contributions to the Mexican Reform, 1855-1857." University of Texas, 1959.

Burks, David D. "The Dawn of Manufacturing in Mexico, 1821-1855." University of Chicago, 1952.

Cadenhead, Ivie E. "González Ortega and Mexican National Politics." University of Missouri, 1950.

Chaney, Homer C. "The Mexican–United States War as Seen by Mexican Intellectuals, 1846-1956." Stanford University, 1959.

Donathan, Carl D. "Lucas Alamán and Mexican Foreign Affairs, 1821-1833." Duke University, 1968.

Falcone, Frank S. "Federal-State Relations during Mexico's Restored Republic." University of Massachusetts, 1971 (?).

Gerrity, Francis X. "American Editorial Opinion of the French Intervention in Mexico, 1861-1867." Georgetown University, 1952.

Gilmore, Newton R. "British Mining Ventures in Early National Mexico." University of California, 1956.

Green, Stanley C. "Lucas Alamán." Texas Christian University, 1969 (?).

Kovac, Alan F. "Catolicismo, Nacionalidad y Orden: Expressions of Mexican Conservatism, 1835-1862." University of Florida, in progress.

Lamar, Quinton Curtis. "The Role of Lucan Alamán in Mexican–United States Relations, 1824-1853." Louisiana State University, 1971 (?).

Leary, Donald Thomas. "The Attitudes of Certain United States Citizens toward Mexico, 1821-1846." University of Southern California, 1970.

Leonard, Glen Milton. "Western Boundary Making: Texas and the Mexican Cession, 1844-1850." University of Utah, 1970.

Lynn, Vela L. "The Political Career of Teodosio Lares, 1848-1867." University of Texas, 1951.

Macune, Charles William, Jr. "A Test of Federalism: Political and Economic Relations between the State of Mexico and the Mexican Nation, 1823-1835." University of Texas, 1969.

Manno, Francis J. "History of United States Naval Operations, 1846-1848: With Particular Emphasis on the War with Mexico." Georgetown University, 1954.

Marti, Werner H. "Archibald H. Gillispie and the Conquest of California, 1846-1847." University of California, Los Angeles, 1953.

Miller, Robert R. "Mexican Secret Agents in the United States, 1861-1867." University of California, 1960.

Niosi, Jerome J. "The McLane Mission to Mexico, 1859-1860." New York University, 1954.

Olliff, Donathon C. "Economics of Mexican–United States Relations during the Reforma, 1855-1861." University of Florida, in progress.

Park, Joseph F. "Activities of United States Annexationists to Acquire Territory in Northwestern Mexico, 1854-1876." University of Arizona, 1967 (?).

Powell, Thomas G. "The Indian Question in Central Mexico, 1867-1876." Indiana University, 1970.

Sanders, Frank J. "Proposals for Monarchy in Mexico, 1823-1860." University of Arizona, 1967.

Schoonover, Thomas D. "The Diplomatic Relations between Mexico and the United States from 1861 to 1867." University of Minnesota, 1970.

Schulte, Josephine. "Gabino Barreda and the Law of Public Instruction." Loyola University, 1967 (?).

Sedgwick, Donna Cook. "The Mexican Government's Attitude toward the California Franciscan Missionary Enterprise, 1821-1846." University of

Southern California, in progress.

Sims, Harold D. "The Expulsion of the Spaniards from Mexico, 1821-1828." University of Florida, 1968.

Sinkin, Richard N. "The Development of Nationalism in Mexico, 1855-1876." University of Michigan, 1971.

Southerland, James E. "The Mexican Reaction to the United States' Foreign Policy, 1850-1860." University of Georgia, 1969.

Stevens, Robert Conway. "Mexico's Forgotten Frontier: A History of Sonora, 1821-1846." University of California, Berkeley, 1964 (?).

Stout, Joseph A. "The Last Years of Manifest Destiny: Filibustering in Northwestern Mexico, 1850-1862." Oklahoma State University, in progress.

Tyler, Daniel. "Manuel Armijo: Last Mexican Governor of New Mexico." University of New Mexico, in progress.

Tyler, Ronald C. "The Age of Cotton: Santiago Vidaurri and the Confederacy, 1861-1864." Texas Christian University, 1968.

Vigness, David M. "The Republic of the Rio Grande: An Example of Separatism in Northern Mexico." University of Texas, 1951.

Vishanoff, John G. "Gabino Barreda and the Educational Reforms of the Juárez Regime, 1867-1872." University of California, Santa Barbara, 1969 (?).

Weeks, Charles A. "The Mexican Constituent Congress of 1856-1857: A Study in Nineteenth Century Mexican Liberalism." Indiana University, in progress.

Winecup, Michael B. "The Conservative Movement in Guadalajara, 1830-1854." State University of New York, Stony Brook, in progress.

THE PORFIRIATO

Albro, Ward Sloan III. "Ricardo Flores Magón and the Liberal Party: An Inquiry into the Origins of the Mexican Revolution of 1910." University of Arizona, 1967.

Anderson, Rodney D. "The Mexican Textile Labor Movement, 1906-1907: An Analysis of a Labor Crisis." American University, 1968.

Aston, B. W. "The Life and Times of José Ives Limantour." Texas Technological University, 1967 (?).

Bryan, Anthony B. "Mexican Politics in Transition, 1900-1913: The Role of General Bernardo Reyes." University of Nebraska, 1969.

Case, Robert Phillip. "Politics during the First Administration of Porfirio Díaz." Northern Illinois University, in progress.

Crossman, Herbert A. "The Early Career of José Ives Limantour, 1854-1886." Harvard University, 1950

Dahl, Victor C. "The Anglo-Mexican Rapprochement of 1884: Its Background and Consequences." University of California, 1959.

Forrest, Jack Lavan. "United States Recognition of the Porfirio Díaz Government, 1876-1878." University of Oklahoma, 1967.

Fraser, Donald J. "The Disposition of Indian Communal Lands in Mexico, 1856-1911." University of Florida, 1969 (?).

Gansel, David Ross. "Political and Economic Impact of the Railroad in Mexico, 1876-1910." University of California, Berkeley, in progress.

Goldsmith, Bernard. "The Ateneo de la Juventud." Clark University, 1969 (?).

Gómez Quiñones, Juan. "Mexican Nationalism: The Formative Years, 1890-1912." University of California, Los Angeles, 1972 (?).

Hart, John M. "Anarchist Thought in 19th Century Mexico." University of California, Los Angeles, 1970.

Howell, Ellen Douglas. "Revolutionary Activities on the U.S.–Mexican Border, 1906-1908." University of Virginia, 1967 (?).

Isaacs, Harold. "United States–Mexican Relations during the González Administration, 1880-1884." University of Alabama, 1968.

Jenkins, Myra. "Ricardo Flores Magón and the Mexican Liberal Party." University of New Mexico, 1953.

Kaiser, Chester C. "John Watson Foster: United States Minister to Mexico, 1873-1880." American University, 1954.

Keremitsis, Dawn K. "Development of the Cotton Industry in Nineteenth Century Mexico." University of California, Berkeley, 1970 (?).

Knowlton, Robert J. "The Effects of the Disamortization and Nationalization of Ecclesiastical Property in Mexico, 1856-1910." University of Iowa, 1964.

Lee, James H. "Porfirio Díaz and the Mexican Ministry of the Interior, 1876-1911: A Case Study of the Porfirian Power Structure." Ohio State University, in progress.

Miller, David L. "Porfirio Díaz and the Army of the East." University of Michigan, 1960.

Morf, Paul. "The Cananea Strike: Case Study in Law Enforcement under Porfirio Díaz." University of Illinois, in progress.

Niblo, Stephen Randall. "The Political Economy of the Early Porfiriato: Politics and Economics in the Consolidation of the First Porfirio Díaz Administration, 1876-1880." Northern Illinois University, 1971 (?).

Perry, Laurens Ballard. "The Dynamics of the Insurrection of Tuxtepec: Mexico in 1876." University of Michigan, 1971.

Raat, William Dirk. "Positivism in Díaz' Mexico, 1867-1911: An Essay in Intellectual History." University of Utah, 1967.

Roehl, Charlotte. "Porfirio Díaz in the Press of the United States." University of Chicago, 1953.

Romney, Joseph B. "American Interests in Mexico: Development and Impact during the Rule of Porfirio Díaz, 1876-1911." University of Utah, 1969.

Schiff, Warren. "German Interests in Mexico in the Period of Porfirio Díaz." University of California, 1957.

Schmidt, Arthur P., Jr. "The Impact of the Railroad in Puebla and Veracruz, Mexico, 1867-1911." Indiana University, 1970.

Secrest, James. "The End of the Porfiriato: General Díaz's Final Year in Office, Sept. 1910–May, 1911." University of New Mexico, 1969.

Schmitt, Karl M. "Evolution of Mexican Thought in Church-State Relations, 1876-1911." University of Pennsylvania, 1954.

Stillinger, Richard. "The Political, Economic and Social Thought of Francisco Bulnes, with Emphasis on his Attitudes toward the Regime of Porfirio Díaz" Columbia University, 1970.

Sumner, Alanson J. "The Rise of the Científicos." Case Western Reserve, in progress.

Suss, Stuart A. "Roots of a Revolution: Labor Agitation in Mexico, 1906-1911." New York University, in progress.

Weatherhead, Richard W. "Justo Sierra: A Portrait of the Porfirian Intellectual." Columbia University, 1964 (?).

THE REVOLUTION

Allen, C. Crosby "Artistic Expressions of the Ideologies of the Mexican Revolution." New York University, 1967.

Anderson, William Woodrow. "The Nature of the Mexican Revolution as Viewed from the United States, 1910-1917." University of Texas, 1967.

Bailey, David Charles. "The Cristero Rebellion and the Religious Conflict in Mexico, 1926-1929." Michigan State University, 1969.

Baldridge, Donald C. "Mexican Petroleum and United States–Mexican Relations, 1919-1923." University of Arizona, 1971.

Balmaseda, Francisco A. "Isidro Fabela: Intellectual Mexican Diplomat." Case Western Reserve, in progress.

Britton, John A. "The Mexican Ministry of Education, 1931-1940: A Decade of Radicalism and Institutional Development." Tulane University, 1971.

Brown, James Chilton. "The Pre-Institutional Roots of the Revolutionary National Party (PNR) in Mexico: The Calles Years, 1924-1928." University of New Mexico, 1970 (?).

Buford, Nick. "Luis Morones, Biography of a Mexican Labor and Political Leader." Louisiana State University, in progress.

Caleca, John. "Francisco Vásquez Gómez and the Mexican Revolution, 1909-1929." University of Nebraska, in progress.

Campbell, High G. "The Radical Right in Mexico, 1929-1944." University of California, Los Angeles, 1968.

Cardoso, Lawrence A. "Migration of Mexican Labor to the United States, 1900-1930: An Analysis of Socio-Economic Causes." University of Connecticut, in progress.

Crowley, Florence J. "The Conservative Thought of José Vasconcelos." University of Florida, 1964.

Dooley, Francis P. "Mexico's Cristeros: Rebels for Religion." University of Maryland, 1969 (?).

Farías, Hector. "Nemesio García Naranjo: Mexico's Minister of Education, 1913-1914." Northwestern University, 1971.

Fowler, Heather. "The Agrarian Revolution in the State of Veracruz, 1920-1940: The Role of Peasant Organizations." American University, 1970.

Giese, Anna Mae. "The Sonoran Revolutionaries: Obregón, Calles and De la Huerta." University of Florida, in progress.

Gilderhus, Mark T. "The United States and the Mexican Revolution, 1915-1920: A Study of Policy and Interest." University of Nebraska, 1968.

Gotshall, Elwood Rufus. "Catholicism and Catholic Action in Mexico, 1929-1941: A Church's Response to a Revolutionary Society and the Politics of the Modern Age." University of Pittsburgh, 1970.

Hanley, Timothy C. "The Role of the National League for the Defense of Religious Liberty in the Church-State Conflict in Mexico, 1910-1929." Columbia University, 1969 (?).

Hansis, Randall C. "Alvaro Obregón: The Mexican Revolution and the Politics of Consolidation, 1920-1924." University of New Mexico, 1971.

Henderson, Peter Van Ness. "Félix Díaz and the Porfirian Military Aristocracy, 1910-1920." University of Nebraska, in progress.

Holcombe, Harold E. "United States Arms Control and the Mexican Revolution, 1920-1924." University of Alabama, 1968.

Horn, James John. "Diplomacy by Ultimatum: Ambassador Sheffield and Mexican-American Relations, 1924-1927." State University of New York, Buffalo, 1969.

Ignasias, Charles Dennis. "Reluctant Recognition: The United States and the Recognition of Alvaro Obregón of Mexico, 1920-1924." Michigan State University, 1967.

Innes, John S. "Revolution and Renaissance in Mexico: El Ateneo de la Juventud." University of Texas, 1970.

Kelley, Sister Marie. "Cárdenas and the Ideology of the Communist Party." Georgetown University, in progress.

Kirshner, Alan M. "Tomás Garrido Canabal and the Mexican Red Shirt Movement." New York University, 1971 (?).

McKechnie, Marian E. "The Mexican Revolution and the National Presbyterian Church of Mexico, 1910-1940." American University, 1970.

Martínez, John R. "Mexican Emigration to the United States, 1910-1930." University of California, 1957.

Masingill, Eugene F. "The Diplomatic Career of Henry Lane Wilson in Latin America." Louisiana State University, 1957.

Mazzaferri, Anthony. "Public Health and Social Revolution in Mexico, 1910-1930." Kent State University, 1968 (?).

Michaels, Albert L. "Nationalist in Mexico, 1920-1940." University of Pennsylvania, 1969.

Nathan, Paul. "Mexico under Cárdenas." University of Chicago, 1953.

Quirk, Robert E. "The Mexican Revolution and the Catholic Church, 1910-1929: An Ideological Study." Harvard University, 1951.

Rausch, George, Jr. "Victoriano Huerta: A Political Biography." University of Illinois, 1960.

Rippy, Merrill. "Oil and the Mexican Revolution." University of Texas, 1950.

Rivera, Feliciano. "Social and Political Aspects of the Mexican Revolution as Seen through the Writings of Mariano Azuela." University of Southern California, 1970.

Roberts, Donald Frank. "A Case Study of Elite Responses to a Developing Social Revolution: Mexico, 1908-1917." University of Pittsburgh, in progress.

Roman, Richard. "Recurrent Issues in the Post-revolutionary Consolidation of Power and Legitimation of Authority: The Case of Mexico, 1914-1924." University of California, Berkeley, 1970 (?).

Rosser, H. Edwin. "Beyond Revolution: The Social Concern of Moisés Sáenz,

Mexican Educator (1888-1941)." American University, 1970.

Rossiter, William M. "Mexican-American Relations, 1913-1920: A Reappraisal." University of Chicago, 1952.

Robertson, O. Zeller. "Mexico and Non-intervention, 1910-1919: The Policy, the Practice, and the Law." University of California, Los Angeles, 1969.

Shepard, Julia. "[A Biography of Francisco Múgica]." University of Connecticut, in progress.

Starkweather, James A., Jr. "El Ateneo de la Juventud: The Change in the Direction of Thought in Mexico: 1880's-1925." University of California, Los Angeles, in progress.

Stegmaier, Harry I., Jr. "From Confrontation to Cooperation: The United States and Mexico, 1938-1945." University of Michigan, 1970.

Vaughn, Mary Kay. "Educational Thought and Program of José Vasconcelos." University of Wisconsin, in progress.

Wakely, Francis E. "The Basis of Conflict of Four Mexican Bishops with the Church-State *Arreglos* of 1929: Profiles of Manríquez y Zárate, González y Valencia, Lara y Torres, and Orozco de Ximénez." State University of New York, Buffalo, in progress.

Watkins, Holland D. "Plutarco Elías Calles: Jefe Máximo." Texas Technological University, 1967 (?).

White, D. Anthony. "Mexico in World Affairs, 1928-1968." University of California, Los Angeles, 1969 (?).

Williams, Peter W. "The Mexican Cristero Rebellion, 1926-1929." Yale University, 1969 (?).

THE CONTEMPORARY ERA

Campbell, Howard L. "Public Law 78 and Mexico: The Impact of the Bracero Program on Mexico." American University, 1971 (?).

Campbell, Ted A. "The National Indian Institute of Mexico, 1948-1968." University of California, Los Angeles, 1969 (?).

Goodman, Margaret Ann. "The Effectiveness of the Mexican Revolution as an Agent of Change in the State of Yucatán." Columbia University, 1970.

Haight, Charles H. "The Contemporary Mexican Revolution as Viewed by Mexican Intellectuals." Stanford University, 1957.

Lux, William R. "Mexico's Conservative Party: The PAN." University of Southern California, 1967.

Mabry, Donald J. "Partido de Acción Nacional in Urban Politics, 1952-1970." Syracuse University, in progress.

McCain, Johnny Mac. "Contract Labor as a Factor in United States–Mexican Relations, 1942-1947." University of Texas, 1970.

Morris, Donald Russell. "Political Violence and Political Modernization in Mexico, 1952-1964." University of Wisconsin, 1971.

Nutt, Katherine F. "Nationalism: A Search for Unity–The Role of Mexican Government in Sponsoring the Fine Arts." University of New Mexico, 1951.

Prager, Kenneth. "The Mexican Sinarquistas, 1937-1945." Indiana University, 1969.

Santoro, Carmela Elvira. "United States–Mexican Relations during World War II." Syracuse University, 1967.

Smith, Arthur K., Jr. "Mexico and the Cuban Revolution: Foreign Policy Making in Mexico under President Adolfo López Mateos, 1958-1964." Cornell University, 1970.

Smith, Kent W. "The American Cultural Crusade in Mexico, 1938-1945." University of California, Berkeley, in progress.

Torrence, Donald Ray. "La Organización Regional Interamericana de Trabajadores (ORIT) and the Latin American Labor Movement, 1959-1969." Northern Illinois University, in progress.

Wollenberg, Charles M. "Land Reform in Mexico since 1940." University of California, Berkeley, 1969 (?).

Appendix A
A Scholar's Map of Mexico City

ARCHIVES ▲
1. Archivo General de la Nación (National Palace)
2. Anexo al Castillo de Chapultepec
3. Archivo de Relaciones Exteriores de México (Secretaría de Relaciones Exteriores de México)
4. Archivo Histórico de la Defensa Nacional (Secretaría de la Defensa Nacional)
5. Centro Cultural de CONDUMEX, S.A.
6. Colección General Porfirio Díaz

LIBRARIES ●
1. Biblioteca Nacional
2. Hemeroteca Nacional
3. Biblioteca Central de la Universidad Nacional Autónoma de México
4. Biblioteca Iberoamericana
5. Centro Cultural y Biblioteca Isidro Fabela
6. Capilla Alfonsina
7. Biblioteca de México
8. Biblioteca del Banco de México, S.A.
9. Biblioteca Central del Instituto Mexicano del Seguro Social

EMBASSIES ◀
1. American Embassy
2. Canadian Embassy
3. British Embassy

SCHOOLS ▜
1. Escuela Nacional Preparatoria
2. El Colegio de México
3. Instituto Politécnico Nacional
4. Universidad de las Américas (Puebla)
5. Universidad Nacional Autónoma de México
6. Universidad Ibero-Americana
7. Colegio Militar
8. Conservatorio Nacional de México

MUSEUMS ■
1. Museo Nacional
2. Palacio de Bellas Artes
3. Museo de Arte Popular
4. Museo Nacional de Antropología
5. Castillo de Chapultepec
6. Museo Anahuacalli (Diego Rivera)
7. Museo de Copilco
8. Museo de Arte Religioso
9. Museo de Historia Natural
10. Museo de la Ciudad de México (Casa del Conde de Santiago)

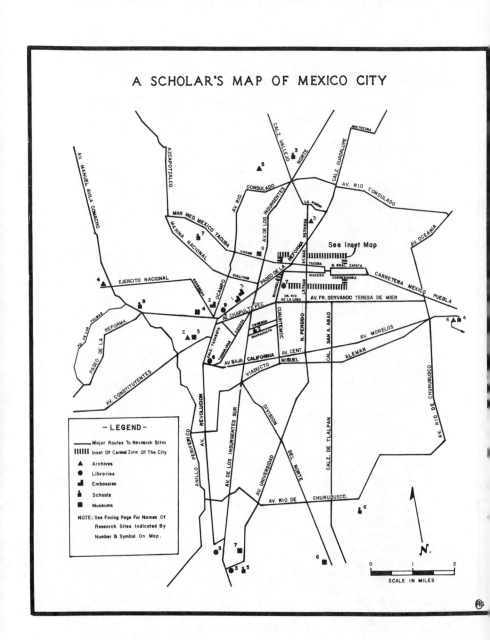

A SCHOLAR'S MAP OF MEXICO CITY

- LEGEND -

▬▬ Major Routes To Research Sites
||||||| Inset Of Central Zone Of The City
▲ Archives
● Libraries
🏛 Embassies
🏛 Schools
■ Museums

NOTE: See Facing Page For Names Of
Research Sites Indicated By
Number & Symbol On Map.

See Inset Map

N.

SCALE IN MILES
0   1   2

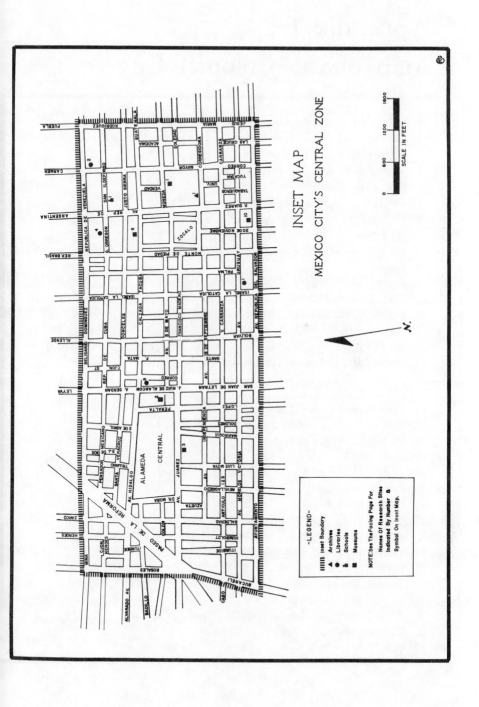

INSET MAP

MEXICO CITY'S CENTRAL ZONE

SCALE IN FEET

0   600   1200   1800

-LEGEND-

IIIIII Inset Boundary
▲   Archives
♦   Libraries
⚓   Schools
■   Museums

NOTE: See The Facing Page For
Names Of Research Sites
Indicated By Number &
Symbol On Inset Map.

Appendix B
Map of the Colonial City

1. Site of one of Moctezuma's palaces, today the Monte de Piedad
2. Cathedral. Be sure to go into subterranean passages to see Zumárraga tomb, etc.
3. Ruin of main Aztec pyramid
4. Site of first university
5. Building that housed first printing press, 1539
6. National Palace; Rivera murals, Juárez museum, AGN, Biblioteca de Hacienda
7. House of counts of Santiago de Calimaya, Museo de la Ciudad de México
8. Hospital de Jesús
9. Majestic Hotel terrace; view of colonial architecture
10. Santo Domingo Church, site of one of Cuauhtémoc's houses
11. Palacio de la Inquisición, eighteenth century
12. House of Nuño de Guzmán, 1530; later residence of Columbus's granddaughter
13. House of Diego Pedroza, first surgeon of Cortés
14. House of Malinche and Juan Jaramillo
15. Home of Juan Suárez, Cortés's brother-in-law
16. Birthplace of Conde Manuel Heras y Soto, eighteenth century
17. Hospital de Divino Salvador for insane women, 1700
18. Residence of Juan de Cervantes
19. Educación Pública; see Rivera frescoes
20. Former National Preparatory School; see frescoes by Orozco and Rivera
21. Academia de San Carlos
22. Casa de Moneda
23. Palacio de Ayuntamiento, originally owned by Cortés's family, destroyed in 1692 riots, rebuilt 1720s. Federal District headquarters
24. Palacio de Justicia, Supreme Court Building; Orozco frescoes
25. Sanborns; facade and interior. Construction begun in 1590 by Condes del Valle de Orizaba
26. Church of San Francisco
27. Torre Latínoamericana; panoramic view
28. Escuela de Minería; stairway and facade
29. Palacio de Iturbide

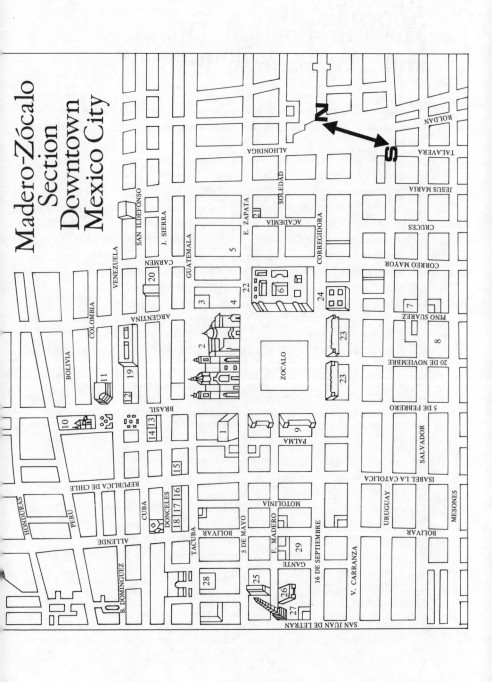

Madero-Zócalo
Section
Downtown
Mexico City

Appendix C
Mexican Political Divisions and Populations, 1970

POLITICAL DIVISION	AREA IN SQUARE MILES	CAPITAL	POPULATION OF CAPITAL CITY BY MUNICIPIO[a]
Aguascalientes	2,500	Aguascalientes	225,000
Baja California	27,800	Mexicali	396,000
Baja Calif. (terr.)	27,800	La Paz	52,000
Campeche	19,700	Campeche	81,000
Chiapas	28,700	Tuxla Gutiérrez	71,000
Chihuahua	94,800	Chihuahua	277,000
Coahuila	58,100	Saltillo	191,000
Colima	2,000	Colima	73,000
Distrito Federal	600	Mexico City (metropolitan zone, 8,850,000)[b]	2,903,000
Durango	47,000	Durango	204,000
Guanajuato	11,800	Guanajuato	65,000
Guerrero	24,900	Chilpancingo	59,000
Hidalgo	8,300	Pachuca	92,000
Jalisco	31,000	Guadalajara	1,199,000
México	8,300	Toluca	24,000
Michoacán	23,200	Morelia	218,000
Morelos	1,900	Cuernavaca	161,000
Nayarit	10,400	Tepic	111,000
Nuevo León	25,100	Monterrey	858,000
Oaxaca	36,400	Oaxaca	116,000
Puebla	13,100	Puebla	533,000
Querétaro	4,400	Querétaro	163,000
Quintana Roo	19,400	Chetumal (capital in municipio of Payo Obispo)	36,000
San Luis Potosí	14,400	San Luis Potosí	268,000
Sinaloa	22,600	Culiacán	360,000
Sonora	70,500	Hermosillo	208,000
Tabasco	9,800	Villahermosa (capital in municipio of Centro)	164,000
Tamaulipas	30,700	Ciudad Victoria	96,000
Tlaxcala	1,600	Tlaxcala	22,000
Veracruz	27,700	Jalapa	130,000
Yucatán	14,900	Mérida	242,000
Zacatecas	28,100	Zacatecas	58,000

Source: Population data developed by James W. Wilkie from unpublished 1970 census material.

[a]Because at present there is no satisfactory manner of listing the population for all capitals in a consistent format, data for *municipios* (roughly analogous to the county in the United States) are used here in order to give some indication of the metropolitan zones which transcend city limits. Thus, the capital city of Puebla was listed at 402,000 in the 1970 census as compared to 533,000 for its municipio.

[b]The metropolitan zone of Mexico City includes the entire Distrito Federal as well as eleven *municipios* in the state of Mexico; see Luis Unikel, "La Dinámica del Crecimiento de la Ciudad de México," *Comercio Exterior*, June 1971, pp. 507-16.

Appendix D
Table of Equivalents

CURRENCY

1 Mexican peso	=	$ .08 (U.S.)
10 Mexican pesos	=	.80 (U.S.)
100 Mexican pesos	=	8.00 (U.S.)
500 Mexican pesos	=	40.00 (U.S.)
1,000 Mexican pesos	=	80.00 (U.S.)
1 U.S. dollar	=	$ 12.50 (Mexican pesos)
10 U.S. dollars	=	125.00 (Mexican pesos)
100 U.S. dollars	=	1,250.00 (Mexican pesos)

LINEAR MEASURE

1 meter	=	39.37 inches
5 meters	=	5.47 yards
10 meters	=	10.94 yards
1 foot	=	.305 meters (approx.)
1 yard	=	.914 meters
5 yards	=	4.57 meters
10 yards	=	9.14 meters
1 kilometer	=	.62 miles
5 kilometers	=	3.10 miles
10 kilometers	=	6.20 miles
1 mile	=	1.609 kilometers
5 miles	=	8.045 kilometers
10 miles	=	16.09 kilometers

LIQUID MEASURE

1 liter	=	1.056 quarts (approx.)
5 liters	=	1 gallon, 1.28 quarts (approx.)
10 liters	=	2 gallons, 2.56 quarts (approx.)
1 pint	=	.473 liters
1 quart	=	.946 liters
1 gallon	=	3.785 liters
5 gallons	=	18.925 liters

WEIGHTS

1 gram	=	.035 ounces
10 grams	=	.35 ounces
100 grams	=	3.5 ounces
1,000 grams (1 kilogram)	=	2.2 pounds (approx.)
2 kilograms	=	4.4 pounds (approx.)
5 kilograms	=	11 pounds (approx.)
1 ounce	=	28.35 grams (approx.)
10 ounces	=	283.50 grams (approx.)
1 pound	=	453.59 grams (0.45 kilograms approx.)

CONVERSION FORMULAS

pesos to dollars	multiply by	.08
dollars to pesos	multiply by	12.50
inches to centimeters	multiply by	2.54
centimeters to inches	multiply by	0.39
miles to kilometers	multiply by	1.61
kilometers to miles	multiply by	0.62
liters to quarts	multiply by	1.056
quarts to liters	multiply by	0.95
pounds to kilograms	divide by	2.2
kilograms to pounds	multiply by	2.2

Centigrade to Fahrenheit: Multiply degrees C. by 1.8 and add 32. For example, $22°$ C. x 1.8 = 39.6, plus 32 = $71.6°$ F.

Fahrenheit to Centigrade: Subtract 32 from degrees F. and divide by 1.8.

Appendix E
Rulers of Mexico

Preconquest Period

Tenoch	?
Queen Ilancueitl	1349-75
Acamapichtli and Queen Ilancueitl	1375-83
Acamapichtli	1383-96
Huitzilihuitl	1396-1417
Chimalpopoca	1417-27
Itzcóatl	1427-40
Moctezuma Ilhuicamina (Moctezuma I)	1440-69
Axayácatl	1469-81
Tizoc	1481-86
Ahuitzotl	1486-1502
Moctezuma Xocoyotzin (Moctezuma II)	1502 to June, 1520
Cuitláhuac	June-October, 1520
Cuauhtémoc	October, 1520-August, 1521

Immediate Postconquest Period

Hernán Cortés	1521-24
Crown Officials	1524-26
Residencia Judges	1526-28
First Audiencia	1528-31
Second Audiencia	1531-35

Viceroys of the Colonial Period

Antonio de Mendoza	1535-50
Luis de Velasco (the elder)	1550-64
Gastón de Peralta	1566-68
Martín Enríquez de Almanza	1568-80
Lorenzo Suárez de Mendoza	1580-83
Pedro Moya de Contreras	1584-85
Alvaro Manrique de Zúñiga	1585-90
Luís de Velasco (the younger)	1590-95
Gaspar de Zúñiga y Acevedo	1595-1603
Juan de Mendoza y Luna	1603-1607
Luís de Velasco (the younger)	1607-11
Fray García Guerra	1611-12
Diego Fernández de Córdoba	1612-21
Diego Carrillo de Mendoza y Pimentel	1621-24
Rodrigo Pacheco y Osorio	1624-35

Lope Díaz de Armendáriz	1635-40
Diego López Pacheco Cabrera y Bobadilla	1640-42
Juan de Palafox y Mendoza	1642-48
Marcos de Torres y Rueda	1648-49
Luis Enríquez y Guzmán	1650-53
Francisco Fernández de la Cueva	1653-60
Juan de Leyva y de la Cerda	1660-64
Diego Osorio de Escobar y Llamas	1664
Antonio Sebastián de Toledo	1664-73
Pedro Nuño Colón de Portugal	1673
Fray Payo Enríquez de Rivera	1673-80
Tomás Antonio de la Cerda y Aragón	1680-86
Melchor Portocarrero Lasso de la Vega	1686-88
Gaspar de Sandoval Silva y Mendoza	1688-96
Juan de Ortega y Montañez	1696
José Sarmiento Valladares	1696-1701
Juan de Ortega y Montañez	1701
Francisco Fernández de la Cueva Enríquez	1701-11
Fernando de Alencastre Noroña y Silva	1711-16
Baltasar de Zúñiga y Guzmán	1716-22
Juan de Acuña	1722-34
Juan Antonio Vizarrón y Eguiarreta	1734-40
Pedro de Castro y Figueroa	1740-41
Pedro Cebrián y Agustín	1742-46
Francisco de Güemes y Horcasitas (subsequently first Count Revillagigedo)	1746-55
Agustín Ahumada y Villalón	1755-60
Francisco Cajigal de la Vega	1760
Joaquín de Monserrat	1760-66
Carlos Francisco de Croix	1766-71
Antonio María de Bucareli	1771-79
Martín de Mayorga	1779-83
Matías de Gálvez	1783-84
Bernardo de Gálvez	1785-86
Alonso Núñez de Haro y Peralta	1787
Manuel Antonio Flores	1787-89
Juan Vicente de Güemes Pacheco y Padilla (second Count Revillagigedo)	1789-94
Miguel de la Grúa Talamanca y Branciforte	1794-98
Miguel José de Azanza	1798-1800
Félix Berenguer de Marquina	1800-1803
José de Iturrigaray	1803-1808
Pedro Garibay	1808-1809
Francisco Javier de Lizana y Beaumont	1809-10
Francisco Javier de Venegas	1810-13

Félix María Calleja del Rey	1813-16
Juan Ruiz de Apodaca	1816-21
Francisco Novella	1821
Juan O'Donojú	Did not assume office

Independence Period and Early Republic

Emperor Agustín de Iturbide	1822-23
Guadlupe Victoria (Félix Fernández)	1824-29
Vicente Guerrero	1829
José María Bocanegra (interim)	1829
Pedro Velez, Luis Quintanar, and	
Lucas Alamán, triumvirate	1829
Anastasio Bustamante	1830-32, 1837-39, and 1842
Melchor Múzquiz (interim)	1832
Manuel Gómez Pedraza	1833
Valentín Gómez Garías	1833, 1834, and 1847
Antonio López de Santa Anna	Variously from 1833 to 1855
Miguel Barragán	1835-36
José Justo Corro	1836-37
Nicolás Bravo	Variously from 1839 to 1846
Javier Echeverría	1841
Valentín Canalizo	1844
José Joaquín Herrera (interim)	1844, 1845, and 1848-51
Mariano Paredes Arrillaga	1846
Mariano Salas	1846
Pedro María Anaya	1847 and 1848
Manuel de la Peña y Peña	1847 and 1848
Mariano Arista	1851-53
Juan Bautista Ceballos (interim)	1853
Manuel María Lombardini	1853
Martín Carrera (interim)	1855
Rómulo Díaz de la Vega	1855

The Reform and the French Intervention

Juan Alvarez	1855
Ignacio Comonfort	1855-58

Liberal Government

Benito Juárez	1855-72

Conservative Government

Félix Zuloaga	1858 and 1859

Manuel Robles Pezuela	1858
Miguel Miramón	1859-60
Ignacio Pavón	1860
Conservative Junta	1860-64
Emperor Maximilian von Hapsburg	1864-67

Post-Reform Period

Sebastián Lerdo de Tejada	1872-76
Porfirio Díaz	1876-1880 and 1884-1911
Juan N. Méndez	1876
Manuel González	1880-84

Revolutionary Period

Francisco León de la Barra (interim)	1911
Francisco I. Madero	1911-13
Pedro Lascurain (interim)	1913
Victoriano Huerta (interim)	1913-14
Francisco S. Carbajal (interim)	1914
Venustiano Carranza	1914 and 1915-20
Eulalio Gutiérrez (interim, named by Convention)	1914
Roque González Garza	1914
Francisco Lagos Cházaro	1915
Adolfo de la Huerta (interim)	1920
Alvaro Obregón	1920-24
Plutarco Elías Calles	1924-28
Emilio Portes Gil (interim)	1928-30
Pascual Ortiz Rubio	1930-32
Abelardo L. Rodríguez (interim)	1932-34
Lázaro Cárdenas	1934-40

Institutional Revolution

Manuel Avila Camacho	1940-46
Miguel Alemán Valdés	1946-52
Adolfo Ruiz Cortines	1952-58
Adolfo López Mateos	1958-64
Gustavo Díaz Ordaz	1964-70
Luis Echeverría Alvarez	1970-

List of Contributors

Elsa Barberena, Associate Librarian, University of the Americas

William H. Beezley, Department of History, North Carolina State University

Bernard E. Bobb, Department of History, Washington State University

Alicia O. de Bonfil, Departmento de Investigaciones Históricas, Instituto Nacional de Antropología e Historia

Lyle C. Brown, Department of Political Science, Baylor University

Anthony T. Bryan, Department of History, University of Rhode Island

Daniel Cosío Villegas, Centro de Estudios Históricos, El Colegio de México

Romeo Flores Caballero, Centro de Estudios Internacionales, El Colegio de México

Charles Gildersleeve, Department of Geography, University of Nebraska, Omaha

Richard E. Greenleaf, Department of History, Tulane University

Kenneth J. Grieb, Department of History, Wisconsin State University, Oshkosh

Charles A. Hale, Department of History, University of Iowa

C. Alan Hutchinson, Department of History, University of Virginia

Robert Knowlton, Department of History, Wisconsin State University, Stevens Point

Eugenia Meyer, Departamento de Investigaciones Históricas, Instituto Nacional de Antropología e Historia

Michael C. Meyer, Department of History, University of Nebraska, Lincoln

Albert L. Michaels, Department of History, State University of New York, Buffalo

Roberto Moreno, Biblioteca Nacional, México, D.F.

Charles F. Nunn, Department of History, University of Richmond

Robert A. Potash, Department of History, University of Massachusetts

William D. Raat, Department of History, State University of New York, Fredonia

James D. Riley, Department of History, Saint Benedict College

Donald Robertson, Department of Art History, Tulane University

Jaime E. Rodríguez, Department of History, California State College, Long Beach

Ramón Eduardo Ruiz, Department of History, University of California, San Diego

France V. Scholes, Emeritus, Department of History, University of New Mexico

Robert J. Shafer, Department of History, Syracuse University

William L. Sherman, Department of History, University of Nebraska, Lincoln

Ronald M. Spores, Department of Anthropology, Vanderbilt University

Stanley J. Stein, Department of History, Princeton University

John C. Super, Department of History, University of California, Los Angeles

William B. Taylor, Department of History, University of Colorado

Berta Ulloa, Centro de Estudios Históricos, El Colegio de México

Paul Vanderwood, Department of History, San Diego State College

James W. Wilkie, Department of History, University of California, Los Angeles

DATE DUE